FENG SHUI

DESIGN

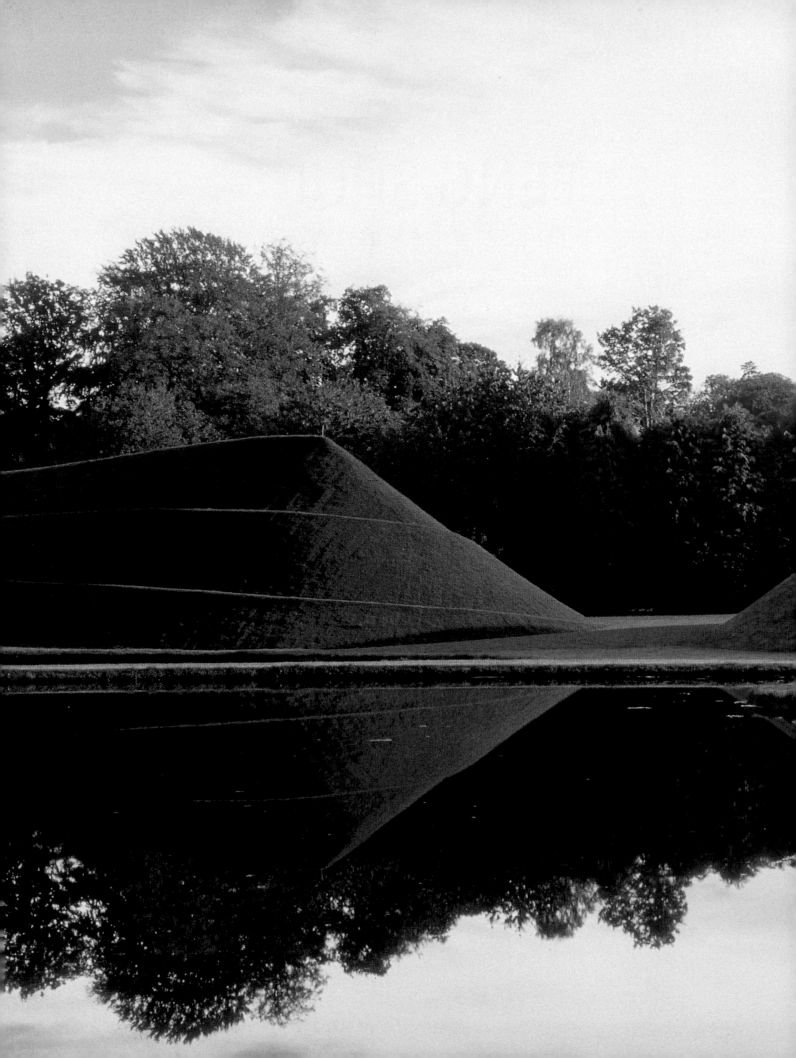

Sarah Rossbach & Master Lin Yun

FENG SHUI
DESIGN

From History and Landscape to
Modern Gardens & Interiors

Viking

VIKING
Published by the Penguin Group
Penguin Putnam Inc., 375 Hudson Street,
New York, New York 10014, U.S.A.
Penguin Books Ltd, 27 Wrights Lane, London W8 5TZ, England
Penguin Books Australia Ltd, Ringwood, Victoria, Australia
Penguin Books Canada Ltd, 10 Alcorn Avenue,
Toronto, Ontario, Canada M4V 3B2
Penguin Books (N.Z.) Ltd, 182–190 Wairau Road,
Auckland 10, New Zealand
Penguin India, 210 Chiranjiv Tower, 43 Nehru Place,
New Delhi 11009, India

Penguin Books Ltd, Registered Offices:
Harmondsworth, Middlesex, England

First American edition
Published in 1998 by Viking Penguin,
a member of Penguin Putnam Inc.

10 9 8 7 6 5 4 3

Line art: Edward Emerson, Lon Cohen
Photography: Daniel Aubry: 7, 11, 19, 24, 81, 91 (top right), 93, 94, 97, 99, 102, 107, 115, 116, 119, 120/121, 123, 126, 127, 128, 130, 132, 136, 137, 138/139, 141, 142, 143 (bottom), 144, 145, 146/147, 148, 149, 151, 152, 154/155, 157, 158, 159, 162, 166/167, 171, 173, 174/175, 176, 177, 179, 180, 181, 183; Penny Coleman: 13, 16/17, 21, 25, 27, 55, 59, 61, 62, 64, 66, 67, 68, 69, 70/71, 72, 73, 75, 76, 77 (top, middle), 78, 79, 82/83, 108/109; 111 (right) courtesy Arquitectonica; 20 (top) Mel Chin, courtesy of the artist; 90/91 (except upper right, 91) Delany, Cochran & Castillo; 2/3, 86 Pieter Estersohn/Lachapelle Representation, courtesy Charles Jencks; 9, 20, 43, 56, 77 (bottom) Kathryn Glenchur; 110 IBM/Kohn Pederson Fox (rendering); 143, 170 interior Jamson Whyte Soho store, New York/Paul Wicheloe; 111 (left) Kohn Pederson Fox; 15 Lin Yun Temple; 14, 100, 101 Thomas Rosenthal; 22/23 Trevira FR/Treviracs

LIBRARY OF CONGRESS CATALOGING IN PUBLICATION DATA
Rossbach, Sarah.
    Feng Shui design : from history and landscape to modern gardens &
interiors / Sarah Rossbach & Lin Yun.
        p.   cm.
    Includes bibliographical references (p.   ) and index.
    ISBN 0-670-88223-2
    1. Feng-shui.   I. Lin, Yun, 1932–   II. Title.
    BF1779.F4R65   1998
    133.3′337—dc21   98-18275

Printed in the United Kingdom
Designed by DW Design, London

Contents

Preface

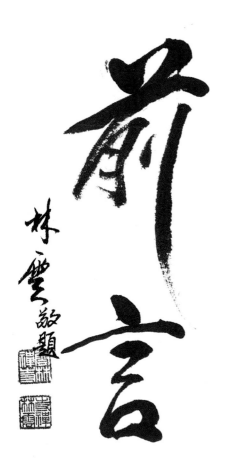

Preface

I have dreamed of writing an illustrated book on feng shui, the Chinese art of placement. Feng shui is a visual art, practice and pursuit, so it is with this approach that we can best understand its impact, be it in the past on the Chinese landscape and architecture, or the present on Eastern and Western architecture and design. My hope is that, equipped with this visual knowledge, the reader can better fathom and apply feng shui rules and cures to home and business, to create more comfortable and harmonious places in which to live and work. And I hope that in doing so the reader will come to enjoy a more positive life.

When I began writing about feng shui in 1978, a pictorial book on the subject was not a possibility. Where was the interest? After all, only a small group of Westerners had heard of it. Funded by a pittance of an advance, my first book was a labor of love, a journalistic challenge to explain an arcane, oriental practice to a Western audience. It was similar to discovering a lost treasure in a grandparent's attic, something that had existed for a long time but that no one—at least in the West—had noticed or valued.

Today, two decades later, the story of feng shui in the West is completely different: interest in the art has burgeoned. Stories appear in such diverse magazines as the *Economist, House Beautiful, Esquire, New Woman, Business Week*. Numerous articles have run in newspapers such as the *New York Times*, the *Washington Post*, the *Denver Post, New York Newsday*, the *San Francisco Chronicle*, the *Los Angeles Times*, the *Wall Street Journal*, and their equivalents all around the world. Cartoons, sitcoms and talk shows refer to it, and it crops up in novels and short stories. Feng shui has become more than a mere curiosity: it is becoming woven into the very fabric of Western life. Property developers are embracing it to attract investors and renters, some executives are using it in their offices as a new tool to gain power and wealth. More and more architects and designers employ consultants or say they factor feng shui into their blueprints, some for design purposes, some for marketing reasons. The roster of those who have purportedly used it reads like a publicist's A-list: Prince Charles, Madonna, Donald Trump, Marla Maples Trump, Rita Wilson (Tom

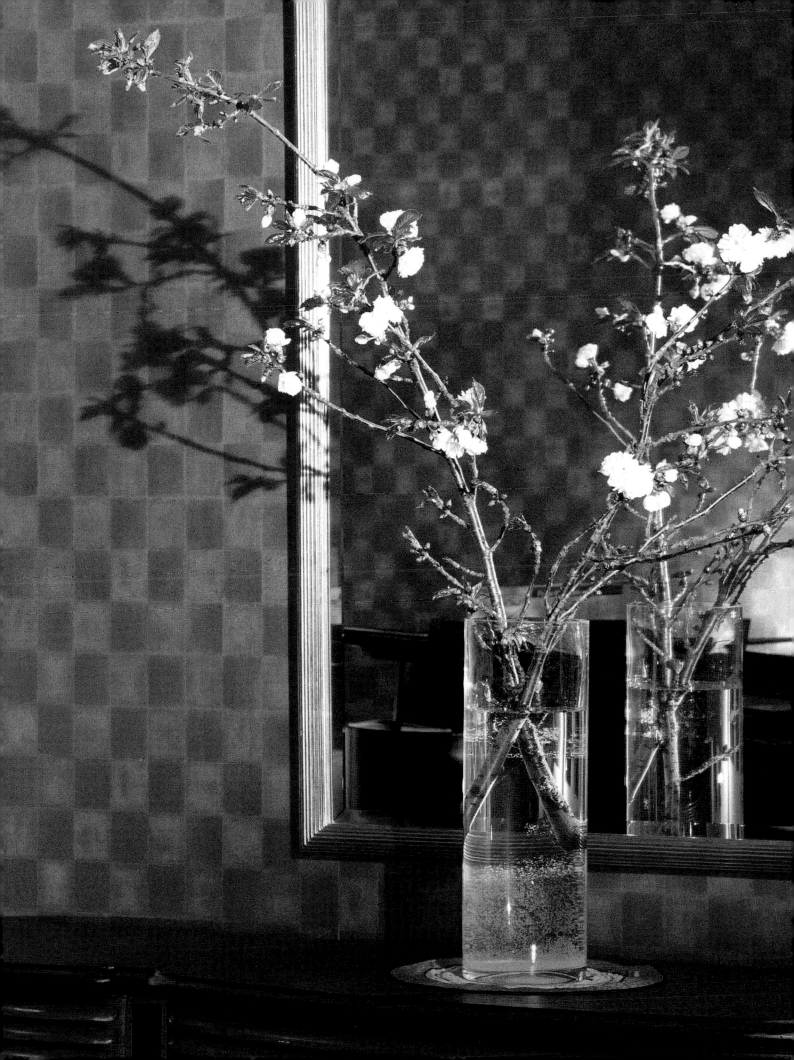

Hanks's actress wife), Eartha Kitt, Lynne Franks, Michael Crichton, the Duchess of York, Michael Ovitz, Sir Richard Greenway of Marks & Spencer—to mention a few.

Feng shui is more than just a New Age quick fix, or a trendy dinner-party topic. If properly applied, it tends to improve interiors, and improved interiors tend to enhance their occupants' lives. There is, however, no guarantee—and feng shui is rarely a source of miracles.

The book, in a sense, is a marriage of both my and Master Lin Yun's lectures. My own talks—given at the Museum of Fine Arts in Boston, the Asia Society, the China Institute, the University of Chicago, Wharton Business School—tend to be historical, and are illustrated by photographs taken by Penny Coleman. While traveling through China, Penny and I documented numerous ancient Chinese sites that were influenced by feng shui. I feel that to fully appreciate the scope of the art, one must return to its origins and chart its development. Its earliest themes—such as the powerful effect of the environment on humans, the influence of auspicious and positive symbolism on our psyches, the balance of nature and ch'i, the landscape as metaphor and the need for protection and guardians, re-creating the calm and peace of nature—recur throughout the practice of modern feng shui.

The modern feng shui guidelines in this book derive directly and indirectly from Master Lin Yun's talks as well as from his replies to my frantic faxes. The earliest of these talks began in 1977 when I was living and working in Hong Kong under a journalism fellowship. At the time, I must admit I thought feng shui was a bizarre yet intriguing custom. I was planning to be a foreign correspondent in Beijing. But fate in the form of Chinese language lessons with a Yale-in-China professor intercepted my original plans. As my language instructor, Master Lin Yun would meet me in a Hong Kong hotel lobby and we would trudge through dogmatic texts of Chinese cadres' heroic exploits over glasses of orange juice. However, we were frequently interrupted by desperate individuals seeking feng shui help. Closing our textbook, Master Lin would ask me not to pay him for the lesson, but to join him on his feng shui rounds: the home of an executive whose young wife had died in childbirth; the grave of the mother of an investment banker with financial problems; the home of a foreign journalist with a strained marriage. Or merely tea with an Asian beauty queen, stewardess or actress seeking advice on which boyfriend to marry.

My own experience with feng shui has been serendipitous. While Master Lin has always encouraged me to consult on feng shui, this was not in my personal life plans. I am, however, fascinated by China and its past, and when I returned to the United States, I wrote a short piece on feng shui for the *New York Times*. The day it ran, I was approached to write a book on the subject, which I researched for three years in Asia and the USA, the result being *Feng Shui: The Chinese Art of Placement*. After it was published, I began to receive calls from artists, cooks, business people, all seeking feng shui advice. This prompted *Interior Design with Feng Shui*, intended as a practical guide for Westerners. *Living Color*, written with Master Lin, followed a few years later. This book, however, is the culmination of my experience with feng shui: a three-decade fascination with China, Chinese customs and culture; over two decades of working and studying with (and haranguing!) Master Lin; more than one decade of consulting for architects and designers, particularly Clodagh; and a conviction that only when one is visually guided through many sites, both ancient and modern, can one fully appreciate feng shui and all its facets.

This book is not just the work of two individuals. Many friends and professionals have contributed their time and help. We would like to acknowledge the efforts of Mary Testa Bakht of the Hong Kong Tourist Association, and Tom Rosenthal, press officer of the Hong Kong Economic and Trade Office. An impressive array of designers and architects were very generous with their time: Bernardo Fort-Brescia and Laurinda Spear of Arquitectonica; Steven Robinson of Steven Robinson Architects; Randy Martin; Rob Whitlock and James von Klemperer of Kohn Pederson Fox; John Kinnear and Kelly Longwell of Janko Rasic Associates; David Van Buren of David Van Buren Architects; Wayne Turett of Turett Collaborative Architects; Susan Aiello; Fred McNeese; Dennis Wilhelm; Alison Hecht; Diana Metcalf; Ellen Sweeney; Charles Jencks; the artist Mel Chin; Topher Delany of Delany, Cochran & Castillo. Clodagh has been a great friend and support, and her partner, Robert Pierpoint, and their staff at Clodagh Design International have also been invaluable. A big thank you goes to friend and colleague Kathryn Glenchur, a designer studying sacred architecture in China. On the corporate side, we would like to thank Elektra Entertainment, Dentsu, Tommy Boy Music, Ginny Kamsky of Kamsky Associates International, Noelle Spa for Wellness & Beauty, Elizabeth Arden, Gerald Peters Gallery, Jamson Whyte, Felissimo, the Hongkong & Shanghai Bank, Art Samansky, the Four Winds Restaurant, Flower Lounge. Individually, we appreciate with all our hearts the help and support of Crystal Chu, Yang Wei, Lin Gu-hu, Ann Rossbach, Howard and Katie Rossbach, Anne and Ernie Munch, Kim Widener, Naoto Nakagawa, Alessandra and Henry Devine, Courtney Beinhorn, Bill and Lucy Bogdon, Diana and Pepe Gomez, Susan Mindham, Martin Marx, Dick Davis, Susan Fowler, Ara and Rachel Hovnanian, An-le Chang, Dary Derchin, Wilson and Tzu-wei Chang, Holly Huang, Ly-ping Wu, Lien Nguyen, Nancy Yang, Frances Li, Shena Huang, Daiana Leung, Jonathan Chau, Mary Hsu, Albert Lu, Camille Jensen, Lauren Graham, Cindy Bruckmann, Kathy Adler, Kathy Woo, Tommy Huen and Liloo Akim of the Four Seasons Hotel, Toronto, Ken Yeh, Doreen and Kenny Wang, Gail and Charles Slingluff, Sandy Henning, Rita and Robert Boyle, Liz and Arvi Sood, Pieter Estersohn. On the home front, SR would like to thank with big hugs her children B and C, as well as her husband D, and for all their support Pauline Greene and the Granny Nanny clipping service of Connie and Ellie. Thank you to Trip Emerson and Lon Cohen for their patient and talented efforts to illustrate the book, and to gifted photographers Daniel Aubry, with the help of his staff, who shot the modern sites, and Penny Coleman, who photographed the historical sites in China. Furthermore, we would like to thank Caroline Press, our agent, for all her hard labor, and our long-distance editor, Gordon Wise, who first approached us to embark on this project.

Sarah Rossbach

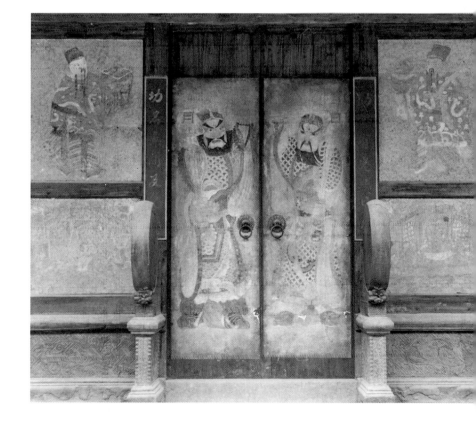

This doorway in China's Cheng Kan province is flanked by "spirit screens" Festooned with door guardians in the form of inscriptions and symbols, they protect the Luo family ancestral hall (Luo Jia Chi Tang).

Introduction

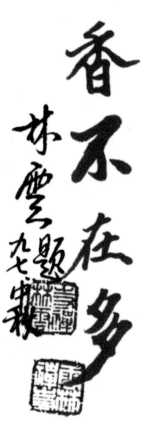

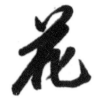

Feng shui has recently become very popular far beyond its native China. New books seem to be published almost in succession, with many schools of thought vying for attention. Perhaps this is because "East winds are felt in the West," as the old adage goes. Another saying has it that "every ten years, feng shui takes a turn." Whatever the case, the ch'i of ancient Eastern culture seems to be slowly but surely permeating the West.

Geomancers from several different countries have told me that it is Sarah Rossbach's three books, *Feng Shui: The Chinese Art of Placement, Interior Design with Feng Shui* and *Living Color,* that have drawn them to the study of Chinese feng shui. This places a lot of credit at the feet of one person, but I can well believe it. Certainly for my part, I am invited all over the world to lecture due to the wide outreach of these books. At the conclusion of each lecture, I invariably find myself presented with the surprising and precious gift of a copy of one of them in the language of that country—whether French, German, Italian, Thai, Vietnamese or Chinese.

Feng Shui Design is our fourth book collaboration. Our aim is to emphasize the use of modern knowledge and modern examples to explain feng shui, while abiding by the evolutionary process of feng shui from ancient times to the present. Hence the book endeavors to explain both ancient gardens and modern landscape gardening, and both traditional homes and contemporary living environments. We have used a wide range of examples, from the design of dining rooms, bedrooms and hallways to the siting of garages, shapes of paths and driveways and the layout of gardens, to clarify how the use of feng shui can and will affect your life. Our abiding principle, however, is that we consider feng shui to be an ancient concept, in existence since the beginning of human civilization, and not merely since the publication of books about feng shui.

When the inhabitants of ancient China were looking for suitable land on which to live and farm, they had already discerned this knowledge and discovered these principles. Over thousands of years, these have been modified, adjusted and refined by succeeding generations; thus feng shui has become a geographic and geomantic art form.

Just as for flowers to be fragrant, there do not have to be many ...

... so for a room to be elegant, it does not have to be large.

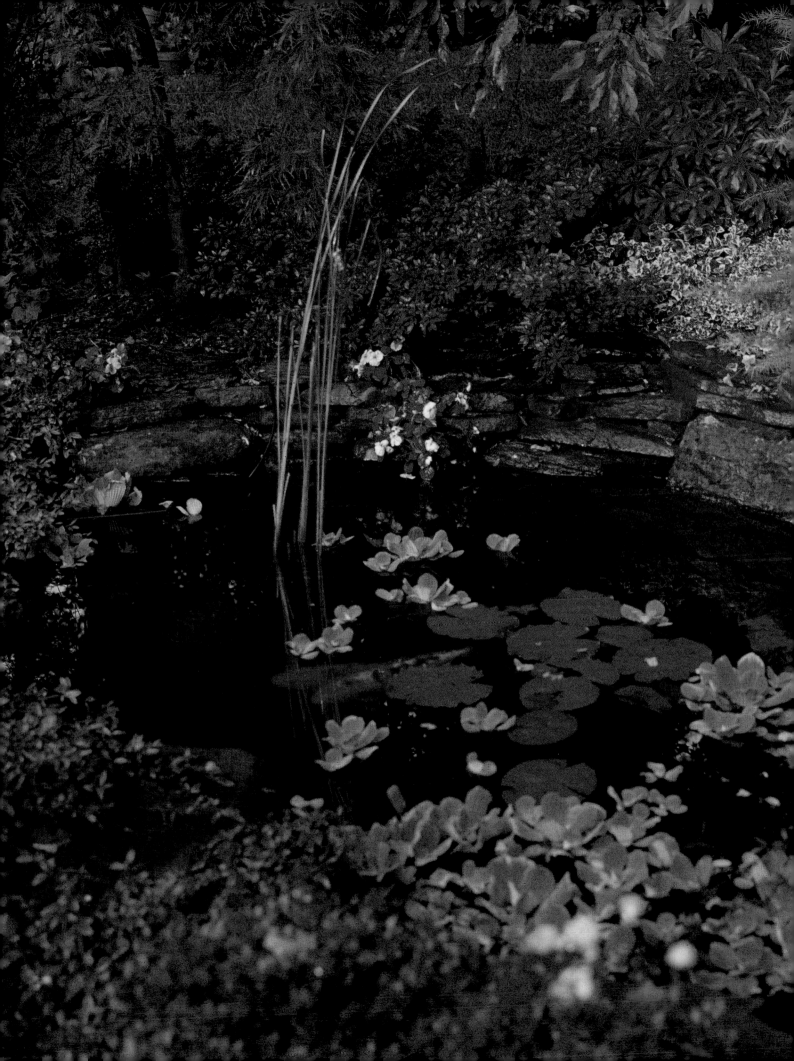

Some people feel that feng shui is nothing more than superstition. We have respect for all points of view, and our aim is not to force others to believe or disbelieve—everything should follow karma. But the new definition I have given feng shui is that it occurs when people, using the knowledge they have available to them at any one point in time, choose, create or build the safest and most suitable living and working environment for their needs. Naturally, this includes landscape design, architecture, bridge-building and road-paving, designing houses for the living, houses for the dead, temples, government agencies, business and industrial buildings, offices—and more. It covers more ritualistic aspects too, such as selecting auspicious dates for certain events, ground breaking for construction projects, erecting a building's main structural beam, installing the stove, blessing a site or a person, expelling evil or sickness, and maintaining wealth and safety.

In the course of this work, we have found that two distinct themes emerge. One is that *the fundamental principles and ideas of feng shui have never changed.* They are the consistent criteria upon which five thousand years of Chinese architectural history and culture are based. In terms of architecture in particular, no matter how styles may change, people are always looking for the safest, healthiest, happiest and most comfortable living situation. So we examine feng shui from the perspective of an ancient culture, in the hope that in this way readers will absorb something of the essence of traditional Chinese geomancy.

On the other hand, we also understand feng shui to be *an art form that is alive.* It is not fixed and immutable, constrained by dogma. Rather, it is a knowledge that never ceases to evolve. In prehistory, some groups of primitive man lived in trees, believing nest-dwelling to be the safest and most comfortable means of shelter. Later, cavemen made fire with branches, and felt that living in caves was the most convenient and most suitable habitat. Now, we live in an age of high technology, with electricity in daily use, computers revolutionizing our existence continually. Architecture is at the vanguard of the high-tech revolution, with construction projects involving bridges that cross the sea, skyscrapers, airports built on reclaimed land, and artificial harbors commonplace. In the footsteps of our predecessors, we use the knowledge available to us to create environments most suitable for living and working in at this point in time. At every stage in history this level of knowledge is different. And so, too, at every stage is mankind's perception of feng shui different. It constantly evolves through changing knowledge.

The *I* ("change") in the *I Ching* (*Book of Changes*) has the implied meaning of both "never-changing" and "ever-changing." This is paralleled in the study of feng shui. It has fixed fundamental principles (never-changing), yet it also has tools, designs and methods that are augmented or updated with the passage of time and further accumulation of knowledge (ever-changing). Thus feng shui progresses, and remains attuned to changing needs governed by geography, geology, ecology, building technology and society. But certain basic tenets, such as mankind's reverence for, and harmonious treatment of, nature, the pursuit of balance and control of natural energy (ch'i), and the acknowledgment that our interior and exterior environments influence our lives, should never change.

However, the balance between mankind and the universe is nevertheless very strained, and achieving it is a formidable task. "Balance" and "harmonious development" are embodied in the Tao, according to the *I Ching*. As this book will explain, the concept of Tao takes everything in the universe and splits it in two, yin and yang. The Chinese universe consists of heaven (yang) and earth (yin). Heaven itself consists of the sun (yang) and the moon (yin). In turn, earth consists of rivers and streams (yang), and mountains and plains (yin). On those mountains and plains, there are people

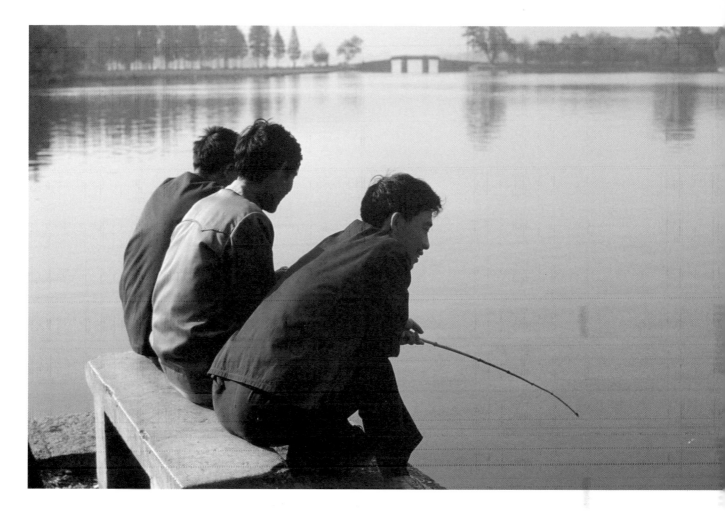

(yang) and buildings (yin). In people themselves, males (yang) and females (yin) possess an exterior (yang) and interior (yin). Through harmony between the yin and the yang, mankind will bond closely with heaven, earth, mountains, rivers, family and office. And the overall interplay between yin and yang forms energy: ch'i.

According to the theories of Black Sect Tantric Buddhism, we have to consider yin and yang when studying feng shui. Visible aspects of feng shui (*sying*, or form), that which can be seen, is yang, whereas the invisible aspects (*yi*, or intuitive), that which cannot be seen, is yin. Things that can be verbally communicated are reasoning; those that cannot, we communicate transcendentally through ch'i.

In the universe, there are many kinds of ch'i. Heaven has heaven ch'i, the earth has earth ch'i, and people have human ch'i. Our lives are formed by our many personal types of ch'i. If we can maneuver and control the ch'i of our surroundings, we can then enhance and fine-tune our internal ch'i and improve our lives and our fates. One of the methods of maneuvering and controlling ch'i is feng shui.

Chinese often say that the five key factors influencing our lives, in descending order of significance, are 1) destiny, 2) luck, 3) feng shui, 4) to do good deeds anonymously (*yin de*), and 5) education. So we should bear in mind that feng shui is but one element of a successful life; the others should be equally stressed, and practiced. However, if we only focus on the other elements, and neglect or abandon feng shui, then it would be equally difficult to achieve success.

As they have for generations and down the centuries, fishermen by West Lake in Hangchow pursue nourishing fish and enjoy the reflective calm of the lake.

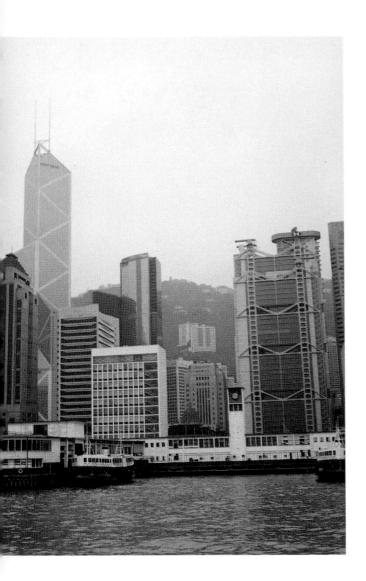

It is very important to have an understanding of these ideals when pursuing our goals in life. In order to become successful feng shui practitioners, I ask that my students and friends possess the following:

◆ *a loving heart, and a willingness to help others;*
◆ *an understanding of how to practice and utilize both physical and more transcendental solutions of feng shui, and to have a full understanding of the basic concepts and methods of these;*
◆ *the willingness to learn and research at any time, and to have a thorough understanding of what is classical, modern, Eastern and Western, as well as to have respect for other religions and schools of feng shui;*
◆ *personal spiritual cultivation.*

Over twenty years ago, Sarah Rossbach began studying Chinese language, folklore and culture with me, which included studying ch'i and feng shui. At that time, she would regularly accompany me to sites, and there learn how to use both practical and transcendental solutions as I worked to adjust feng shui for my friends. Our visits included appointments with companies, at factories, offices, administration buildings, restaurants, hotels and banks, as well as at houses for the living and houses for the dead. Sarah is best described as the kind of person who, in the words of an ancient Chinese saying, "Whenever drinking water, think of the source." According to traditional Chinese folklore, feng shui and divination, it is very important to emphasize

The Bank of China towers over its Hong Kong neighbors, who claim that its sharp mirrored angles point at them in a threatening manner, their reflections appearing at a distorted disadvantage.

who your teacher is, and from where your wisdom comes. It seems that nowadays too many people forget their teacher once they begin to achieve even a little fame and success for themselves.

Sarah also has a sincere heart. Having carefully studied Eastern culture, her desire is to introduce others with a good heart, sense of knowledge, good fortune and karma to those aspects which she has ascertained to be beneficial to the West, so that they in turn may propagate them further. Our belief is that people living in all countries of the world will attain more happiness, health, wisdom and success in their daily lives through good feng shui and positive ch'i cultivation.

Sarah's contribution to this book has been much larger than mine. I have found it difficult to find someone who is truly able and truly willing to help me, even among my many students, friends and people with the same ideals. While some are willing and offer moral support, what they know is limited. Others who are able have already started their own schools, and are reaping in their own fortunes. Further, someone who at once embodies spiritual cultivation, compassion and patience is a rare find. In my experience, some people with psychic or spiritual powers are sometimes arrogant, intolerant and selfish. However, Sarah is a most suitable collaborator, and we have always enjoyed a very fruitful partnership.

So *Feng Shui Design* reflects a vital modern form of an ancient tradition. It emphasizes the balanced and harmonious concept of Tao, yet uses contemporary knowledge, sympathy with modern lifestyles and awareness of new inventions to unite Eastern ideologies and Western concepts, while blending together wisdom, theories and practicality. From the yin perspective, there is the stable, never-changing, deeply rooted knowledge of ancient traditions. From the yang, there is preparedness for never-ending changes to match the needs of our time.

This book was written with the intention of assisting readers to achieve a broader and deeper understanding of the study of feng shui. It may therefore be very different from many others now available, although our aim is not to provoke contradictions, but to explain and present our reasoning. We welcome your comments and suggestions.

Master Lin Yun

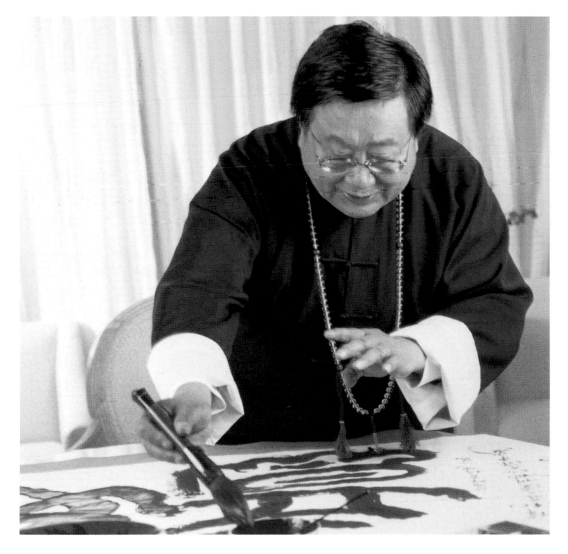

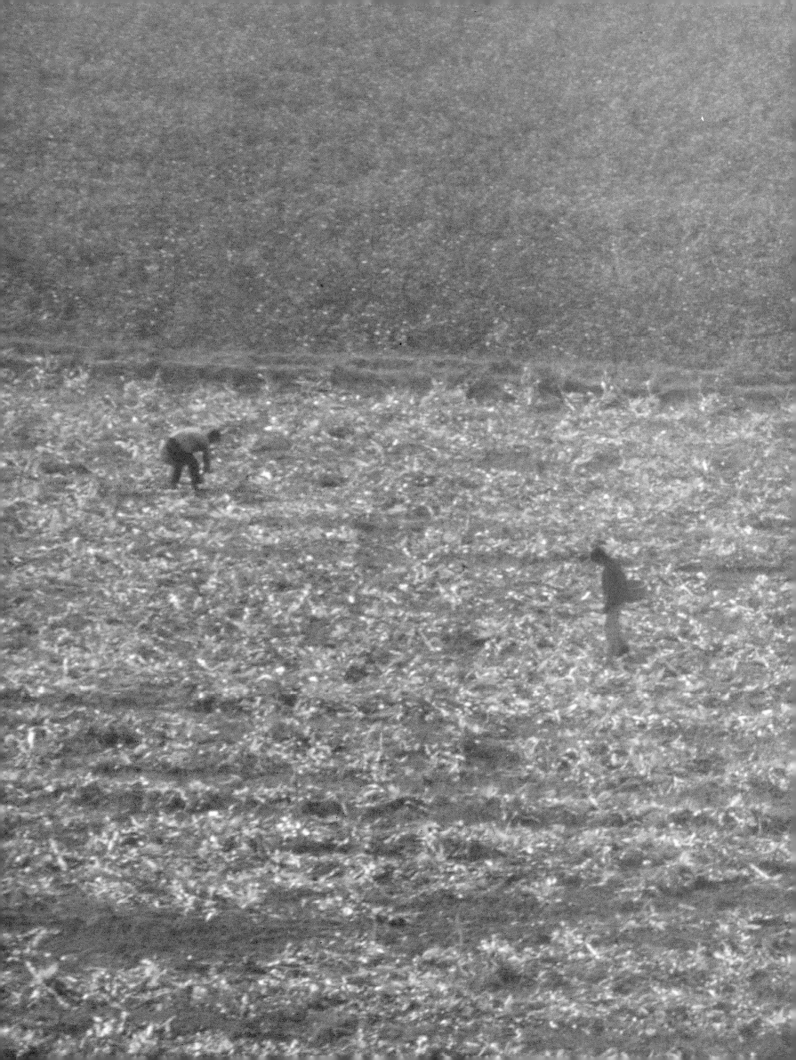

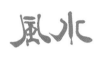

FENG SHUI'S HISTORICAL ROOTS

Feng shui was born out of China's agrarian tradition. Farmers' struggle to survive and eventually prosper depended on understanding the changes and forces of nature. Feng shui was—and still is—the study of how we are affected by the environment, and how to manipulate our surroundings to enhance our lives and our fortunes.

CHAPTER I

Feng Shui Today

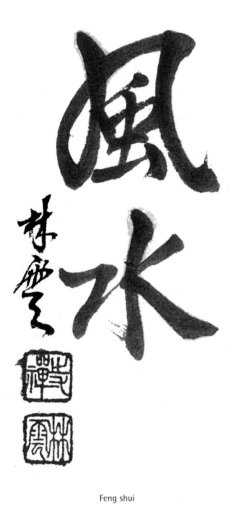

Feng shui

In the United States, a family hangs a cut-glass crystal ball in the corridor leading directly from the front door to the back of their home, hoping to stem loss of clients and revenues in the husband's business. In Hong Kong, a developer altered the position of his new high-rise's front door to ensure a stable and full occupancy rate. In London, Marks & Spencer has executive offices appraised by a feng shui expert to enhance British business prospects in the way feng shui improved profits in its Asian stores. And in New York, Donald Trump has installed a large metal globe in front of his new Trump International Tower and Hotel on Columbus Circle, to soften the negative effect of strong ch'i created by frenzied traffic patterns and the intersecting fast roads that aim at the building like so many sharp pins in a cushion. These are only a few recent examples of people worldwide employing the ancient art of feng shui to enhance their health, wealth and lives.

Feng shui, pronounced "fung shway," literally translates as "wind" and "water" and traces its roots back thousands of years to the beginning of Chinese agrarian life, when early settlers sought harmony with natural forces to survive. The Chinese deduced that humans are affected for good or ill by their environment, that every hill, river, tree, wall, window or corner has an effect. They concluded that if you changed your surroundings you could change your life. One result of these early observations was feng shui, the practical, yet sacred, art of positioning humans within a vast, beautiful and untamed universe. And the ideal was to locate a home, farm or city in harmony with natural forces and the universe so that good fortune would befall its residents.

Feng shui encompasses many areas, ranging from aesthetic appreciation to a complete metaphysical design system. Its uses can range from siting an entire city to placing a vase of flowers in a room. The aesthetic of feng shui is the sense of balance that one experiences when gazing on, or living in, a particularly harmonious environment. Its metaphysics is that it links humans with their environment. Its philosophy is that balanced surroundings positively affect the health, fortunes and lives of inhabitants, and is based on ancient observations that if you can improve your environment, you can improve your life.

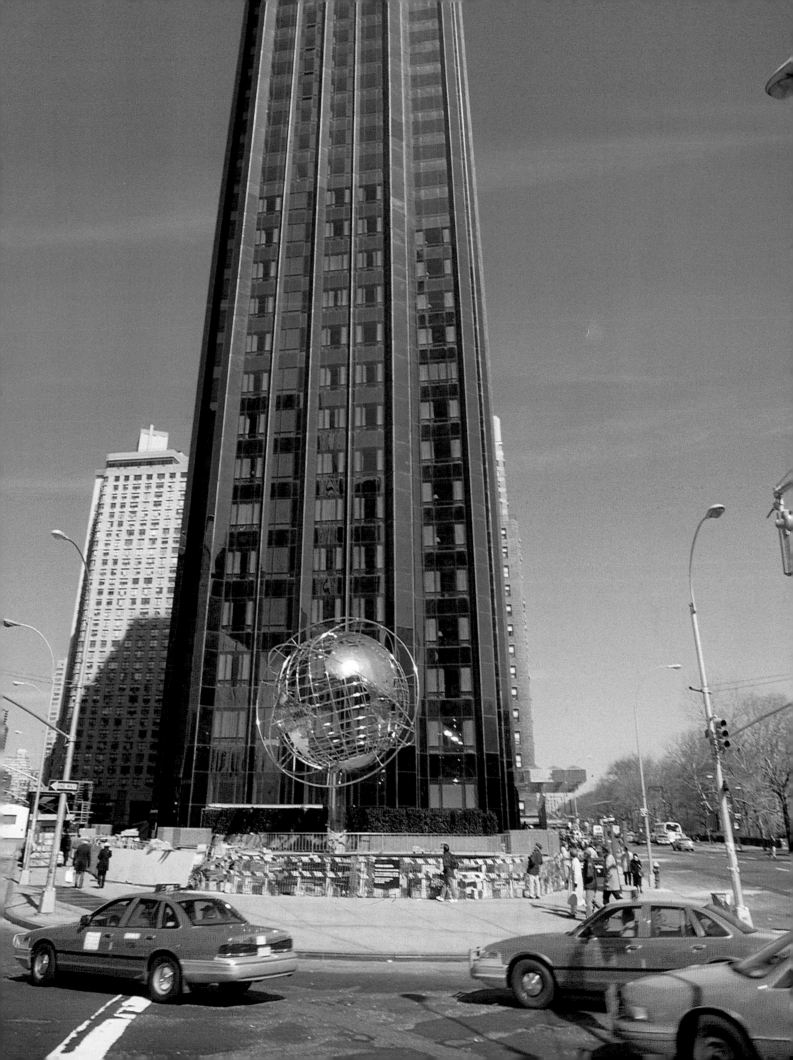

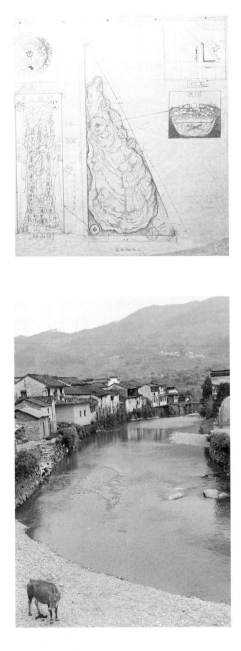

Over the millennia, feng shui grew to have a profound effect on Chinese architecture, city planning, landscaping, interior design and even the planning and placement of graves. For thousands of years, emperors used it to maintain and to increase power: palaces and imperial cities were sited and laid out to best tap into nature's positive forces, and to create a harmonious site on earth that helped the emperor both to mediate successfully with heaven in order to bestow positive growing conditions and abundant harvests, and to govern wisely and powerfully on earth. Villages and farms were sited to best tap into nature's forces to aid human survival, comfort and endeavors, to bring about in their turn good health, good crops and good fortune.

Today, feng shui is the experience of living or working in any environment, interior and exterior, natural or man-made. Its goals echo the aims of ancient Chinese practitioners. It still seeks to decode the silent dialogue between humans and their surroundings, a language articulated through natural forms and phenomena, man-made structures and symbols, and by the continual patterns, changes and cycles of nature and the universe. All existence, according to feng shui, is interrelated, bound by a common, yet shifting, cosmic energy or spirit: ch'i. Translated as "breath," this is a life force that links humans to their surroundings, the energy that undulates waves, creates mountains, breathes life into plants, animals and humans and propels us along a life course.

There are three major interrelated themes that run through feng shui, whether one is considering an early Chinese palace, a farmhouse or a twentieth-century home or office:

◆ *The first is that humans are affected by their surroundings. The siting of a building, landscaping, views, shapes of homes and businesses, color and lighting, structure and furniture arrangement all shape our outlook and moods, our habits and personalities, our physical and mental health, our performance at home and work, our personal and professional relationships—and ultimately our lives and destiny. In ecological terms, human destiny is certainly linked to the environment.*

◆ *The second is that feng shui is a language of symbols: it interprets how the color of a leaf, the shape of a hill or a house, the position of a bed or a desk, the direction of a road or a river, the decoration on a building or in a home*

Top, artist Mel Chin's design for an urban regeneration scheme in New York's Chinatown. The shape of the site on which the park was to be sited was interpreted as being like an oyster. Below, an auspiciously sited village in An Hui province, backed by mountains and facing a meandering river to the south.

become messages that influence and shape our lives. Ancient Chinese masters of the art would analyze and interpret feng shui by identifying the meaning of mountain shapes, and scrutinizing the configurations of lakes, rivers and streams.

◆ *The third theme is that feng shui is a form of literal metaphysics. It emerged through the centuries as an eclectic mixture of Chinese philosophy, religion, folk cures and early science. Through ch'i, human life is linked to nature and the rhythm of the universe. And by understanding the workings of ch'i and nature, the feng shui master seeks to maintain or create balanced living environments that replicate the harmony of nature. Ultimately, feng shui is used to improve human ch'i by adjusting, enhancing and balancing environmental ch'i.*

Over feng shui's long life, what has it become? Ironically, in China, the land of its origins, it is officially, if unsuccessfully, condemned and suppressed by the government. Yet in town after town locals still seek feng shui advice when building a home, moving into a new shop or burying a member of their family. Some villages are being rebuilt using the advice of local feng shui masters. And here and there, new horseshoe-shaped graves are sprouting up on hillsides, although more likely as evidence of superstitious tenacity than political defiance. It is unclear whether a new museum constructed in Shanghai along the lines of ancient Chinese architecture incorporated feng shui vernacular and design on purpose or inadvertently.

In Hong Kong, in spite of the former colony's reversion to Chinese rule, business people fall silent when asked about feng shui, yet when Tung Chee-hwa, its first Chinese leader, went office-hunting, he brought his trusty feng shui master with him. (The master wisely advised him not to step into his predecessor's shoes and move into the colonial government house, but to seek new and more auspicious quarters.)

Throughout Asia, where the largest building boom of the 1990s is taking place, the ancient practice of feng shui is often a major consideration for any architectural firm or property developer in the design of the ubiquitous ultra-modern high-rises. But perceived benefits aside, it has also become a technical issue with some Western insurance companies who, after insuring a building, discover that the owners will make feng shui alterations that break building codes and affect insurability. In

Even today in Hong Kong, thousands of graves seem to occupy the most prime real estate, with auspicious views out to the South China Sea and its islands. Some are constructed in a horseshoe shape to embrace good fortune and good opportunities for succeeding generations; others use Western-style headstones to absorb good luck for offspring.

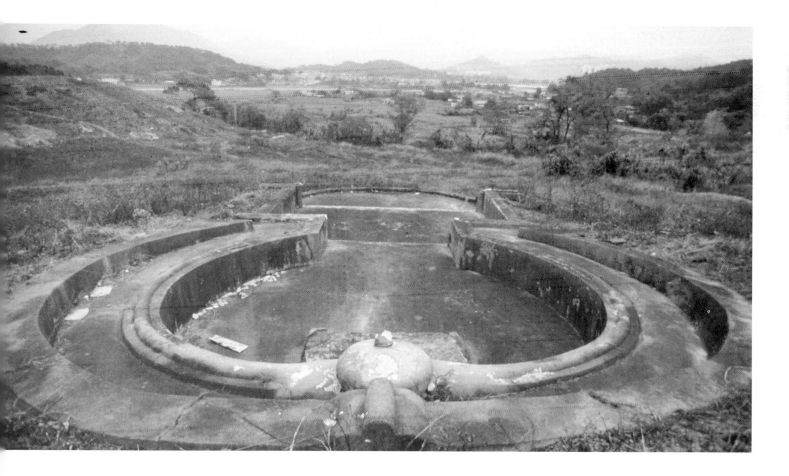

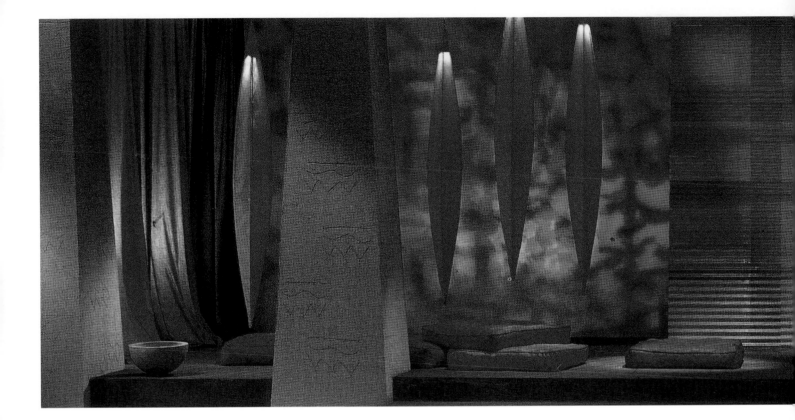

This installation was created by Clodagh for the fabric company Trevira, for a Brussels trade fair. It takes into account feng shui principles, such as use of water, light, color, movement, sound and scent, to provide an oasis away from the stress and strain of a long day at the fair.

Singapore, architects and developers have to address both stringent building codes and feng shui.

And now, feng shui has entered the West and Western consciousness. There are those who have known about it for decades. Edmund Bacon, author of *Design of Cities*, commented during an informal chat that when he was studying architecture in China in the 1930s, he and a fellow student coined nicknames for each other: one was "feng" and the other was "shui." He went on to say that he was influenced by feng shui's use in classical Chinese city plans. For years, Western expatriates have used it in offices to appease Asian employees. Some repatriated converts have sent detailed plans of offices or homes to a favored master in Asia, hoping to ensure that their new location in the West is harmonious. But today in the West there are many different practices of feng shui, all of which have been altered to suit modern-day life. There is traditional feng shui: the Nine Star School, the Yin-yang School, the Compass School, etc. And there is the less traditional Black Sect feng shui, which supplies the rules in this book. There is also Western feng shui, a new development, which seems to be an interpretive practice embracing both practical and "mystical" means, some derived from other cultures and traditions. Its consultants sometimes are not well schooled in, or ignore, Chinese beliefs. For example, an article in British *Vogue* featured a couple who had built their "feng shuied" house with lovely glass walls on a site overlooking a graveyard—which any Chinese knows is bad feng shui. (The Chinese studiously avoid any death-oriented symbolism such as coffin-shaped driveways, or views of smokestacks that remind them of the incense used to appease the dead.)

While change is important and necessary for a custom to survive and meet modern needs, some Westerners have taken liberties that run counter to feng shui precepts, and seek to help

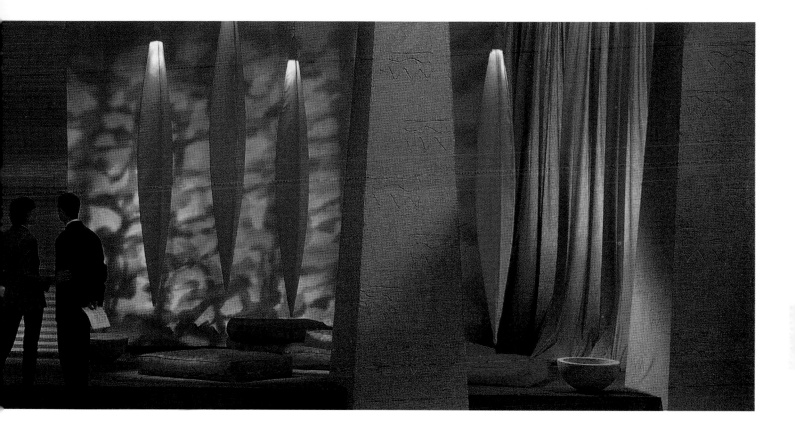

themselves rather than their clients. Western feng shui also differs from its Chinese counterpart in that in China the expert did not market himself, but relied on his reputation. In the West, there are feng shui conferences and symposiums, feng shui tours and cruises, "accreditation" courses, feng shui institutes, feng shui consultants armed with publicists and groupies, countless Internet pages and Web sites. Indeed, feng shui has become a marketing gimmick be it for Northwest Airlines or for the *Asian Wall Street Journal*.

Today in the West there is no real quality control with regard to feng shui. It is practiced on many levels, by people of varying knowledge, talents and purposes. They may range from masters—though only a few exist in the West—to an individual using basic rules out of a book to create comfortable living quarters. In between are architects and designers who may use feng shui to inform their designs, and active students ranging from those who have only taken a weekend course in feng shui, to serious full-time practitioners. Some of these advanced students are so well schooled in feng shui ritual that they are able not only to help to auspiciously rearrange the physical environment, but also to create more positive energy through blessings.

Consultation fees range from a couple of hundred dollars to, reportedly, a couple of hundred thousand dollars for some large Asian projects. One international hotel in China paid $50,000 to a Hong Kong consultant for a single day's work, and the general manager reports that business has not improved.

Feng shui is an inexact art/science. Each practitioner brings his or her own insights, knowledge and personality into a space. When deciding on a consultant, get references and spend time talking to him or her. Find out where and how they studied. Enlisting the help of a feng shui consultant is like looking for a wise and capable doctor: look at your home or office interior as you would at your health. One consultant might suggest the equivalent of an operation while another might know a less intrusive cure. When Molly O'Neill interviewed four feng shui professionals for a *New York Times* story, she found that the "less experienced consultants called for more expensive solutions." (This discrepancy seems to echo that in ancient China, where feng shui "experts" encompassed a range from charlatan to wise man. Some of the cures were so bogus that "feng shui professor" became a term for "liar.") Indeed, a consultant with only a little knowledge can create further problems for a place by offering facile and expensive cures involving major structural work, when a simpler cure such as a well-placed mirror might not only remedy the problem, but also encourage further benefits (see page 40). Knowledge mixed with intuition, imagination, sensitivity, personal discernment and good judgment are all important characteristics when seeking to examine and harmonize a site.

Like its name, "wind-water," feng shui is fluid. There are basic rules of application, but cures and how to exercise them to create positive feng shui will vary from consultant to consultant. Even experts with similar training use their own discretion and creativity in different ways. Perhaps even more important is the client, with whose tastes the consultant must harmonize. Along with knowledge and spiritual training, compassion and instinctive awareness of the client's needs are crucial attributes for the expert to bring to any site.

The interest in feng shui in the West is spurred by Westerners seeking to improve their lives by "balancing" their homes and offices, as well as by a growing number of real estate agents and developers who are finding it good business sense to embrace feng shui. The latter are seeking to build homes for Westerners now aware of feng shui's precepts, as well as for Asians looking for homes, offices and capital investment opportunities in the West. "We keep feng shui's basic design parameters in mind when going forward with a community," comments Ara Hovnanian of K. Hovnanian, the ninth largest home-builder in the USA. "We use a summary of feng shui's basic design elements, such as door and window placement, and lucky or unlucky street numbers. It is particularly used in our southern Californian communities, which attract Asian home buyers." On the east coast of the United States, the company has also held a feng shui seminar for its contractors.

There are three basic components to the feng shui consultation: the place, the expert and the client(s).

The client should ideally be involved in the process. While it is unnecessary for clients to divulge personal information, problems or hidden desires—often the expert will intuit these—they should be ready to participate in the process, if only to express disagreement with a proposed cure, which may not go with their space or taste.

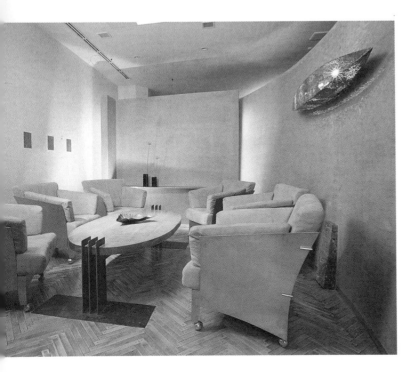

Feng shui in a corporate setting—and its totality underlined by the fact that here is Chinese wisdom deployed by a Western designer in a Japanese setting. This informal basement meeting room, by Clodagh for the Tokyo advertising agency Dentsu, appears to enjoy natural light through the use of a back-lit screen. Curving walls soften the subterranean setting, and the use of natural wood finishes provides grounding warmth.

Properly installed, feng shui can go with any taste—be it French, Japanese, modern or bad. Often, a client reveals hopes and fears, and the consultant optimally serves as a facilitator and healer by manipulating the space and flow of ch'i, thus bringing a sense of well-being to the site. No matter what the practice, the aim of any good feng shui consultant should be to create a comfortable and harmonious space.

This book covers feng shui and its contribution to design. It seeks to help the reader to fully appreciate and understand its concepts, rules and sensibility—an awareness that we are affected by our environment. We trace feng shui's journey from ancient Chinese siting and building practice to its new role as a modern Western design tool. It is important to note that with the enormous variety of modern design, a book cannot cover every possible example and cure. However, if one grasps the basic concepts behind the examples and cures discussed, one should be able to adapt them positively to any appropriate situation.

Millennia-old themes from Chinese sacred architecture and landscaping recur in modern feng shui rules; ancient Chinese sensibility can inform the visual as well as the tactile experience of a place. As Kathryn Glenchur, a designer studying sacred architecture in China, comments, "Feng shui addresses the experience of changing perspective, alignment, scale and balance. It can be helpful today. For example, some architects design buildings to be viewed from a distance, but these buildings don't hold up well when viewed close up." The chapters on philosophy, history and landscaping seek to explain the concepts, rules, considerations, sensibilities and perspective behind the feng shui tradition. The modern architecture chapter addresses the evolution of feng shui to meet modern design needs, as well as its adaptation to soften the collision of Eastern and Western design practices.

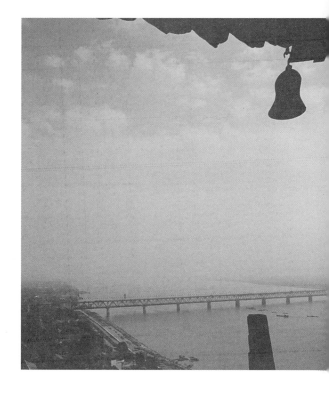

Feng shui experts may use small, symbolic gestures to seek to bring balance and improve a site. For example, this bell on the Pagoda of Six Harmonies in Hangchow could symbolically adjust ch'i flow, or wind and water currents.

Feng shui themes recur on an interior level where perspective, alignment and balance continue to be crucial elements to the experience of a place. Clodagh, a designer who since 1985 has employed a feng shui consultant on her projects, explains, "In a sense, it is mystical, but in fact it is practical and helps harmonize design. It makes one aware of line-ups and flow—what stops the eye and what makes you feel comfortable." The chapters on interior design focus on how feng shui principles and practice can be translated into positive modern design.

The key to feng shui is to tap into the energy of the environment in order to work and live to one's fullest potential. It both provides concrete rules and addresses the soul and spirit of a place; sensitive and visual, it explores the emotional content and messages of a space, or the objects within it. Through feng shui, design metaphor and symbolism, and the structure and layout of a place, reinforce our experience of that space, as well as reinforcing our hopes, intentions and destiny.

As this book seeks to help readers understand and appreciate feng shui today, it is first necessary to have an overview of its long journey through time and space. Through this we can come to understand how it evolved from an ancient Chinese art of placement to a modern design practice used in both East and West.

CHAPTER II

Philosophy and Divination

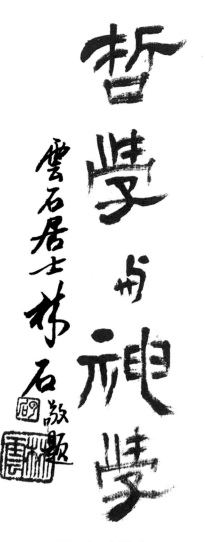

Philosophy and divination

China boasts some of the world's most impressive landscapes: massive mountains rising out of serene valleys; plateaus and plains bisected by rivers and streams. For thousands of years the Chinese have been inspired by these monumental, rugged mountain ranges and jagged peaks emerging over and into ethereal mists that float above green fields and rice paddies, fed by snaking rivers. Their awe and reverence of nature, as well as their ever-watchful eye towards its patterns and the fluctuations of its forces and forms, link, feed and inform nearly every pursuit.

Poets glorified nature's harmony, extolling its peace and beauty and celebrating such joys as still, moonlit lakes and the green hills of spring. Painters long sought to capture the expanse, energy, serenity and power of nature. On silk scrolls, they created nature in miniature: towering mountains, tall, rocky cliffs, straight waterfalls cascading like veils through clouds of misty voids into pools and streams crossed by bridge or forded on foot by the diminutive figure of a hermit sage or weary traveler. Taoist philosophers, ever observant of nature's patterns, sought harmony and identity with Tao, the "way" of the universe. From this awe and observation of nature grew early Chinese philosophy and religion, science (astronomy, geology, alchemy, magnetism), superstition (astrology, shamanism, fortune-telling), and feng shui, an art and science which weds all three.

Feng shui, like many Chinese disciplines ranging from calligraphy and landscape painting to martial arts, is a product of Chinese philosophy and religion, so a basic grasp of some Chinese concepts will help the reader understand how best to apply it. For example, the tie between humans and the universe (and the need for humans to harmonize with the universe) evolved from the concept of Tao.

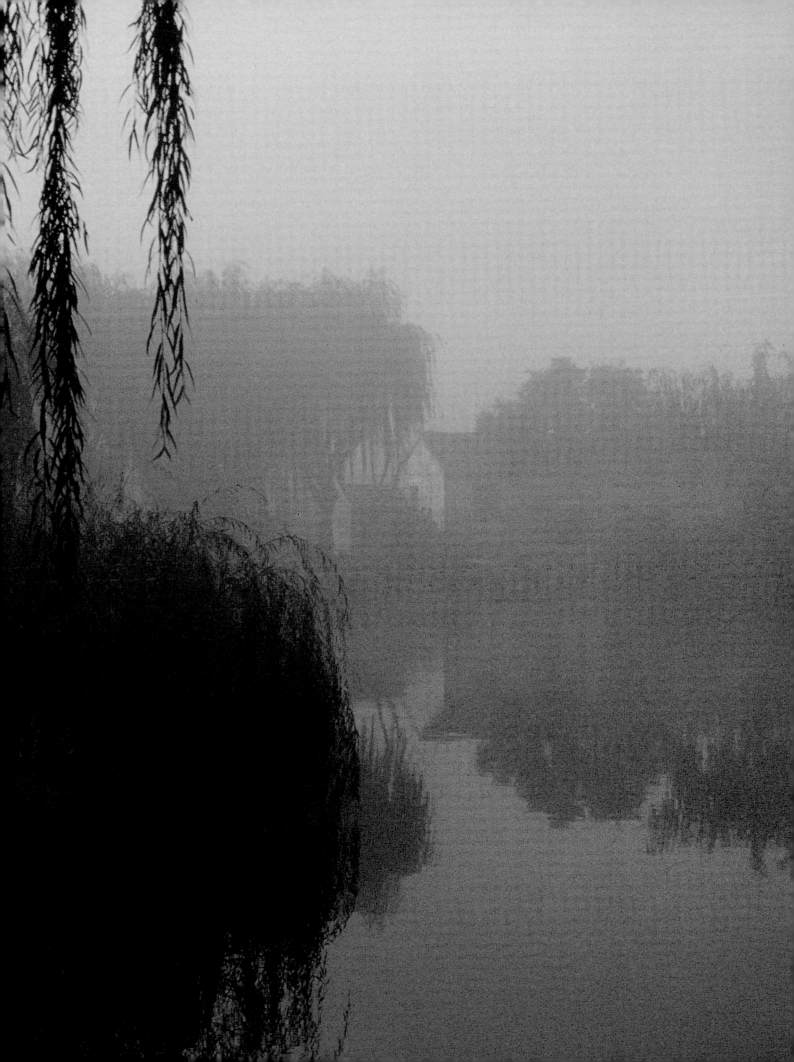

TAO

Tao, which translates as the "way," "path" or "principle," is both a concept and a process. As a concept, it is the way of nature, evoking the natural rhythms and balance of the universe. As a process, it is a continually moving pattern of the cosmos, a cosmos in constant flux. Tao also provides a pattern for man, for man and nature follow the same laws and paths. Man should mirror nature.

The story of Liu Ling, a third-century sage, reveals the strength of this identification with nature. Liu Ling occasionally lolled naked in his room. On greeting some shocked visitors, the sage commented, "I take the whole universe as my house and my own room as my clothing, why then, do you enter into my trousers?"

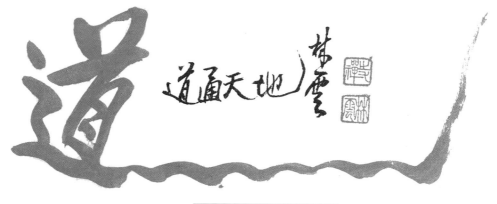

TAO—TAO UNITES HEAVEN AND EARTH

Tao also represents the wholeness of the universe. From observing the continual seasonal changes, the Chinese saw that opposites continually spawned each other, creating a whole, or Tao. Winter gave way to spring, summer and fall, only to have the cycle recur, year after year. Similarly, the sun at daybreak replaces the moon which, in turn, rises again at sunset, day after day. These were all noted as universal opposites, giving way to each other and creating a totality: Tao.

YIN AND YANG

Out of Tao come yin and yang, two forces that govern the universe. They are complementary opposites: yin is night, yang is day; yin is interior, yang is exterior; yin is feminine, yang is masculine. When united, they create the dynamic harmony of Tao. Like the positive and negative charges of a magnet or a battery, they express opposite sides of, and contribute to, the same thing.

Yin and yang are interdependent. Without the concept of dark (yin), the concept of light (yang) would not exist. Without the negative concept (yin), there would be no positive (yang).

Yin and yang also exist within each other. For example, within a man there exists a feminine side and within a woman there exists a masculine side. Nothing is totally black or white. The circular symbol of Tao, Tai-chi, epitomizes this concept: black and white halves are divided by a wavy line, and the interior of each contains a small circle of its opposite (see page 37). Everything is interrelated and interdependent.

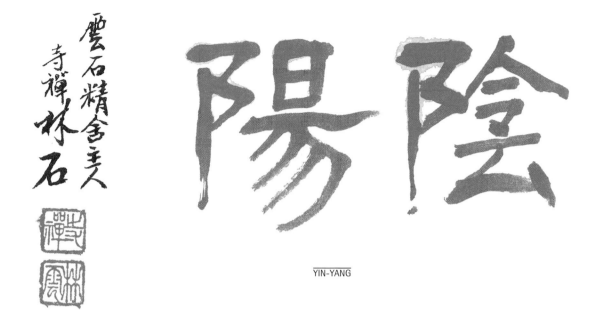

YIN-YANG

Ideally, yin and yang should naturally exist in a dynamic state of balance, the way of Tao. This harmony is expressed in feng shui in a number of ways: the balance of heaven (yang) and earth (yin), mountains (yang) and rivers (yin), homes of the living (yang) and homes of the dead (yin), homes and offices (yang) and people who live or work in them (yin). Feng shui is ultimately about manipulating the exterior world around us (yang) to maintain or create a balance within ourselves (yin).

CH'I

The most important concept in achieving good feng shui is ch'i. Translated as "breath," ch'i is a life force or cosmic energy. This ch'i is thought to ripple waves, create mountains, breathe life into plants, animals and humans and propel us, for better or worse, along a life course. Ch'i's vital force animates all things. Without ch'i's energy plants and trees would not bloom, mountains and hills would not form, rivers and streams would not run, animals and humans would not exist.

Ch'i circulates within the earth, spiraling around, constantly shifting, always pulsating. Sometimes it exhales towards the earth's surface creating a mountain or hill. If it is too strong, its force can push through the crust and erupt into a volcano. Sometimes, it inhales so far from the surface that the land is parched, flat and devoid of life. Ideally, ch'i should circulate so close to the earth's surface as to be nearly brushing it, causing hills to form, trees to grow and branch out, grass to be lush and green, air to be clear and fresh, water to be clean and accessible, flowers to blossom and humans to live healthy, happy and comfortable lives. If ch'i recedes too far from the earth's crust, water and earth dry up, pollution and illness abound and human life suffers. And while all things in the universe inhale or absorb ch'i, they also exhale it, thus affecting their surroundings.

As a concept, ch'i is a force present in many Chinese pursuits, ranging from landscape painting and feng shui to medicine and martial arts. It is the energy that links the mind to the heart to the body to our surrounding world. In Chinese painting, ch'i is a creative force that links the artist's inspiration through his body along his arm to his hand and brush to create a desired brush stroke. In Chinese

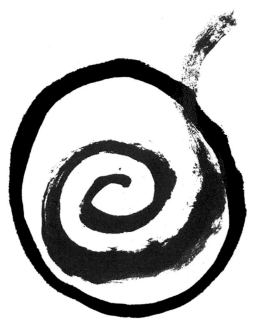

CH'I OF THE EARTH

martial arts, such as *gung fu* or *tai chi ch'uan*, ch'i is the controlled and concentrated power that is propelled through the body in blows, kicks and general movements. In Chinese medicine, the doctor or acupuncturist seeks points and flow of ch'i to analyze and cure patients. And in feng shui, the practitioner analyzes the exterior and interior of a home or an office to see how best to channel and enhance environmental energy, thus to improve the ch'i of occupants.

There are countless varieties of human ch'i. As the energy that circulates in our bodies it both moves us and motivates us, and sets our personalities and individual cadences as well as determining our potential and destiny. From the moment we are born, it flows throughout the body moving muscles and bones, stimulating emotional and physical reactions. It is our life force; without ch'i, we cannot live. While ideally ch'i should flow smoothly throughout every part of the body and up to the top of the head, few individuals have attained that balanced state. But if ch'i cannot flow to our legs, our legs cannot walk. If ch'i does not flow to our hands, we cannot touch or grasp. And if ch'i leaves our bodies, we cease to exist.

Ch'i determines human personalities. For example, a shy person who cannot express thoughts and feelings might have "choked" ch'i, which is caught in the throat, so that feelings and ideas are swallowed. A person who talks a lot without thinking might have ch'i that flows up to the mouth and out without touching the brain. A rigid person who can never compromise might have "bamboo" ch'i, which is as inflexible as its namesake.

The Chinese traditionally employ both exterior and internal means to adjust human ch'i through meditation, rituals, acupuncture, *ch'i gung* (exercise) and feng shui. In feng shui, experts try to manipulate surroundings so that the flow of environmental ch'i enhances and adjusts human ch'i, so that people can live more positive, healthy, fortunate and prosperous lives.

Feng shui offers three basic ways to adjust ch'i:

1 THE CONNECTING CH'I METHOD attracts ch'i that lies too deep below the earth's surface, or too far from a building. By installing a hollow pole in the ground with a light on top, for instance, ch'i can be siphoned up from deep in the earth. If a house is "missing" a corner in feng shui terms (see page 46), the Connecting Ch'i Method can also be applied by laying a brick or stone walkway, or building a loggia that connects the house to a nearby shed. This will symbolically square off the seemingly incomplete house shape by drawing the shed back into it.

2 THE BALANCING CH'I METHOD adjusts an awkward layout to create a harmonious environment. A landscape or structural addition to an awkwardly shaped building or site can balance the shape as well as bring it in harmony with other external elements.

3 THE OUTSTANDING CH'I METHOD can improve and channel ch'i flow. For example, a wall that closely faces an entry door will seem oppressive and block the residents' ch'i. As a result, when they enter they will feel that they are coming up against a "brick wall" in life. By installing a mirror or a landscape painting on the wall—creating an appearance of greater depth—the occupants will have a sense that a new road has opened up, with increased possibilities instead of a dead end, and their ch'i will feel less blocked.

THE FIVE ELEMENTS

Out of the interplay of yin and yang come the five elements. These manifestations of ch'i are the powers or essences of all matter, symbolized by metal, wood, water, fire and earth. In Chinese thought, each of these essences is associated with specific colors, matter, moods, tastes, organs of the body and variations of time and space. For example, metal corresponds to white, west and autumn; wood is associated with green or blue, east and spring; water is black (the deeper the water, the darker it gets), north and winter; fire is symbolized by red, south and summer; earth, meanwhile, corresponds to yellow or brown or orange, mid-autumn and the center.

Further, the five elements can affect each other in a prescribed cyclical order, creating or destroying each other in a fixed sequence. The creative cycle goes like this: fire creates earth (ash); earth produces metal (mined from the earth); metal creates water (while water rusts metal, it will form on the outside of a metal cup holding cold water); water cultivates wood (trees need water to grow); wood feeds fire.

The destructive cycle, in spite of its name, is not seen as negative. Similar to the creative cycle, it expresses constant regeneration through change, an eternal recycling. The sequence goes as follows: wood upheaves earth; earth obstructs water; water puts out fire; fire melts metal; metal chops down wood. In feng shui, when the five elements are superimposed on the ba-gua (see pages 44–45, 50), they can instruct us on how to use their associated colors to enhance our surroundings and life.

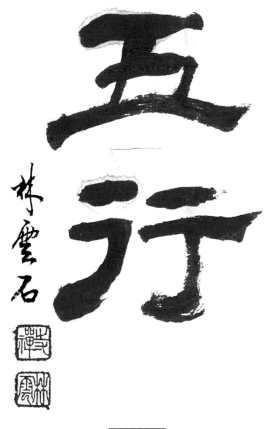

FIVE ELEMENTS

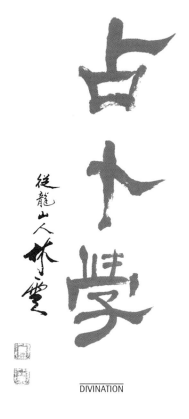

DIVINATION

DIVINATION

Divination and ritual are important components of feng shui. The early Chinese looked to the sky and earth for signs and guidance on how to perform sacrifices, whether to wage war, where to farm or build an imperial city, and when was the most auspicious time to do it.

Heaven (as represented by the sky) and the configurations of its constellations informed what became both astrology and early astronomy, as well as various aspects and schools of feng shui. Some say that a third-century B.C. Chinese imperial palace was built along a cosmological plan. Its form was said to follow the shape and path of the Plough or Big Dipper, a constellation that revolves around the stationary Pole Star, which is seen as the heavenly symbol of the emperor's centralized position of power on earth.

On earth, topography, vegetation and animals instructed early feng shui experts on where best to build. Further, records from the second millennium B.C. show that court diviners used ancient methods of prophecy, such as tortoise shells and oracle bones (ox-shoulder bones which, when exposed to fire, cracked in various "yes" or "no" formations), to help the emperor decide on the advisability of war, the siting of an imperial palace or cemetery, or the prospects of hunting or fishing expeditions.

I CHING

Out of the oracle-bone tradition, as well as observation of nature, came the *I Ching, The Book of Changes*, considered the mother of Chinese thought and practice. The *I Ching* codified natural elements and forces to impart wisdom, philosophy and the ability to tell fortunes to the user, thus further linking man's fate to nature. The Chinese interpreted omens, knowledge and guidance from trigrams of broken (yin) or solid (yang) lines formed by tossing yarrow sticks, wooden blocks or, more recently, coins. The resulting trigrams (or *guas*) symbolized natural forces and formations: ☰ heaven; ☷ earth; ☳ thunder; ☶ mountain; ☲ fire; ☴ wind; ☱ lake; ☵ water. The analogies of the trigrams were expanded to include other important concepts such as family relations, cardinal directions, time and the fluctuations of life and nature.

By its very nature, the *I Ching* also expresses the basic Chinese philosophical concept of constant, cyclical change, the belief that the universe and all things within it are constantly changing, and that human fortunes are ever-shifting. Life is never frozen in a state of good luck or bad; fortunes are eternally shifting, and humans float with the ebb and flow of nature's tides.

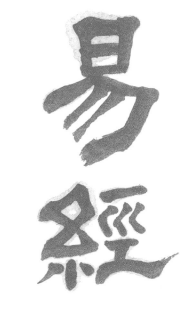

I CHING

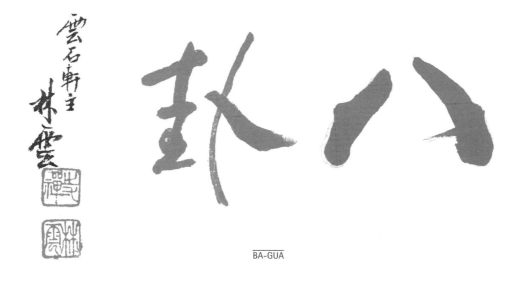

BA-GUA

BA-GUA

The collective image formed by the eight *I Ching* trigrams creates the ba-gua—literally translated as "eight trigrams"—a symbol of cosmic energy and wholeness. In feng shui, this is a basic tool to analyze an environment and prescribe cures in order to enhance the occupant's life. It is used both as a lucky charm to ward off bad luck and attract good fortune, and as a mystical compass to set the client along a nicely charted life course. While this chapter speaks of the lofty intent of feng shui to mirror the rhythms and harmony of nature, although emerging from these deeply philosophical roots, feng shui more often serves practical goals such as improving one's life, health and fortunes.

Various ba-guas arose during China's oracular, philosophical and cultural history. They differ in the position of different trigrams and, in addition, the application of the ba-gua varies from practice to practice. In "traditional" feng shui, the ba-gua is a static template. The individual trigrams are always set in fixed positions, and then superimposed on a building, property or room. For example, the trigram *li*, or "fame," may always lie in the south, and thus the wealth position is always in the south-east corner.

The ba-gua in this book—that of the unorthodox Black Sect of Feng Shui—deviates from this application. It is neither stationary nor set according to cardinal directions. It should be noted that while ba-gua applications vary, their ultimate goal—to raise the ch'i of a location and to improve its occupants' lives—remains the same. The next chapter will explain how to apply the ba-gua to a plot of land, a building or a human body.

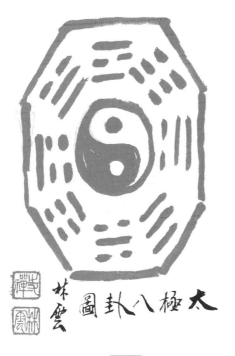

BA-GUA

LUO-PAN

Traditional feng shui experts perform a sort of astrology of the earth that calculates the optimal orientation of an individual's front door, bed and desk and factors in the client's birthday, using a beautiful and intricate cosmic compass known as the luo-pan. The luo-pan is thousands of years old—most feng shui manuals trace its invention to the legendary Huang-ti, or Yellow Emperor, in the third millennium B.C. In fact, the Chinese were the first to invent a compass, purportedly in order to use it for feng shui purposes.

The luo-pan is a simple compass surrounded by all the elements of the Chinese universe, charted in concentric circles. These rings include elements of heaven—the twenty-eight constellations of the moon's orbit, the twelve signs of the solar zodiac, the nine stars, the ten heavenly stems, and the five planets and their corresponding five elements—and the components of earth—the twelve earthly branches, as well as the ba-gua and the *I Ching* hexagrams, the sixty-four possible combinations of its eight trigrams.

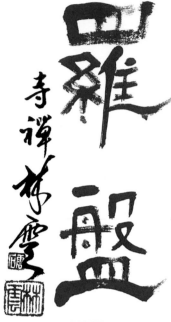

LUO-PAN

Today in Asia, some traditional feng shui experts also rely in part on computers to speed up calculations. One expert in China explains that, far from bucking tradition, "the luo-pan is the true ancestor of the computer." This book relies on an internalized compass, the ba-gua (see page 44), so the cardinal directions are important only in discerning the effects of wind, sun and other natural elements.

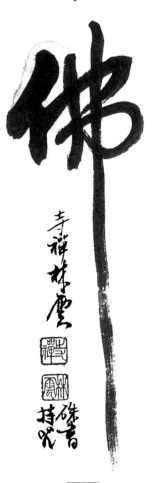

BUDDHA

BUDDHISM

The religious and philosophical roots of feng shui are intertwined. While it is indigenous to China, it absorbed and was absorbed by a foreign import—Buddhism. Feng shui combines deep Taoist philosophy with an unusual combination of folk cures, mysticism, early science and common sense. To this eclectic mixture was added Buddhism. Chinese Buddhism is the product of its long trek from India through Tibet and into China. In each country it adopted local teachings and practices. From India, it brought a church organization replete with meditations, yoga, chants, the concepts of dharma and compassion and the tradition of a master transmitting sacred knowledge to a student. In Tibet, native mystical charms and the chants of the Bon tradition were incorporated. And in China, Buddhism adopted indigenous thought and practices: the *I Ching*, Taoist, Confucian and Neo-Confucian thought and folk religions, customs and remedies—not the least of which was feng shui. The result is a union of complementary opposites: a practical and intuitive approach to the environment that offers an array of useful, sensible and mystical cures.

THE WORLD
OF THE SPIRIT

To the ancient Chinese the everyday world was a literally spiritual experience; one full of ancestors, spirits, demons and gods. Folklore and customs imbued their life and the afterlife with creatures and feats of exceptional powers. The earth itself was in legend born of a god figure, Taoist immortals populated mountains, caves and islands, and early emperors were endowed with great strength, power and longevity. Certain gods could intercede on behalf of a household, and the emperor, who was considered semi-divine, was the overall mediator between heaven and earth. A whole world of smaller spirits and demons coexisted with humans on an everyday basis, sometimes interfering in their lives. The Feast of the Hungry Ghosts is but one ceremonial day for quelling and quenching the needs of the more restless beings, when feasts are left outside to sate their appetites. If the spirits will not bless the house, they will at least spare it. At Chinese New Year, the face of the kitchen god is smeared with honey to ensure that when he returns to heaven he reports only good things about the household.

In feng shui, spirit screens and guardians act as protective devices against the forces of the spirit world. Many people still have spirit houses and others burn incense. There is also still a demand for exorcisms.

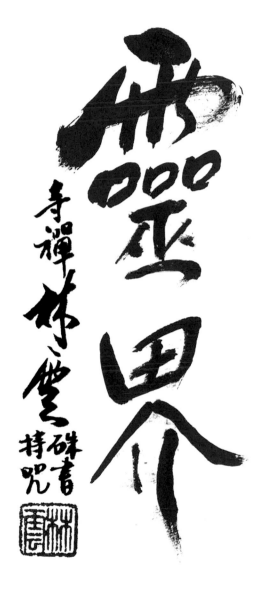

SPIRIT WORLD

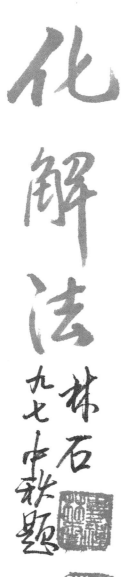

CURES

CURES

Ritual and superstition have their place alongside the more practical approaches and aspects of feng shui. The power of feng shui lies somewhere between common sense (in Chinese, *ru-shr*) and superstition or un-common sense (*chu-shr*). Ru-shr encompasses all that is within the scope of our experience and knowledge. It is rational, reasonable and easily accepted, proven and understood. Chu-shr is that which falls outside the sphere of accepted knowledge. It is irrational, illogical, mystical—beyond reason.

The cures put forth in this book are both ru-shr and chu-shr. The ru-shr aspects coincide with good design sense, scientific logic and modern medicine. The chu-shr approach goes beyond our known physical world to encompass the enormous expanse outside proven knowledge. It works on a more personal level, tapping our subconscious and often producing better results than more rational means. It could be said that chu-shr encompasses the mysteries of today that may become tomorrow's facts: it covers the vast area of what is yet to be discovered, understood or envisioned. Illogically, the chu-shr remedies are often the most effective.

There are many different schools of feng shui. The cures in this book follow the dynamic of the Black Sect Tantric Buddhism: an eclectic, mystical yet practical approach—a complementary mixture of opposites like feng shui itself. It is constantly evolving, yet respectful of tradition. It is a marriage of old and new and, more and more, a combination of East and West. This is not a religious book, but one that focuses on feng shui's practical cures, drawing on both ancient philosophy and modern means to achieve a harmonious result.

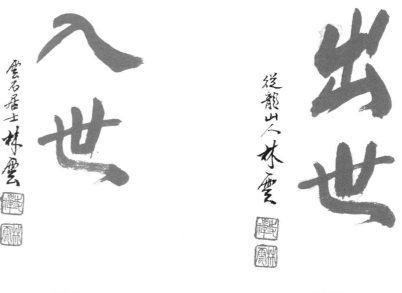

RU-SHR

CHU-SHR

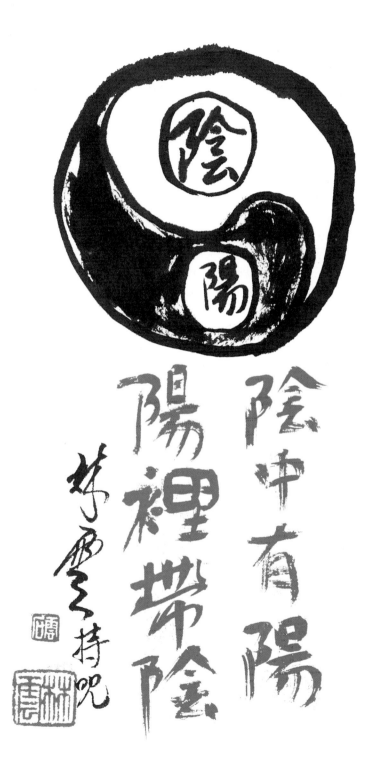

陰中有陽
陽裡帶陰

Yin-yang, a central tenet of Taoist philosophy. Within yin exists yang, within yang exists yin—in a balance feng shui strives to reinforce or emulate.

CHAPTER III

Feng Shui Tools
Understanding Its Components, Cures and the Ba-gua

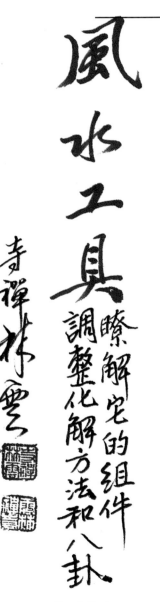

Feng shui tools

P art of the appeal of feng shui is that for nearly every design problem there exists a cure. The cures can range from the practical to the psychological, the mundane to the mystical, the obvious to the obscure and the arcane to the up-to-date.

SYING AND YI CURES

Feng shui cures operate on two complementary levels: *sying* and *yi*. Sying, translated literally as "form" or "appearance," encompasses the tangible and external elements and experience of our environment. It deals with how we visually, emotionally, physically and intellectually respond to our surroundings. By analyzing earth ch'i (see pages 29, 56–59), the shape and layout of buildings, door and window alignment and furniture placement, the feng shui expert can interpret how surroundings affect the occupant.

Yi, which translates as "wish," "will" and "intention," represents both the intangible and intuitive aspects, and the cures of feng shui. It is a vital, spiritual process that encompasses blessings and rituals—visualized or visual—designed to adjust and enhance ch'i. It reflects the positive intention of the practitioner to overcome barriers and negativity, to heal physical and emotional illness, to cultivate compassion, insight and awareness, and to produce a space in which to live a more productive, healthy and happy life.

Together, sying and yi work on a physical and metaphysical level, and can positively adjust both environmental and human ch'i. The table opposite shows how they can be categorized.

Of all the aspects of sying and yi listed in the table, the one that affects our lives the most is "others," the subtle signs and rituals that identify and determine our destiny. In sying, the strategic placement of a mirror might make all the difference in balancing an awkward interior. In yi, a simple ritual repeated over time might help harmonize and heal a person's body and mind. While this book does not promise miracles, one family reports a story about the healing of a young boy who at eighteen months had suffered brain damage after choking on some food. "Our son was in a coma for almost two

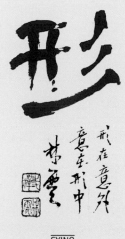

SYING
The form of sying is outside yi,
but yi is within sying

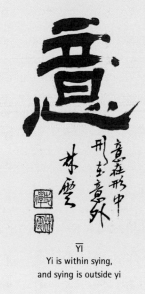

YI
Yi is within sying,
and sying is outside yi

SYING

Earth ch'i (see pages 56-59)

Earth shapes (see pages 73, 87-89)

Building shapes (see pages 107-113)

Room positions (see pages 168-169)

Others (see page 38)

Internal Factors

Stove position (see pages 173-176)

Beams (see pages 129-130, 164-165)

Stairs (see pages 130, 162-163)

Columns (see pages 129, 165)

Doors (see pages 129, 160-161)

Desk—study (see pages 180-181)

Dining table (see pages 176-178)

Desk—office (see pages 130-134)

Wall and furniture colors
   (see pages 52, 135, 157)

Lighting (see pages 136, 157)

Others (see page 38)

External Factors

Road direction (see pages 94, 104)

Bridges (see pages 94-95)

Trees (see pages 78, 87, 90-93, 96-97)

Rooftop (see pages 57, 67, 68-69, 111)

Corners (see pages 97, 104-105)

Outdoor temple or shrine
   (see pages 63-65)

Water (see pages 59-61, 81-85)

Utility poles (see pages 80, 96-97)

Exterior colors (see pages 52, 66-67,
   113-115)

Others (see page 38)

YI

Three Secrets (see Chapter IX)

Ba-gua (see pages 33, 44)

Tracing the Nine Stars (see Chapter IX)

Eight-Door Wheel (see Chapter IX)

Yu-nei; internal method of adjusting
   house ch'i (see Chapter IX)

Yu-wai; external method of
   adjusting house ch'i (see Chapter IX)

Constantly Turning Dharma Wheel
   (see Chapter IX)

House history (see pages 80, 103,
   Chapter IX)

Sealing the Door (see Chapter IX)

Others (see page 38)

weeks. When he regained consciousness, he was blind and immobile. Paralyzed vocal chords necessitated a tracheotomy, with a feeding tube inserted into his neck," recounts his father. However, a friend of his, who knew about feng shui, helped the parents to hang mirrors and gave them a drawing of the Constantly Turning Dharma Wheel. She would also often *guan chi*, which translates literally as giving a ch'i transfusion, supplying the boy with extra energy to recover. "Within a year the feeding tubes were removed. He is now at school, and much of his sight and mobility has returned. He enjoys computer games, takes classes in karate, and sings in a choir!"

THE NINE BASIC CURES

1 Bright or light-refracting objects: lights, mirrors, crystal balls

2 Objects that make sounds: wind chimes, bells

3 Living objects: plants (real or artificial), bonsai, flowers, an aquarium or fish bowls/tanks

4 Moving objects: mobiles, whirligigs, fountains, waterfalls, windmills

5 Heavy objects: stones, statues, rock gardens

6 Electrically powered objects: televisions, stereo systems, air conditioners, computers

7 Bamboo flutes

8 Colors

9 Others (see page 38)

THE NINE BASIC CURES

When resolving feng shui problems related to sying, the most commonly used remedies are the Nine Basic Cures. A compendium of everyday objects, they can resolve unbalanced shapes, adjust and improve ch'i flow and improve the areas of the ba-gua and their related situations. Each remedy possesses its own healing properties. A cut-glass crystal hung in a western window may symbolically refract the oppressive glare of the afternoon sun, as well as creating the positive image of a rainbow on walls; a mobile hung in a long hallway will disperse strong ch'i; a flute hung properly on an overhead beam might lighten its overbearing effect.

Here's how the cures work:

BRIGHT OBJECTS

Lights Can be used to solve both interior and exterior feng shui problems. They can resolve awkward shapes: outside an L-shaped building, a spotlight or lamp can square off the shape; inside a space with an acute angle, a light can encourage ch'i circulation. If a property is on a steep slope, a light installed at the bottom of the hill will recirculate ch'i and stem the flow of money rolling away from the site. Interior lights—representing the nurturing power of the sun—generally improve the ch'i of a space and, as a broad rule, the brighter they are the better.

Mirrors Known as the "aspirin of feng shui," mirrors alleviate a host of feng shui ills resulting from slanted or oppressively close walls, awkward room shapes or poorly sited beds, desks or stoves. Used since ancient times, they also deflect negative outside influences. Thousands of years ago, the armor worn by Chinese warriors was inlaid with mirrors to reflect back the enemy's ferocity and protect the wearers. The deflective use of mirrors continues today: they are hung outside many modern Chinese homes to deflect the negative impact of anything from bad views, unpleasant neighbors or oncoming traffic to churches, funeral parlors or police stations, to name a few examples (see page 105).

Interior mirrors serve many purposes. A general rule is the bigger the better. Never hang one so low that it cuts off the top of someone's head, creating tension and headaches, or so high that it makes the occupants feel uncomfortable, as though they do not measure up. Avoid mirror tiles, as these can distort the image. And dark or smoky mirrors seem oppressive and can lower ch'i.

Properly hung mirrors draw in the beneficial effects of the outdoors—good views, good ch'i and light. They also help to create a sense of depth when a space is confined or a wall is obstructive, or will reflect someone entering a room when its occupant is working or cooking with his or her back to the door or sleeping in a position where the door can't be seen. They symbolically straighten a slanted wall or correct awkward spaces and create an addition wherever they are hung, and can also enhance any ba-gua life situation. Popular areas for enhancement are wealth, career and family.

OBJECTS THAT MAKE SOUNDS

Wind chimes and bells Used inside and outside, wind chimes moderate the circulation of ch'i, dispersing strong or malign energy (such as the effects of a long corridor or a road that may aim directly at a house). Hung on the eave of a home, a bell or a wind chime will symbolically improve the house's ch'i and its residents' finances. Hung on the outside of business premises, they attract ch'i, clients and profits. Hung near the entrance, they provide a simple security system, warning those within each time anyone enters.

LIVING OBJECTS

Plants and flowers Symbolic of growth and development, as well as nature's beauty and life force, plants and flowers—be they living or artificial—purvey nourishing ch'i within a space. Outside, they are indicators of good ch'i: if vegetation flourishes in a certain spot, so will the human residents. Inside and out, they can balance a plot of land, the shape of a building or a room. Plants not only give hope to an interior's occupants, but can also help resolve sharp corners that jut into a room, awkward, acute angles and slatted stairwells. Within, and flanking the entrance to, a store or a restaurant, healthy plants and flowers are subtle beacons attracting clients, business and ch'i.

Fish bowls and aquariums Symbolic of water's nurturing role in nature, fish bowls are positive interior cures evoking nourishing and money-enhancing ch'i. Because the presence of water is essential for crop cultivation and aquaculture, water and views of water symbolize wealth-endowing properties and are seen as enriching a home or a business. In locations lacking visual access to water, fish tanks become symbolic reminders, imbuing a place with money-making possibilities.

Live fish function in several ways: as fruit of the sea they further enhance the symbol of water's property of endowing riches. They are also seen to serve as sort of aquatic scapegoats, absorbing bad luck and accidents that might have affected the human occupants of the space. (When a fish dies, replace it immediately.) Fish bowls and aquariums with aerators further enhance the ch'i of a location, and the aerators are considered the best solution for keeping the water fresh.

MOVING OBJECTS

Whether wind-powered or electrical, moving objects such as mobiles indoors or windmills, whirligigs and weather vanes outdoors are used to deflect or disperse the negative effects of "killing ch'i" (a risk in long hallways or when facing arrow-like roads and overbearing neighboring buildings or landscape features such as an overhanging outcropping). Water fountains, man-made geysers and waterfalls—all microcosms of ch'i-enhancing and wealth-producing water—create active, positive ch'i too, as well as enhancing finances for both family and business.

HEAVY OBJECTS

Heavy objects such as stones and statues, when properly placed according to the ba-gua, can harmonize unbalanced shapes or stabilize unsettling or elusive situations ranging from maintaining a job to maintaining a marriage.

COLOR ASSOCIATIONS

 Purple, deep red or plum are auspicious, the colors of nobility, richness and power.

 Red is auspicious, the color of happiness, fire and passion, fame, strength and power.

 Pink denotes love and pure intent, joy, romance and happiness.

Peach stands for romance and attraction.

Orange is auspicious and denotes happiness and power.

 Yellow stands for tolerance, patience, wisdom, perspective, power, earth and loyalty.

 Green evokes hope, development, family, tranquillity, spring and growth.

Blue-green is less auspicious than green; in fact, blue is a secondary mourning color, but it can also stand for growth and new beginnings.

Black or deep dark colors convey spirituality, psychological and intellectual depth, wisdom and perspective, but also depression and lack of hope.

Gray denotes frustration and hopelessness; also the marriage of opposites such as black and white—and thus the creation of balance and resolving conflict.

 Brown stands for stability, depth, something long-established and enduring, elegance, autumn, the passage of time and heaviness.

Tan or café-au-lait evokes new possibilities: after disappointment comes a successful beginning.

ELECTRICALLY POWERED OBJECTS

Electrically powered machines can stimulate interiors. They are useful in adjusting areas of a resident's life by adjusting the corresponding areas—according to the ba-gua—in a home or a business. For example, a sound system in the wealth area of a bar will amplify profits, or an air-conditioning unit in the fame area of a business will raise the business's profile.

BAMBOO FLUTES

Because bamboo flutes were used in ancient China to announce peace and good news, they are symbolic of safety, peace and stability. Hollow and segmented, they are also seen as funneling up the ch'i of a location, section by section. They can symbolically penetrate an oppressive beam: two flutes with red ribbons tied around them are hung slanting inwards on a beam, creating a partial octagon which both evokes the ba-gua and pumps ch'i upwards, lightening the beam's effect. Flutes resembling swords are also protective, and are hung in Chinese homes, stores and restaurants to guard the establishments against robbers and evil spirits. When shaken, they are said to drive away bad ch'i, bad luck and bad spirits; when played, their sound can bolster weak ch'i and low morale.

COLORS

As colors define all that we see, feng shui experts pay attention to them. Their use is symbolic—sometimes part of a mystical color scheme (see pages 50–53), sometimes emotional, sometimes cultural. Some Chinese color associations are shown on the left.

Mind over matter, as well as the choice of tones, is important in order to benefit from the positive connotations of colors that may also carry negative associations. In other words, positivity is in the mood and spirituality of the beholder.

THE BA-GUA

Along with rules and intuition, the ba-gua is an integral part of improving the feng shui of a location.

It is a potent, mystical tool. Its octagonal shape, and the eight *I Ching* trigrams that define it, signify the perfection and power of the Chinese universe. For centuries, the Chinese have placed this mystical octagon on plots of land, houses, rooms and even faces and palms to divine a person's fate. They say that by making some minor adjustments to a space they can change the occupant's life for the better. This section will explain how to apply the ba-gua to a site, building or room. It will reveal how to tell if a shape is lucky or not. And then, it will show how to enhance a positive shape or resolve an unfortunate one.

Basically, the ba-gua is a map (see page 44) of eight life situations: fame, marriage, children, helpful people, career, knowledge, family, wealth. These generally reflect universal aspirations and concerns. However, some of them reveal ideas that are culturally Chinese. For example, "helpful people" means those in both higher and lower stations who can help a person. This is a form of *guanshi*—literally, "relationship"—someone who can patronize, a particularly helpful underling or even a good connection to aid one in achieving one's goal. The scope of the "knowledge" area encompasses the whole Chinese concept of learning, including not only wisdom and book-learned knowledge, but also experience from life and travel—worldliness—as well as deep spiritual cultivation and enlightenment. In addition, the octagon is affixed with the Five Elements and their associated colors, organs and seasonal intervals. The ba-gua is employed in a number of ways. As a more ritual and mystical process of feng shui practice (yi), it is both a method of divination and a system of improving and enhancing a resident's luck.

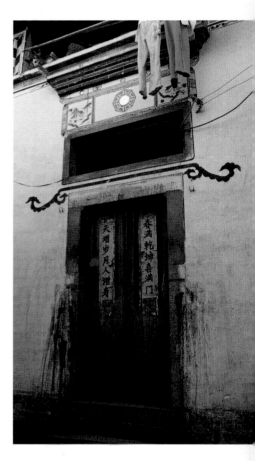

This ba-gua mirror over a door in a rural Chinese town deflects the negative effects of an oncoming road.

The octagonal shape of the ba-gua is sometimes invoked in Chinese design as an auspicious talisman and force, as it is seen as a protective and forceful symbol. Ba-gua mirrors hang outside many Chinese homes to ward off what are considered negative sights and influences and deflect bad luck and bad ch'i so that residents do not have to move elsewhere. The ba-gua symbol is also used to improve the ch'i and luck of a place. For example, a Chinese Canadian hotel owner spent hundreds of thousands of dollars renovating the lobby of his new hotel. The overhaul was in part for feng shui reasons, because the hotel had previously changed hands a number of times but had never enjoyed good profits. To create a more positive and profitable environment, one of the improvements was to install a recessed ceiling in the shape of a ba-gua. A popular suburban Chinese restaurant has a recurring ba-gua theme: ba-gua banquettes, ba-gua interior waterfall and a ba-gua-shaped plant container by the slanted entrance (see page 145).

To intuit the positive and negative areas of occupants' lives, the eight life situations of the ba-gua are superimposed like a template on a property, the floor plan of a home, apartment or business (and even on rooms, desks or beds), to indicate the inadequacies and benefits of the location and their effects on its residents' lives, and then serve as a guide to curing or enhancing them. The diagnosis strangely tends to be quite accurate. Perhaps it works because of happy—or unhappy—coincidence, because life generally is imperfect and the life situations of the occupants are vague (and most honest

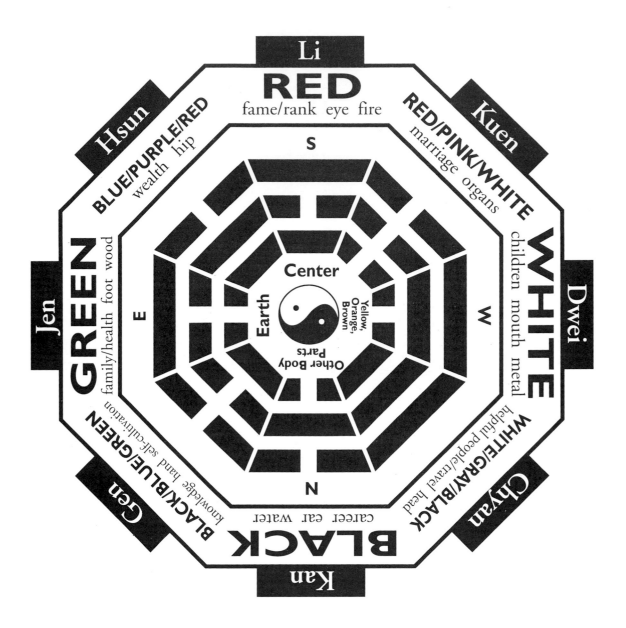

The mystical octagon of the ba-gua incorporates the eight trigrams of the *I Ching*. A fundamental feng shui tool, simply align north (irrespective of the true compass alignment), black or kan with the entrance side of a plot, building or room to discern the corresponding areas in your site, and use this book to see how these may be cured or enhanced in design terms.

people can pinpoint something—be it minute or overwhelming—that is missing or frustrating in nearly all areas of their lives). Or, perhaps, there is something more to it. For example, a couple with a country house hired a feng shui expert who noted it was missing the helpful people and children areas. In fact, they had encountered great difficulty enlisting contractors and workmen for their renovation scheme. And, more painfully, they had just suffered a miscarriage. (After they had cured the house shape with landscaping, help with their renovation materialized and the couple also gave birth to a healthy boy.)

Many stories circulate about people altering their fate by adjusting the ba-gua of a site. For instance, the advertising executive who put a red vase in the fame area of her desk and soon received a promotion. Or the student who adjusted the knowledge area to improve his performance in examinations. Or the couple who enhanced the marriage area—also associated with internal organs—

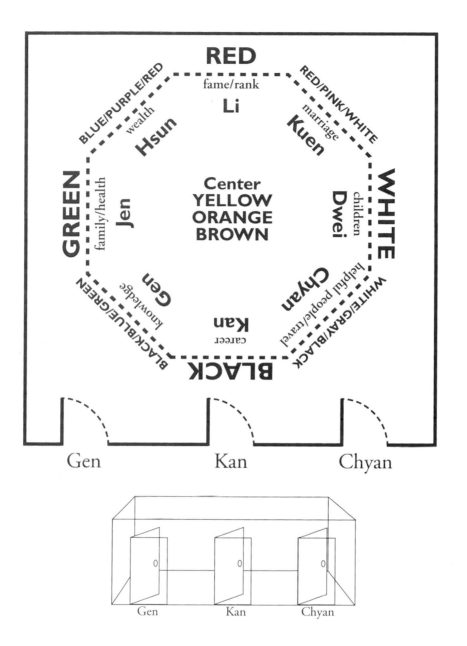

so that their young child's kidney disorder was successfully cured by doctors. Or the couple who planted flowers in the helpful people position and found excellent domestic help.

The method of applying the ba-gua to a property, building or room is quite simple and is called the Three-Door Ba-gua. First, identify the main entrance or *ch'i kou*, translated as "mouth of ch'i." Next, overlay the entry point with the ba-gua octagon, matching up the entrance with the side that has *gen*, *kan*, and *chyan*, the knowledge, career and helpful people areas respectively. (No one entrance, or *gua*, is better than another.) If when you face into a room the entrance is in the center, it lines up with kan or career. If it is to the left, it is at gen or the knowledge area. An entry to the right sits in the chyan or helpful people area. No matter where the entry lies, the wealth area is always in the far left corner of the room, the marriage position is in the far right corner and the fame area is between wealth and marriage in the center of the wall opposite the entry door. The family area is in the center

The Three-Door Ba-Gua is a practical means of clearly superimposing the ba-gua onto a plot of land, building or room, taking into account where its principle entrance actually lies. Align kan with the center of the entrance side, gen on its left, and chyan to its right. The ba-gua areas will lie as shown above; imagine the octagon lying at the center of the space you are considering.

45

THE IMPLICATIONS OF IRREGULAR SHAPES

The diagrams below are examples of irregular shapes, both positive and negative. Always consider the shape from the position of the principle entrance.

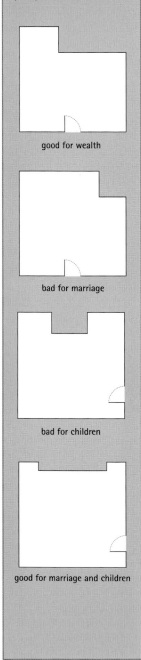

good for wealth

bad for marriage

bad for children

good for marriage and children

of the wall to the left and the children position lies in the middle of the wall to the right.

Eight physical aspects of the body can be associated with the octagon. For example, the ear is associated with kan, the career gua, and the head is represented by chyan, the helpful people gua. Eyes are associated with li, the fame gua. So a house missing the chyan area might be home to migraine sufferers. Adjusting the helpful people area might help ease the pain and frequency of the headaches.

To adjust the ba-gua, one can employ any of the objects listed in the Nine Basic Cures (see page 40): colors, mirrors, plants, fountains, lights, heavy objects, mechanical instruments, etc. These remedies are generally interchangeable, but should be appropriate to the design and use of the space. For example, an advanced stereo system in the wealth position of a recording executive's office suite will enhance his or her fortunes. Or a tree planted in the marriage area of a property might not only block out an unwanted view but also enhance the residents' relationship. Even humor can come into play. One banking executive installed his collection of plastic back-scratchers in the helpful people position of his desk, thus ensuring encouragement from his corporate superiors and cooperation by all.

Another facet of the ba-gua is created by the overlay of the five elements. These are superimposed on it so that their individual properties and associated colors can be engaged to cure and enhance a site. For instance, a design store installed a fountain in the career area, which is associated with the water element. As clients entered they were greeted with the pleasant trill of moving water. The fountain not coincidentally became a popular item, and kept selling out almost as quickly as it was replaced. A restaurant stove might be placed in the fame area—associated with the fire element—to cook up more business. In a home, a sofa upholstered in coral or red—the color allied with the fire element—and positioned in the fame area of a living room could both work with the decor and enhance the residents' careers and renown. You can work to reinforce many areas, but it is best to focus on those that are most relevant to your life.

Shapes

The ba-gua can also be used to determine whether a room, building or property shape is lucky or unlucky. Discerning whether it is positive or negative is generally pretty clear-cut. If a shape is regular or "whole"—a square or a rectangle—it is deemed complete and balanced. If, however, it is irregular—such as an L-, T- or a U-shape—further inspection will indicate whether it is missing something or enjoying an addition. If the shape is found to be lacking, a corresponding area of its occupants' lives may suffer.

Analyzing the proportions of the shape will determine whether it is fortunate or not. If the "missing" area is less than half the width and length of a space, the shape is incomplete, and residents may find they are lacking in one, two or three life situations. If, on the other hand, a "missing" area is greater than half the length and width, the remaining wing is considered an addition, with positive connotations.

Often, a room is missing a gua because a corner, column, closet or bathroom juts into it. Pay attention to where the bathroom sits, because it can have a negative effect on the corresponding area of the occupants' lives. If it is in the wealth area, family profits may be flushed away. (If, on the other hand, the kitchen sits in the wealth area, food and finances will flourish.) A master bedroom in the marriage area of a house, or a bed positioned in the marriage area of a room, is positive for a couple's relationship.

However, it is important not to panic if a home or an office is missing a gua, or if the bathroom is in the wealth area. For example, a family hired a feng shui consultant who correctly told them that the bathroom of their new home was in the wealth area, eating into the space, and meaning that the house had an important area "missing." But he incorrectly suggested moving it—a drastic and expensive undertaking. Panicked, the family called in another consultant who correctly suggested a less expensive cure: hanging a mirror on one side of the bathroom wall to create a symbolic *plus* in the wealth area. Other remedies would have been to hang a crystal ball or a wind chime by each side of the corner, or to train a vine to grow up it.

CURING PROBLEMATIC SHAPES

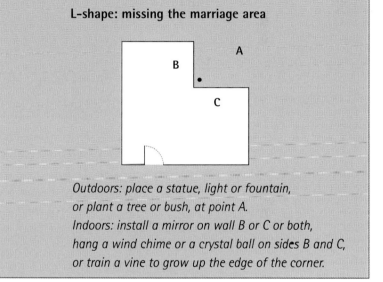

U-shapes: missing the career area

Where a door opens immediately onto the missing area, hang a mirror on the wall of the missing area, next to the door (A). Or, to resolve the shape when you do not view the missing area on entering, lay red bricks outside the area to fill in the missing area (B). Where an outside door is sited in the middle of a missing area, flank it with bushes (C & D).

L-shape: missing the marriage area

Outdoors: place a statue, light or fountain, or plant a tree or bush, at point A.
Indoors: install a mirror on wall B or C or both, hang a wind chime or a crystal ball on sides B and C, or train a vine to grow up the edge of the corner.

Irregular shapes with missing guas can be resolved by adjusting either the interior or exterior of a building. Again, one of the Nine Basic Cures (see page 40) can complete—and enhance—the shape. The table above shows examples of how to balance an awkward shape and thus create harmony and positive influences for occupants.

Slants

A slant is doubly troublesome. In addition to creating an incomplete shape that indicates a missing area in the occupants' lives, it is considered structurally unlucky and unbalancing for any office or home. Slants portend unexpected events—usually bad—or even disaster. In addition, certain slanted walls can affect ch'i flow. For example, ch'i can get trapped in the acute angles created by some slanted walls. The diagrams on page 48 show some cures for these situations. The addition of a light, crystal or plant can symbolically circulate the stale ch'i (A). Exterior lights or plants can square off a

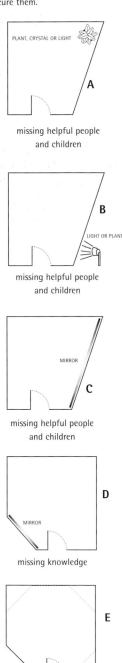

CURING SLANTS

Slants signify something unexpected happening. Here are some preventative ways to cure them.

PLANT, CRYSTAL OR LIGHT

A

missing helpful people
and children

B

LIGHT OR PLANT

missing helpful people
and children

MIRROR

C

missing helpful people
and children

D

MIRROR

missing knowledge

E

missing knowledge

slant (B). Mirrors are also excellent antidotes to the visually unbalancing effect of slants, as they correct the unresolved shape and provide visual comfort for the eye (C and D). And a slanted fifth wall of a room can be made into an auspicious octagon by adding three more slanted walls to the room (E).

The ba-gua and personal goals

Once you have identified the life situations associated with a space, you can enhance the specific area and thus improve the corresponding areas of your life. For example, a couple hoping to improve their marriage might enhance the marriage area of their bedroom with a bouquet of nine (an auspicious multiple of three, see page 115) red or pink roses—good colors for that area. Or a person seeking to enhance his or her career or find a new job might adjust the career area of the home by hanging a mirror—symbolizing a new road or opportunity opening up—or by installing a plant or light to nurture the area. (But then again, some people choose to enhance all areas of their lives by adjusting each of the eight areas of the ba-gua. Of course, attention must be given to design when doing so or the result can be quite humorous: wind chimes here, flutes or whirligigs there, a crystal or two, a fish bowl, and *voilà*, you have a feng shui dream or nightmare.)

The ba-gua can also be employed to adjust a child's behavior and prospects. A bed or a crib placed in the children area will facilitate personal growth. Something white, such as a white bureau or white flowers, as well as a lamp, mobile, whirligig or mirror will also do the trick. One mother of a rambunctious preschool boy periodically places nine flowers on a bureau in the child area when he seems more active than usual. After nine days, she reports, his activity is more focused.

An anxious parent hoping to help a child get into a good school, college or university can also use the ba-gua. Place a flute vertically in the gen or knowledge position of the child's bedroom. If there is a door behind it, you can hang the flute by the side of—or horizontally above—the door. In addition, you can hang a mirror in the chyan (helpful people) position, while you visualize the assistance of a benefactor who can guide and teach the child.

In an office, the ba-gua can improve the corporate visibility of an employee if the fame area is adjusted with a plant, a light or something red. The result may be a promotion. Other useful areas that can be adjusted in an individual's office are helpful people, career, wealth and knowledge. On the advice of a feng shui expert, the principal managing the business side of a medium-sized advertising agency placed himself in the wealth area of the entire office, so that his position would embody financial success for the company. The controller of a billion-dollar hedge (high-risk) fund in New York also sits in the wealth area, to ensure profits in an up-and-down business.

MING T'ANG

Ming t'ang is the ninth area of the ba-gua octagon—the center—and is associated with the occupant's physical and mental health and stability, as well as the earth element and center position. Ming t'ang, translated literally as "bright hall," is a term of spatial definition, a cosmic

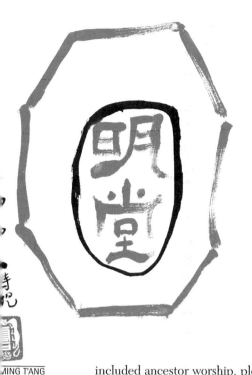

MING T'ANG

court. Originally it described a space, and then a building. Every aspect of Chinese space has a name and a meaning. Ming t'ang, *sze-he-yuan* (four-sided garden) and *guo-bai* (the framed perspective) are but a few. Ming t'ang describes the place that connects man with heaven, where they communicate. Historically, it described a number of constructions. In the legendary Hsia dynasty it was a garden where the most important sacrificial ceremonies, celebrating the unifying relationship between man and nature and heaven and earth, were held. Under the Chou dynasty, it was the hall used for sacrifices to heaven; and the term given to an imperial ancestral hall as well as one in which the emperor received feudal princes. It also describes an open space before a grave, as well as the center courtyard of a home, and is also the central point between auspicious mountains on which to build. Within the emperor's domain, the building called the ming t'ang (a ritual structure) sits at the hub of the compound. It was considered the center of imperial power, and the rituals performed there by the emperor included ancestor worship, ploughing of the sacred plot and spring and autumn audiences, as well as observation of clouds and weather, sacrifices and some transactions of government. The ming t'ang even predates China's legendary emperor Fu-hsi, who is credited with writing down the *I Ching*—tradition claims he found authority for the hall in its text. The ming t'ang itself is a sacred shape, generally made up of units of nine. The Temple of Heaven with its series of nine steps is one example.

Today, feng shui experts seek to create this same sense of a balanced environment and physical well-being for occupants by enhancing the center of the shape of the structure they are dealing with. This can be done simply by placing a plant or light symbolizing growth, or hanging a crystal symbolizing physical purity, strength and lucidity, at the center and then blessing the site (see Yu-nei, Chapter IX).

THE THREE HARMONIES

The Three Harmonies is an additional tool to further balance and enhance the ba-gua of a business or home. It can improve or enhance either bad or good feng shui. It takes an addition to a room, home or plot of land and then creates two more positive areas. The Three Harmonies are in fact four possible mystical triangles that can each be superimposed on the ba-gua, as shown on page 50. (These four triangles, *in toto*, create all 12 stems of the Chinese zodiac.)

The Three Harmonies represents the balance of heaven, earth and man: heaven being the highest, earth being the lowest and man, who is in between, being the connection between heaven and earth. It represents heaven's cyclical time schedule, the benefits and fruits of earth and the harmonious relationships among humans. The heavenly time schedule—which refers both to seasonal

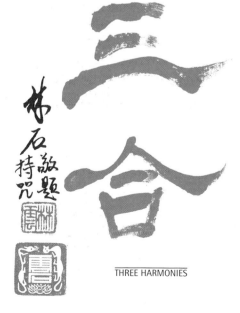

THREE HARMONIES

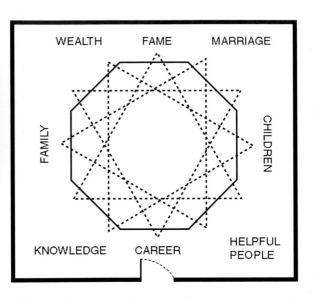

WEALTH   FAME   MARRIAGE

FAMILY

CHILDREN

KNOWLEDGE   CAREER   HELPFUL PEOPLE

Applying the Three Harmonies. Superimpose the octagon on your site, whatever its shape, and where an area is missing or needs improvement, reinforce its matching two other angle points as shown.

changes and to the constant change from day to night—reflects the balance and interrelationship of yin and yang. The benefits or fruits of the earth refer to existence and the value of all things on earth and their harmonious interrelationship. (This part of the Three Harmonies also means mountain and river. Mountain represents ground and river represents water. When ground and water are in balance, everything else coexists harmoniously.) Humans exist between heaven and earth. They recognize, and know how to utilize, the heavenly time schedules and earth's bounty. Those who live in moderation exist harmoniously between heaven and earth.

The Three Harmonies can be used in two ways. It can be applied to augment a room or a building that has a wing by enhancing its matching angle points. It can also be used to enhance the gua of a space by adjusting the complementary angles, thus enhancing the corresponding guas. These measures can rectify a negative space or enhance a positive one. See the diagram on the left for how to apply the Three Harmonies—use a cure in each of the three corners (each of which relates to an area of the ba-gua) of any of the triangles to improve the areas in question.

THE FIVE ELEMENT BA-GUA COLOR SCHEME

The Five Element Ba-gua Color Scheme is another way to enhance the ch'i of a room, a home, an office or a plot of land. In fact, it is one of the Nine Basic Cures of feng shui (see page 40). It works like this: each area of the ba-gua and the corresponding areas of residents' lives can be enhanced by a specific color. To determine the best one for an area, merely refer to the chart on page 44.

The most fortuitous colors are determined by the five elements and their corresponding colors on the ba-gua. The colors are symbols of different aspects of ch'i and correlate to the five elements. Metal is white and enhances the children area. Wood is green or blue and enhances the family gua. Water is gray or black and enriches the career area. Fire is red and enhances the fame position. Earth is brown, tan, yellow or orange and enriches the center, ming t'ang and health. For the other four guas, helpful people is white, gray or black; knowledge is black, blue or green; wealth is blue, purple or red; and marriage is red, pink or white.

Thus a person who is seeking to further his or her career might put a black-and-white photograph in the career area. A student who is hoping to improve examination results might place a green plant in the knowledge area. And a couple with marital problems might install something red or pink in the marriage area of their bedroom.

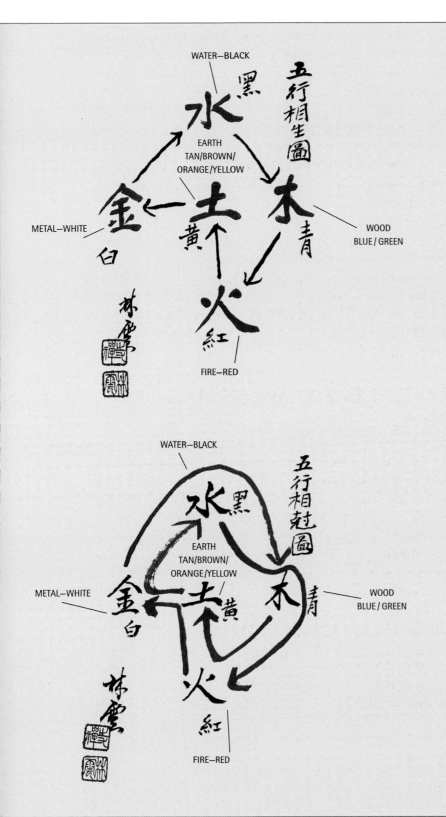

The Five Element Creative Cycle

Once you have identified an area's element, you can also use other effective colors to enhance the area's life situation. These additional alternatives derive from the Five Element Creative Cycle. This dynamic color scheme makes use of the color of the element that creates a gua's element, as well as the color the gua's element creates.

For example, if you want to enhance the fame area you might use the color of its element, fire (red), or the color of the element fire creates, earth—yellow, orange or brown (fire produces ash)—or the color of the element that produces fire, green or blue—for wood. Or if you want to help your career, simply place something black or dark gray—for water—in the career area. The other good colors to use with this are white (for metal, created by earth, and which creates water—condensation appears on cold metal) and green or blue (for wood—which water feeds).

The colors can also be used if you are considering changing a room's color scheme. For a more dynamic cure, follow the cycle in progression, from the floor upwards, employing three, four or five colors in turn.

The chart on page 52 will help you to identify the appropriate sequential colors for the Five Element Ba-gua Creative Cycle.

The Five Element Destructive Cycle

This can be used in a similar way to the Creative Cycle, employing three to five colors in sequence, each overpowering the next. Despite its name, the cycle is not considered negative: these mutually destructive relationships connote eternal recycling: metal chops down wood, wood upheaves earth, earth obstructs water, water puts out fire, fire melts metal, and so on. Like the Creative Cycle colors, these can also be used cyclically in a room's color scheme for a more dynamic cure, but start at the top of the room and work down for the Destructive Cycle.

The chart on page 52 will help you to identify the appropriate sequential colors for the Destructive Cycle.

USING THE FIVE ELEMENT COLOR CYCLES

THE FIVE ELEMENT CREATIVE CYCLE: THREE COLORS

3	tan/brown/orange/yellow	pink/red	blue/green	grey/black	white
2	pink/red	blue/green	grey/black	white	tan/brown/orange/yellow
1	blue/green	grey/black	white	tan/brown/orange/yellow	pink/red

THE FIVE ELEMENT CREATIVE CYCLE: FOUR COLORS

4	tan/brown/orange/yellow	pink/red	blue/green	gray/black	white
3	pink/red	blue/green	gray/black	white	tan/brown/orange/yellow
2	blue/green	gray/black	white	tan/brown/orange/yellow	pink/red
1	gray/black	white	tan/brown/orange/yellow	pink/red	blue/green

THE FIVE ELEMENT CREATIVE CYCLE: FIVE COLORS

5	tan/brown/orange/yellow	pink/red	blue/green	grey/black	white
4	pink/red	blue/green	gray/black	white	tan/brown/orange/yellow
3	blue/green	gray/black	white	tan/brown/orange/yellow	pink/red
2	gray/black	white	tan/brown/orange/yellow	pink/red	blue/green
1	white	tan/brown/orange/yellow	pink/red	blue/green	gray/black

THE FIVE ELEMENT DESTRUCTIVE CYCLE: THREE COLORS

1	tan/brown/orange/yellow	gray/black	pink/red	white	blue/green
2	gray/black	pink/red	white	blue/green	tan/brown/orange/yellow
3	pink/red	white	blue/green	tan/brown/orange/yellow	gray/black

THE FIVE ELEMENT DESTRUCTIVE CYCLE: FOUR COLORS

1	tan/brown/orange/yellow	gray/black	pink/red	white	blue/green
2	gray/black	pink/red	white	blue/green	tan/brown/orange/yellow
3	pink/red	white	blue/green	tan/brown/orange/yellow	gray/black
4	white	blue/green	tan/brown/orange/yellow	gray/black	pink/red

THE FIVE ELEMENT DESTRUCTIVE CYCLE: FIVE COLORS

1	tan/brown/orange/yellow	gray/black	pink/red	white	blue/green
2	gray/black	pink/red	white	blue/green	tan/brown/orange/yellow
3	pink/red	white	blue/green	tan/brown/orange/yellow	gray/black
4	white	blue/green	tan/brown/orange/yellow	gray/black	pink/red
5	blue/green	tan/brown/orange/yellow	gray/black	pink/red	white

The Five Element Color Cycles

The charts on the left show the sequences in which the five element colors should be used, if you are following the dynamic Creative and Destructive Cycles to enhance ch'i. In either, you can employ three, four or five colors.

For the Creative Cycle, consider the lowest area first—whether floor, skirting, path, lawn or roadway. Then use the colors in sequence progressing upwards to the highest point—cornice, ceiling, roof, chimney, or other roof installation. Use three, four or five colors, depending on how many areas you have to consider, or how many accents you want to use. Each color represents an element (see previous page), each of which creates the next.

For the Destructive Cycle, the process is the same, except that you should consider the highest point first, and the Destructive Cycle sequencing offers a further range of color scheme options. Remember that in this context "destructive" is not a pejorative term; rather, it connotes eternal recycling, each color representing an element (see previous page), and each element consuming the next.

Further auspicious color sequencing

Besides the color cycles, you can use all the colors associated with the five elements to improve ch'i. You can also employ the Six True Colors, a recurring cyclical sequence starting at white, progressing to red, yellow, green and blue, and ending in black—only to continue to white again. In practical terms, this would mean an ornament with these colors progressing around it, or an arrangement of furniture and household objects in a hexagonal relationship. Or use the rainbow's spectrum of seven colors in sequence for a potent cure. Each of these colors can also be used to enhance a specific area of the ba-gua.

Feng shui can thus be applied in a number of ways. Sometimes it physically improves a place; sometimes it acts as a symbolic gesture. Here the will-to-believe comes into play, creating a sense of a positive environment and a positive approach to life by its occupants. This book seeks to serve as a visual guide to applying feng shui to your surroundings, thus improving your home, life and the sense of design around you.

Read on to see how feng shui has worked for thousands of years in China, and how it continues to be used today worldwide.

CHAPTER IV

Heaven, Earth and Man

The Pursuit of Harmony and Survival with the Forces of Nature

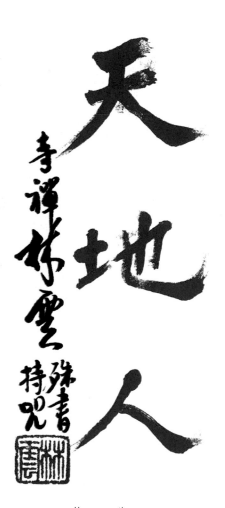

Heaven, earth, man

The basic premises of feng shui originated in early agrarian China—a country slightly larger than the United States—when man's fate was closely intertwined with the workings and cycles of heaven and earth: survival and fortunes depended on whether the earth was fertile or barren, the weather was gentle or cruel, and whether water and sunlight were plentiful. As a victim and benefactor of nature, man observed it closely.

Feng shui also grew out of a sense of place. Its rules and concepts arose from the topography, philosophy, culture and customs of China, and went on to have an enormous impact on building projects, architecture and homes, be it for the living or the dead.

Place has always been an important concern in China. From the time when early farmers sought to settle along the Yellow and Wei River valleys, the Chinese emphasized an almost religious experience of space. They saw themselves unified with the earth, nature and cosmos. They looked to the sky, stars, earth formations and vegetation to inform them on where to live and create order amid seemingly chaotic natural forces. As a study of space, feng shui seeks to identify how the fates of man and nature are closely intertwined, how any change in nature may be reflected in residents' lives and well-being. Where could early man settle and position himself so that farming and animal husbandry would coexist with nature's wild, awesome and, at times, inhospitable terrain? With endless choices, trial and error brought about a repeatedly workable model, a place where settlers not only survived but actually began to thrive and prosper. That ideal location was in concert with the natural forces such as wind and water, sun and earth. That spot seemed significant and blessed, a place of sacred harmony between heaven, earth and man.

To divine these sacred spaces on earth, this early society began to rely on wise men, or experts in this art of auspicious placement. These proto–feng shui practitioners seemed to possess a special knowledge of the interrelated fates of man and nature. They knew that human destiny hinged on the natural fluctuations of the universe. They held the key to understanding the mystery of the powerful and continual interplay of nature's forms and forces with human

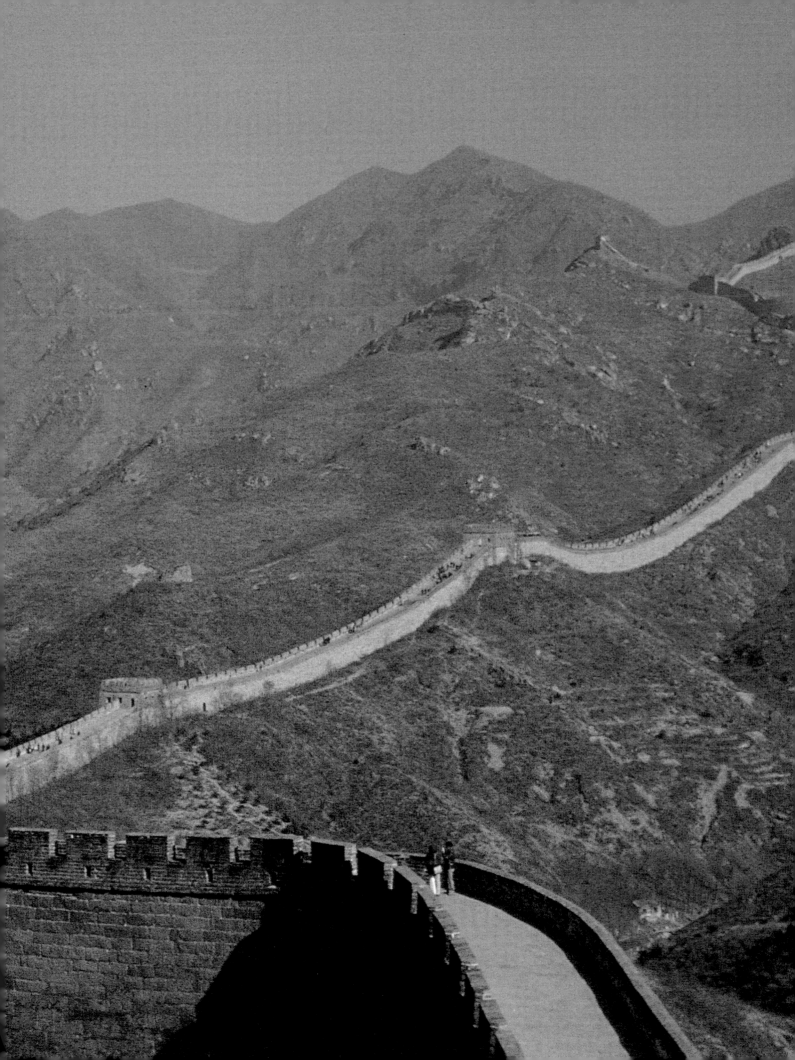

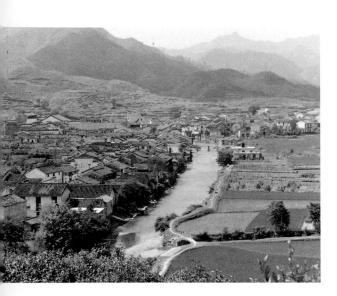

Well-sited Cheng Kan village in Anhui province prospered and grew so much that it actually moved its river to the south, in order still to be able to build new houses with a good aspect on the north bank, protectively backed by mountains.

destiny. Scrutinizing and observing nature, they understood that the color of a leaf or the texture of soil, the shape of a mountain or stream, the configurations in the sky or the position of a palace or hut all have an effect. It was thus that the rules, theories and practices of feng shui arose.

Feng shui is a language full of signs and symbols that direct us along a life course. Feng shui masters operate as decoders and interpreters of the cryptic messages and omens conveyed by natural forms and forces. The early experts would search the heavens and earth for signals of good harvests and warnings of disaster. They looked to the stars, moon and sun for indications of good weather for planting. They examined the earth—mountains, watercourses, vegetation and soil—for signs of fortuitous places to build, work, plant and raise animals. Nature held the clues to all men's fates: to the farmer, nature indicated whether a harvest would be fruitful or devastating; for the emperor, what was good for the farmer was good for the empire. What was disastrous for farmers might mean that the emperor had lost his contract with celestial powers—the Mandate of Heaven.

From ancient times to the present, the key to discerning good feng shui has been the ability to detect, analyze and harmonize with the breath or energy of the earth and cosmos—ch'i. The art of feng shui is therefore twofold: first, to detect the earth's pulse, determining where best to live a happy, comfortable and prosperous life without disturbing the earth's circulation; second, to read and interpret the visible and invisible signs of the universe and channel its positive forces.

Mountains and rivers together create a Chinese landscape, in reality, image and terminology: the word for landscape painting is *shan-shui*, which translates as "mountain-water." Their significance is further underlined by the term *shan-he*, which translates as "mountain-river," referring to the destiny of a country.

MOUNTAINS AND HILLS

The Chinese ascribed human and animal properties to nature. Natural shapes symbolically delineated its power, and the landscape was one expansive metaphor, animated by bodies of earth or snaking waterways as discerned by the feng shui expert. A mountain, for example, might be an awesome but benevolent dragon, an overhanging cliff a tiger's jaw. An entire branch of feng shui, called the "school of forms," interprets the landscape by detecting shapes. Dragons, the most frequent mountain symbol, are said to protect many Chinese villages. It is easy to see that different parts of a mountain mass might embody aspects of a dragon: a line of ridges are his vertebrae, ridges to the side spread into arms and legs. Streams and springs are his veins and arteries, pumping the earth's ch'i.

The Chinese went to great lengths to avoid tampering with the earth or severing a dragon's head or vein. The Great Wall, one of the emperor Ch'in Shih Huang-ti's many building projects to unite the empire in the third century B.C., was constructed to serve as a boundary binding together the nation to the south while fortifying it against incursions of barbarians from the north. It was built with great sensitivity to the terrain—following the rises and dips in its contours—in order to enhance feng

AUSPICIOUS HILL OR MOUNTAIN SITING		
Rounded, gentle hills	A gradual slope with good drainage	Facing out from the hill

	PROBLEMATIC HILL OR MOUNTAIN SITING	DIAGNOSIS	CURE
	On a square butte	A stunted or broken, incomplete shape. Residents are calm, but not motivated; they become more and more lazy and their business has less and less custom.	Install a flagpole or a spotlight to siphon up ch'i.
	On a steep slope	Ch'i and money flow away. Can be a victim of mudslides and danger.	Hang a convex or regular mirror inside the house, facing the outside.
	On or below an overhang—known as a "tiger's jaw"	If the house is below the overhang, residents will be sick, go bankrupt or die prematurely. If the house is on top, they will find their business and career on a precipice—in danger, unstable— or that it is powerful, but dangerous, like drug dealing. The Chinese have a saying, "Riding on a tiger is hard to get off."	If the house is on the bottom, install a spotlight or a flagpole with an arrow whirligig pointing upward. If the house is on top, put a fan on the roof, facing the sky to elevate ch'i.
	On a cliff	Residents may be prone to nervous breakdowns, heart disease and insomnia.	Place a spotlight on the cliff to return ch'i. Plant ivy to hold on to the house, or install a lattice screen with vines.
	On top of a hill—particularly a steep one	Ch'i, good luck and opportunity blow away. Residents will be lonely and friends and relatives will diminish in number.	Install spotlights that point higher than the roof in four corners.
	On a mountain with jagged sides	This terrain is not inhabitable for the living, but fine for graves.	Plant different types of trees in the garden.
	Facing a hill	Bad for wealth and career.	Install a flagpole or spotlight at the rear of the backyard. Aim the light at the roof.

shui and not disrupt it or the nation's luck. However, shortly after the wall's completion and Emperor Ch'in's death, feng shui became central to a devious and successful plot to wrest political power from the heir apparent and General Meng T'ien, who had overseen the construction of the wall. Before the heir and general heard of Ch'in's death they received a forged letter, apparently from the emperor, but in fact from his scheming eunuch adviser Chao Kao, accusing them of treason. According to imperial records, the general bemoaned the accusation, but realized—before he took his life—that he had betrayed his country by supervising the construction of the Great Wall which, he said, cut the veins of the land and thus endangered the nation. Shortly after his death, the dynasty fell.

China offers seemingly endless varieties of mountains, from rugged ranges north of Beijing to the knife-like outcroppings of Kueilin. They loom large in the feng shui landscape, and earth shapes in general, from mountains and hills to slight undulations in the terrain, were seen as outcroppings and indicators of ch'i. Important components of a good feng shui site, they were viewed as centers of cosmic energy, where earth and heaven meet. Some mountains to the west were said to be home to the Taoist Immortals. China itself was topographically defined by Five Sacred Mountains, thought to stand like the poles of a tent at the four corners and center of the Chinese universe and hold up the canopy of heaven. To confirm the validity of their reign—considered to be the Mandate of Heaven—and to ask for celestial blessings on behalf of their country, emperors periodically scaled one of them, Mount Tai (the largest mountain east of Sian, the first capital of China), armed with offerings and prayers. A Han dynasty (202 B.C.–A.D. 221) history, anxious to discredit the preceding Ch'in dynasty (221–207 B.C.)—and justify the Han right to rule—chronicles several failed attempts by Emperor Ch'in Shih Huang-ti to scale Mount Tai, proving him to have been unworthy to rule. In contrast, the Han dynasty Emperor Wu is reported to have successfully ascended the mountain on numerous occasions.

Along with their sacred purposes, mountains were also considered to improve feng shui because of their strategic importance. Barriers against the northern barbarians, they also served to block harsh, chilling winds from the Mongolian steppes in the north.

Hills, like mountains, were regarded as outcroppings of positive ch'i and considered to be the best places to live. Flat, featureless terrain was avoided, as it was considered to lack good ch'i. Hills, as large earth shields, served to protect a home from northern winds as well as provide elevation from floods. When the land lacked hills, berms, which enhanced both the landscape and the feng shui, were constructed.

The shape and slope of a hill or a mountain could help form the fate of residents. Here, symbolism comes into play, with life literally imitating nature. For example, on an island near Hong Kong, a cliff resembling an aroused naked man was said to spur flirtatiousness in the girls of the village it faced. On the other hand, a mountain or hill shaped like a calligraphy brush-stand is said to encourage high scholarly, social and political achievement. In nineteenth-century China, feng shui experts blamed failed crops on nearby rat-shaped hills that they said were devouring the harvest. No sooner did residents construct a large "rat trap" gateway than the fields yielded abundant produce.

Ideally, a gently contoured round hill that gradually dips into a meandering river valley is best. Even better is if it is flanked by slightly lower hills, and fronted by a foothill to the south. This classic feng shui mountain arrangement is described in metaphoric terms—the hills are given animal characteristics, as well as being aligned with the five elements. A house should be sited on a black tortoise mountain which protects it from northern winds, and face south, with a white tiger hill to the west (blocking the sun's glare), and a green dragon hill to the east to make sure the tiger stays in line.

A lower red phoenix foothill should rest to the south. This hill juxtaposition was also described as a "mother embracing child" or "dragon protecting pearl" formation. A mountain or a hill resembling a lion's head or the calm, compassionate face of a Bodhisattva is also auspicious.

If a hill does not seem to be endowed with any positive identifying features, minor additions can be made to create a complete and auspicious shape. A hill resembling a hapless headless dragon, for example, can be empowered and balanced by building a house on the "neck," improving both the site's and the residents' ch'i. Positioned at the "brain" of the hill, the house gives its occupants more control over their lives.

RIVERS AND WATERWAYS

The Chinese word for landscape is shan-shui—mountain-water. In the feng shui landscape, moving rivers (yang) balance the mountain's yin. Mountains and rivers were seen as interdependent and eternal. As Tu Fu, an eighth-century poet, wrote, "The state may fall but hills and streams remain."

For centuries, Chinese painters and poets alike praised the stimulating power of rivers, the calm beauty and spiritual depth of lakes and ponds, in landscape paintings and poems. When court life proved stressful or dangerous, poets and painters, scholars and bureaucrats sought the safety and peace of mountains and water, turning away from civilized life. For their part, farmers needed both access to water and ways to control its flow by irrigation in order to grow healthy, plentiful crops—thus water itself became a symbol of money. And the feng shui expert would analyze the strength and flow of ch'i by observing the flow of water—ch'i moves water.

The seventh-century Grand Canal continues to link many of China's cities with its countryside as well as aiding irrigation.

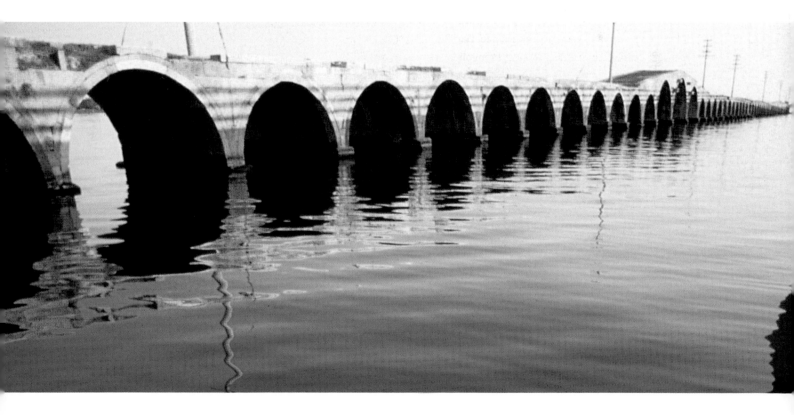

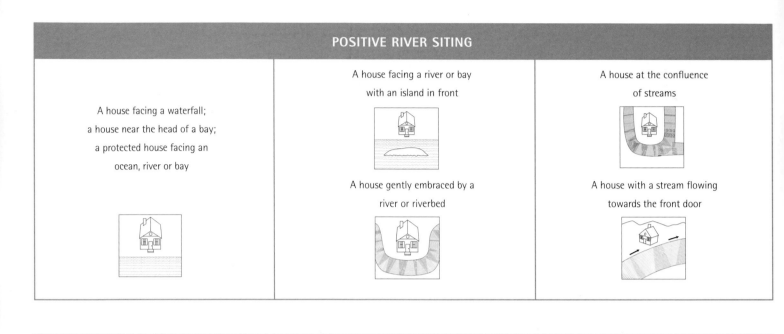

POSITIVE RIVER SITING

A house facing a waterfall; a house near the head of a bay; a protected house facing an ocean, river or bay

A house facing a river or bay with an island in front

A house gently embraced by a river or riverbed

A house at the confluence of streams

A house with a stream flowing towards the front door

PROBLEMATIC RIVER SITING	DIAGNOSIS	CURE
A house facing away from a river or bay	Residents will not be able to grasp money and opportunity.	Install a mirror inside the house facing the water.
A house sited where a river bends away from it	As above.	As above.
A house too close to a river—less than twice the house's height	The family's—and the house's—foundation will be undermined—ill health.	Place ju-sha in a vase or incense burner, in the bedroom or an important room such as a study or dining room.
A house with a river flowing away from the front door	Residents will suffer financial loss.	Install a mirror inside the house facing the water, to balance out the loss.
An overexposed house on a peninsula	Residents will be unable to hold on to money.	As above.

In terms of form and function, water's natural power and force was embodied by water dragons. These symbolized active rivers and lakes, and animated water like moody Loch Ness monsters. The water dragon controlled weather, tides and water levels. When controlled and appeased, he nourished fertile fields. If unchecked, he wreaked havoc or even death on humans. (The dragon image was so vivid in the Chinese mind that one sixteenth-century account reported a dragon sighting during a disastrous flood. It tells how one entered a home in northeastern China, only to make a violent exit by bursting through a wall leaving a wake of water and hail.)

As with mountains, there are many feng shui rules on the configurations and orientation of waterways. In the fourth millennium B.C., when Chinese farmers first cultivated rice, they discovered that a location near to water was desirable—it impacted on mere subsistence. The ideal was a river or stream that gently snaked along the landscape as a natural blessing, nurturing fields and rice paddies and dispersing positive ch'i in its meandering. Straight, torrential rivers, on the other hand, could be problematic, threatening life, wealth and fortunes. But, by altering the surrounding terrain, feng shui can positively reroute a dangerously straight watercourse to curve and wander through fields and countryside, improving irrigation and thus health and profits.

The power and value of watercourses were at once practical and symbolic. The Chinese erected towers on foothills flanking both sides of a river to symbolically modulate its flow and guard against floods. An old Chinese saying goes: "He who controls water, controls the Empire." Indeed, Emperor Sui Yang-di (A.D. 604–618), who ordered the construction of China's Grand Canal, was considered a great unifier of China. The canal in itself united the country physically, by running north to south and linking the great rivers that flowed from west to east. In doing so it added to China's prosperity by opening a great new avenue of trade, and reinforcing the emperor's image as supreme ruler.

Fed by water, vegetation has also long been an indicator of ch'i. A lush, verdant site possesses good ch'i. A barren, parched area indicates a poor flow of ch'i. Crucial to nurturing crops and irrigating rice paddies, water was an essential element in lower-lying areas.

This Hangchow dike creates visual poetry, as well as a safeguard for the city against floods.

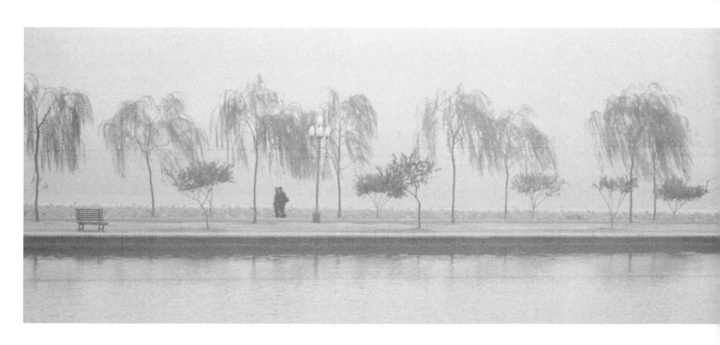

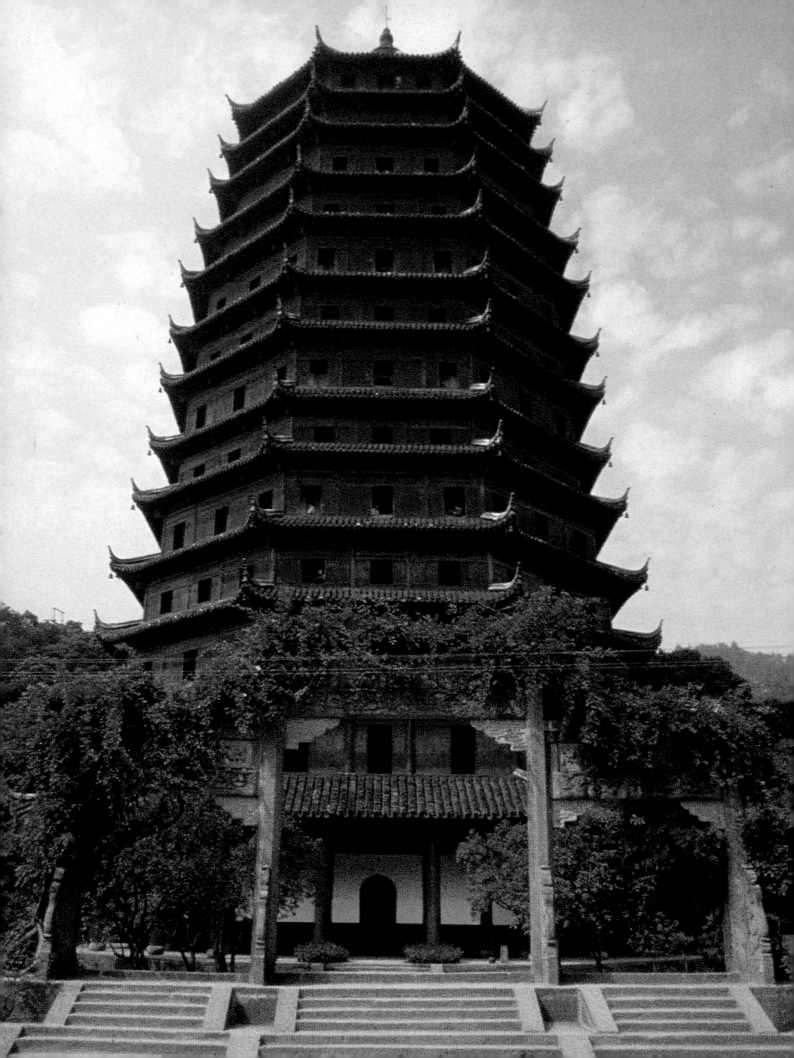

EARLY STRUCTURES IN CHINA

Most sacred and important shrines, tombs and temples in China indicate that great thought was given to the surrounding topography and scenery as well as the approach to the site. The "build-up" of the processional way was instrumental in inspiring awe and appreciation. At measured intervals, the site was framed in a new way to create the effect of unrolling a landscape scroll and achieve a new perspective at every turn. This was known as the guo-bai, translated literally as "pass-through." Even the area of sky that visually existed between frame and site was considered important, for there should be a standardized balance between void and the concrete world—between emptiness and being. At each interval in the approach to a site, harmony was important. The perspective at every turn should be balanced—not too close and not too far away. The art and science of the approach was not just happenstance or aesthetics, but the product of following strictly measured guidelines as put forth in the ancient Chinese classic text of rituals, the *Chou Li*. The measurements of the *Chou Li* indicated where, say, a gate should be built, or a bridge oriented, to create new vistas for a procession to appreciate as it approached the destination site and structure. Great thought was given to any building project. For example, Emperor Ch'in Shih Huang-ti had 50-foot-wide roads, flanked by trees at 30-foot intervals.

The feng shui expert would attempt to select an auspicious site on which to build by taking the surrounding features into account. Once it was selected, the owner, carpenter and feng shui expert combined to plan, build and orient the structure. For his part, the expert would determine what direction a home should face to enjoy the best that nature could offer, such as sun, pleasant breezes, a good view, natural protection. The ideal house should be halfway up a hill facing south or east, with a view and access to water in front, flanked by lower hills on either side and with an even lower hill in front of it.

An ode in the *Book of Songs* goes:

> To give continuance to foremothers and forefathers
> We build a house, many hundred cubits of wall:
> To South and East its doors.
> Here shall we live, here rest,
> Here laugh, here talk ...

Just as the Chinese have long associated their destinies with that of their natural surroundings, they saw the forms of structures as molding the lives and fates of their occupants. The shape of a house was important for feng shui reasons, too. Rising from the earth, the traditional home represented a universe in itself. From a foundation of tamped soil, timbers rose to link earth symbolically with heaven. For thousands of years, the Chinese used the "four-sided courtyard" (sze-he-yuan), a housing unit of a number of buildings grouped around a courtyard—preferably a garden. If the family was wealthy, they merely added more of these units. With an entrance ideally to the south, the house enjoyed warm sun in the winter and was shielded from the northern winds.

This shape and grouping of buildings, as well as their orientation, seem to geometrically mimic the ideal protective feng shui topography of mountains—the mother-embracing-child or dragon-protecting-pearl formations.

Temples, pagodas and shrines were built to inspire and protect local residents as well as to provide refuge for the worship of ancestors, shelter for travelers, and a blessed site for rituals. Pagodas were

The Pagoda of Six Harmonies. This Sung dynasty (960–1279) pagoda was built on a hill above West Lake to protect Hangchow from the tides of the equinoxes. It also enhances the city's luck and ch'i. The shape of the twelve tiers is a particularly potent form.

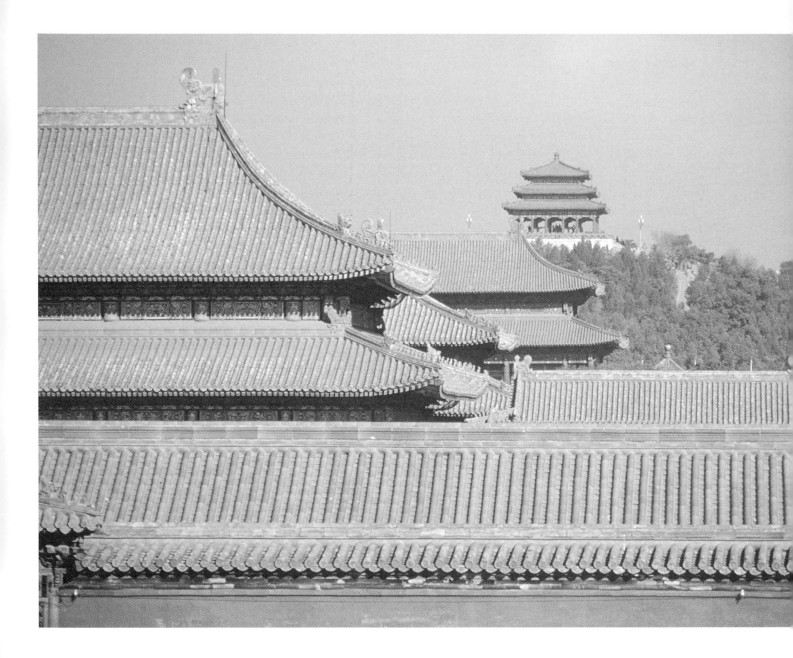

Since the thirteenth century, Coal Hill has been a man-made berm that serves to protect the Forbidden City from harsh northern winds—but it did not protect the Sung dynasty emperor from Mongol invasion and overthrow.

architectural symbols of the Confucian concept of higher learning, and were placed to attract and increase scholarship for one area. Sites were sought that allowed these sacred buildings to harmonize with the local topography and endowed their structures with positive natural forces and defenses, such as protection from wind and water, as well as inspiring if awesome views. Sometimes they would be at the *shui-kou*, or "mouth of water," where a river entered a city or a town, in order to moderate ch'i and water flow. Sometimes they were built on a low dragon mountain to make it seem higher than a ferocious tiger mountain.

These temples and pagodas populate China's hillsides and mountains like lightning rods of good ch'i, sited to visually and spatially enhance their surroundings as well as the luck of local residents.

One example is the 200-foot-high Pagoda of Six Harmonies above Hangchow, the capital of the Southern Sung dynasty (A.D. 1127–1279). While the city of Hangchow, built in the third century B.C. during the Han dynasty, harmonizes with its natural surroundings, it is threatened twice a year by flooding from West Lake, a tidal estuary. The Pagoda of Six Harmonies was built to enhance and protect the area from these floods. (On a more physical level, the city governors—two of whom were famous poet-bureaucrats, Su Tung-po and Po Chu-yi—had two aesthetically pleasing dikes constructed, thus enhancing both the scenery and the feng shui.)

Sacred buildings were constructed in auspicious shapes. Some pagodas were octagonal, symbolizing the complete perfection of the ba-gua and the universe. The Temple of Heaven, south of the Forbidden City in Beijing, is a classic example of the use of auspicious shaping. Here, generations of emperors proceeded to the temple to pray for a good year, abundant crops and the reaffirmation of the Mandate of Heaven. Built on a square plot, symbolizing the earth, the temple progresses into a round form symbolizing heaven.

ANCIENT CHINESE CITIES

The layout and position of early Chinese cities were also affected by feng shui. Through a symbolic system, urban design was linked to religion, politics, astrology and art. The position and shape of a capital city, when aligned with the forces of the universe, empowered the emperor to rule wisely and effectively at the center of the nation, and ensured the country's well-being. For the emperor to govern well he needed to mediate properly between heaven and earth. It was crucial that he sit at the center of the capital, the country and the cosmos. His throne was placed where "earth and sky meet, where the four seasons merge, where wind and rain are gathered in and where yin and yang are in harmony." A nearly square-shaped capital city reflected both the Chinese symbol of the earth and the five elements that define all matter in the cosmos—the four sides with the emperor positioned at the center. Historical records from the second millenium B.C. report that early planners employed various forms of divination, including animal sacrifices, oracle bones and feng shui to ensure and enhance earthly imperial power. An ode in the *Book of Songs* notes:

> The plain of Zhou was very fertile ...
> Here we will make a start ...
> Here notch our tortoise ...
> It says "stop" ...
> "Build houses here."

This sense of being attached to a universal order was further reinforced by metaphor. The Chinese named imperial cities and buildings after celestial bodies: in Peking, the emperor's domain was named Tzu-chin Cheng, "Purple Forbidden City," after the Pole Star Tzu-wei. And within the Forbidden City, the emperor's official meeting room was named "heaven." The three main government halls were called Chong Yang Du, which translates as "middle of earth." In addition, certain imperial buildings were aligned and named for a Fu Hsi formation of the *I Ching* trigram (see page 32). For example, during the Ming dynasty, the emperor resided in the chyan area, Ching Gung (the Palace of Heavenly Purity), named for the gua or trigram chyan—three yang lines—which represents the yang principle and the south. The empress lived in the Kuen Ning Gung (the Palace of Earthly

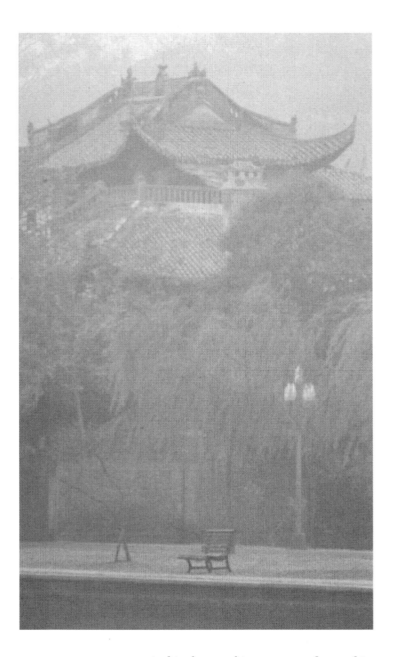

This structure, slightly above Hangchow's West Lake, is well sited to have access to water, but elevated enough to avoid biannual floods.

Tranquillity) named for the gua kuen—three yin lines—which symbolizes yin and the north.

Imperial palaces and capital cities were highly ordered. They were sited south of a mountain and north of water or surrounded by natural or man-made moats. They were constructed along a north-south and eastwest axis with a prescribed placement of walls, gates, towers and markets. The Forbidden City contained a water system—to cool and provide drainage for the palace—that entered from the north-east corner and exited from the southwest corner. A man-made river wandered in the southern section, to protect an area associated with fire—south was aligned with the fire element. Even cemeteries had their place, positioned north or west of the capital in the quadrants that symbolized winter and autumn, seasons of death and decay.

The siting of the emperor, the "Son of Heaven," was important. A feng shui expert would divine where he should sit and face to exert the most power, control and righteousness over the realm. If he was well placed he would rule wisely and the empire would prosper. Generally this meant facing south. One emperor was said to change his sleeping site each night—perhaps for feng shui, perhaps for security.

China was viewed as the center of the universe. *Chung-guo*, the term for China, means "middle kingdom." To reinforce this image and his power, the emperor, who arbitrated between heaven and earth, ruled at the hub from which all power emanated. While his private quarters were sited in the east, his empress and concubines were appropriately sited in the northwest corner of the Forbidden City to reflect their role and position—the yin and female quadrant. For millennia, the imperial city and urban society were also arranged along class lines. For their part, the elite resided in fortified areas, both for their own safety and for the protection of the emperor, whose spies could keep a better watch over potential usurpers.

Color was another decorative method to further enhance the environment and the emperor's authority. Yellow, for example, was associated with power and earth. The emperor wrapped himself in golden silk robes and his residence, the Forbidden City, was roofed primarily with yellow tiles symbolizing his position at the center of the empire, and thus his ability to arbitrate between heaven and earth and rule with authority over the realm. The imperial library roof, however, was black, the color of the water element, and thus acted as a symbolic fire hydrant to protect the archives from fire. Position, both physical and political, was expressed and reinforced by color. For example, one imperial statute decreed that a prince's home could be three courtyards large with his door painted gold and green roof tiles. A duke's home could also have three courts and a gold door, but his roof tiles were to be black. An official of first or second rank was only entitled to two courtyards, and a green door and a black roof.

The importance of positioning the ruler lasted beyond the dynasties. While feng shui was, and is still, officially suppressed in the People's Republic of China, Mao's private doctor wrote that Mao's "compound was located in the heart of Zhongnanhai, in the centre of the old imperial grounds … facing south, in the manner of emperors."

Just as in the countryside, mountains were also an important feature in the landscapes of China's capital cities. Sited to the north, they served as huge earth shields protecting them from harsh winds and barbarians sweeping down from Mongolia. When not naturally occurring, mountains were sometimes manufactured. Such is the case with Coal Hill, an artificial hill that rises 300 feet high directly north of the Forbidden City. Its origins are traced to the birth of Genghis Khan in the

Design details expressed real concerns. Peaked roofs like these in the Forbidden City (left) served to please visually, modify the internal temperature and protect occupants from demons; the animals atop the roof are said to guard against fire. This little creature on a roof in Macao (below) guards the home.

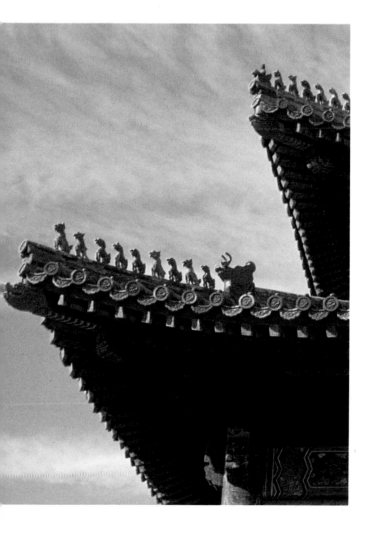

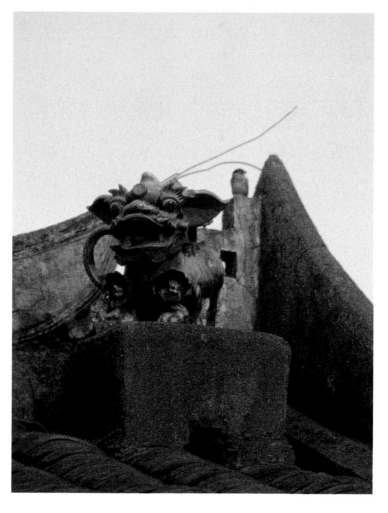

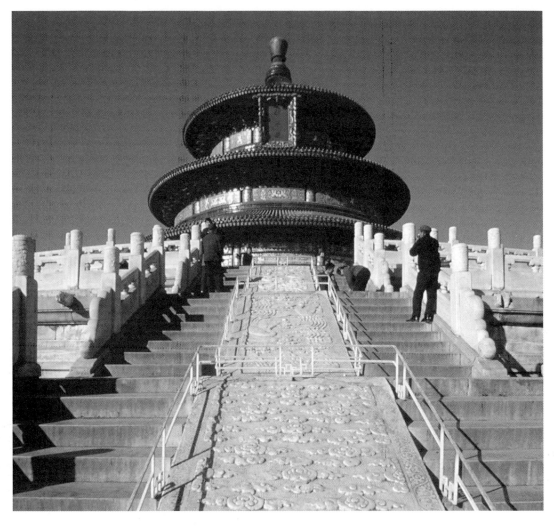

The Temple of Heaven, south of the imperial palace in Beijing, is propitiously shaped to symbolize the emperor's periodic ascent from earth (the square plaza), carried up steps arranged in auspicious variables of three and nine, to heaven (the round shrine), where he sacrificed and prayed for a good harvest and luck for the empire. During his measured ascent, he was carried over this stone plaque, the base of which is carved with mountains, rising into a sky of stylized clouds.

thirteenth century. When court geomancers prophesied that a hill to the north possessing a "king-making vital force" would destroy the dynasty, the emperor lavished gifts on the northern Mongols in order to acquire the hill and move it south to Peking, where it was rebuilt. Shortly after the hill was completed, depleting the work force and imperial coffers, the Mongols, under Genghis Khan, attacked and established their own rule.

Rivers also played an important part in the siting of cities, towns and villages. During the Ch'ing dynasty, a prosperous village even moved its river south. New homes could then be built on its north side, but still be backed by mountains and have an auspicious view over water to the south.

MOTIFS, METAPHORS AND SYMBOLS

Design motifs and metaphors are recurring elements in feng shui visual vernacular. Traditional ornamentation and structure reflected real needs and fears. Upswept roofs were embellished with creatures that guarded and protected residents. Dragons—powerful and versatile mythic creatures thought to be capable of growing miles in length and shrinking to the size of a dragonfly—figure prominently in Chinese art, symbols and legends. A 5,000-year-old grave was decorated with both a tiger and a dragon. Early legendary emperors were said to descend from dragon fathers, and in the third century B.C., Ch'in Shih Huang-ti adopted the dragon as an official imperial emblem. A symbol and a talisman, it was carved into thrones and embroidered into golden imperial silk robes.

While these design details might seem superstitious, Chinese superstition often holds a hidden science. Sloped roofs are said to protect the home from devils falling from the sky: when they pounce, they will slide and be sent skywards again. The spiked eaves serve to impale them should they dare to descend again. But the slope also has a more tangible, practical purpose: it allows maximum sun to enter in winter and minimal sun in summer. The roofs are less peaked in the north, allowing the strong and chilling winds to flow over them unobstructed.

"Spirit screens" in front of doors and gates also had their practical and superstitious uses. While they kept harsh wind and dirt out, they also blocked any demon hoping to enter—demons fly in straight lines. Some screens were armed with the ba-gua or even mirrors, which scared the demon away with the sight of his own face.

A dragon adorns a screen within the Forbidden City in Beijing to adjust ch'i.

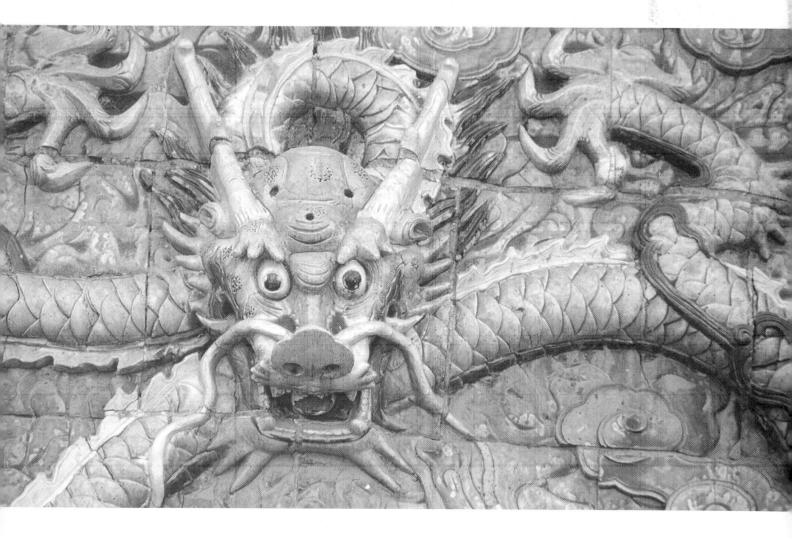

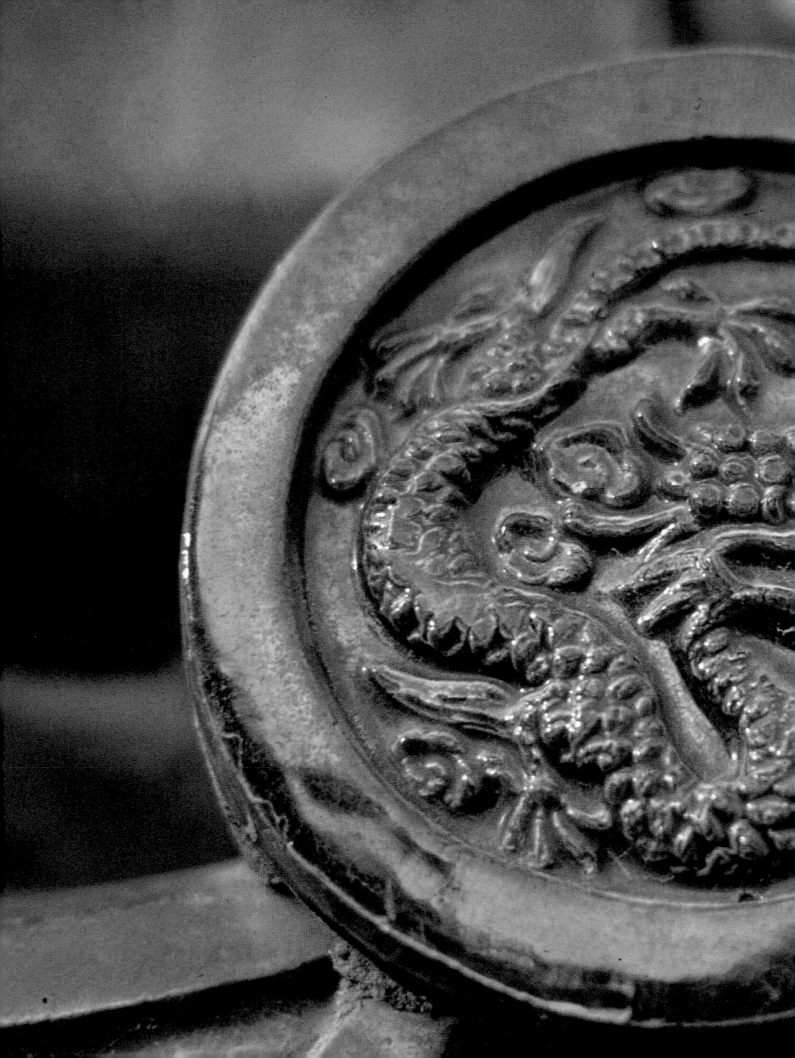

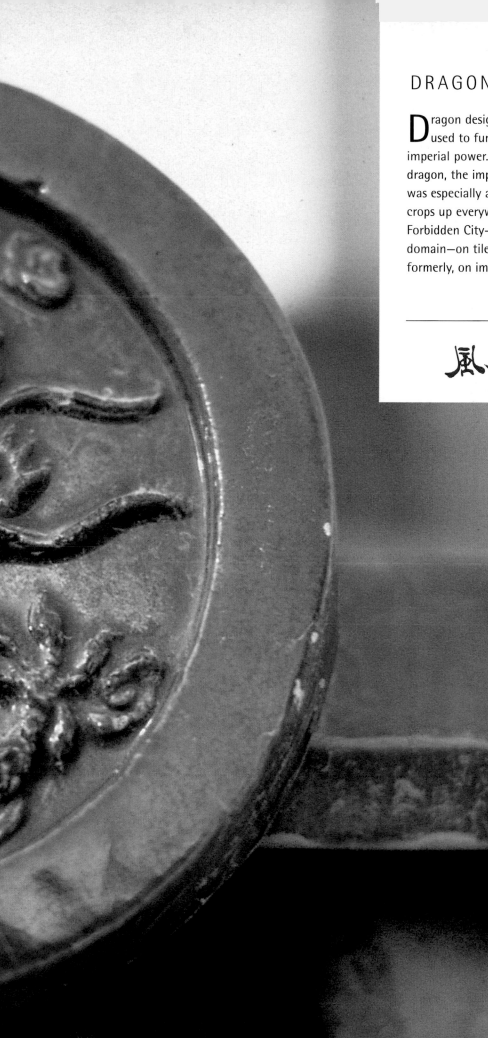

DRAGON MOTIFS

Dragon design motifs were used to further reinforce imperial power. The five-toed dragon, the imperial emblem, was especially auspicious and crops up everywhere in the Forbidden City—the emperor's domain—on tiles, screens and, formerly, on imperial robes.

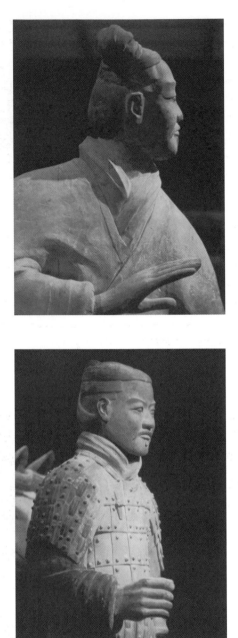

These life-sized terra-cotta figures, two of scores with varying facial attributes and expressions, represent individuals in Ch'in Shih Huang-ti's army—a vastly more humane resolution than earlier methods of guarding and staffing the emperor's heavenly home with the bodies of favored retainers.

GRAVES

Some think feng shui originated with grave siting. For millennia, the Chinese took great pains when burying their dead. As a Confucian offshoot of filial piety mixed with Taoist ritual, it was believed that if one's ancestor reposed eternally in a comfortable, well-positioned and even opulent resting place, one would be rewarded in this life, reaping wealth, many sons, good health and perhaps high office. If not, one's descendants would suffer. So everyone, from emperor to manual laborer, tried to ensure prosperity and luck in this life by creating a fortuitous hereafter for their ancestors. Long-held beliefs die hard: many accredit both Sun Yat-sen's and Chiang Kai-shek's rises to power to the auspicious grave sites of their respective mothers, and blame Generalissimo Chiang's downfall on Communists digging the grave up.

The ideal position for a grave site was similar to that of a well-sited home: halfway up a hill facing south looking out to the sea. However, the location of a grave should be drier than that of a dwelling for the living. When this optimal arrangement was unavailable, the ancient Chinese created their own good grave feng shui. On flat plains, such as those near Ch'ang-an, the ancient capital of China now known as Sian, small hills were created within which to bury royalty, generals and high-ranking officials.

Viewed as the fathers of their country, deceased Chinese emperors were buried in a similar manner to the pharaohs of Egypt, surrounded by comforts, wealth, executed enemies—even ill-fated favored servants, horses and guards who were essential to the expired ruler in the next world. This national form of filial piety served to ensure good luck for offspring and country alike.

The grave of Ch'in Shih Huang-ti, the first emperor to unify China, is one example. Arranged along a north-south axis, this man-made berm was protected by a life-sized terra-cotta army. Constructed by an incredible 700,000 laborers, the tomb's interior symbolized a microcosmic, harmonious universe, replete with heavenly constellations, earthly mountains and mechanically run quicksilver rivers and oceans, as well as a miniature palace.

The creation of emperors' underground palace tombs continued until the fall of the Ch'ing dynasty in 1912. From beginning (site selection) to end (burial ceremonies) the process was imbued with ritual to ensure the comfort of the deceased ruler and the longevity and health of the dynasty and nation. At the core, or best point, of the burial palace sat the "golden well." During the emperor's lifetime, at an auspicious time, soil was extracted from the well by a prince or senior official, with a golden shovel, and deposited in a yellow silk and satin bag inscribed with the time and date. The bag was stored in the Forbidden City until the emperor's death. As the burial ceremony commenced, the soil from the golden well was mixed with jewels, and teeth the emperor had lost during his lifetime, then returned to the well.

Today in Hong Kong, thousands of graves seem to occupy some of the best sites in the area. They enjoy a number of the best views out to the South China Sea and the local islands. Some are constructed in a horseshoe shape to embrace good fortune and opportunities for generations of descendants. Others have Western-style headstones but are still placed to absorb good luck for offspring. After 1997, all this may be moot. Burial is an issue in the People's Republic, which advocates simple cremations partially for reasons of space and partially to discourage superstitious practices. In 1996, two officials in the Beijing government were disgraced when they were discovered burying their ancestors according to the ancient rites. (*Asia Week* carried an advertisement touting a graveyard with the "best feng shui in the Bay Area." It encouraged offspring to exhume their ancestors and rebury them safely south of San Francisco.) Inland, burial urns containing dried and scoured bones mine would-be development areas like booby traps; large payments are sometimes elicited from developers for their proper removal and ritual re-siting and burial, or families may interrupt road or building construction.

Feng shui is a consideration even in Christian cemeteries. Here, the plot shape is important. While a square is best, a "dustpan" shape—with a wider entrance—also serves to sweep in good ch'i and luck for the offspring. A plot with a narrowing front, however, foretells narrowing prospects for descendants, affecting careers, finances and lives in general.

When siting a grave or yin site, the family of the person who had died sought optimal feng shui locations in the hope that good luck would befall them. The best topographic formation was similar to that of a house—the "mother-embracing-child" formation. But when mountains were not a natural local asset, the Chinese created them. Such is the case with these Han and T'ang dynasty tombs of high officials, rising in cornfields near the ancient capital of Sian.

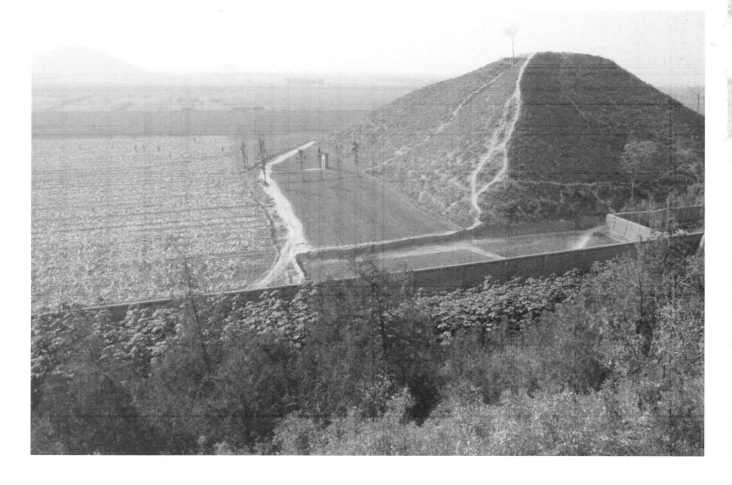

Over the centuries,
Kuelin's scenic
limestone outcroppings
rising above the snaking
Li River have inspired
poets, artists and
garden designers.

CHAPTER V

Man and Nature
The Art of Landscaping and Siting

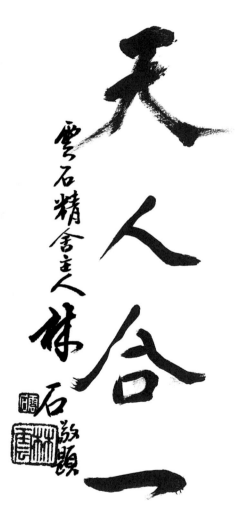

Heaven and man are one

As Chinese civilization grew, feng shui developed into an environmental system that was both an art and a science. It also evolved to meet new concerns and new surroundings, and the Chinese concept of landscape was translated into smaller spaces. In placing a building or adjusting natural settings, feng shui experts soon became early landscape designers, seeking to enhance nature and not disturb it. Like their earlier counterparts they sought harmony with nature, but on slightly different terms. While nature still affected—if not dominated—human life, it was realized that humans also had their own effect on their natural surroundings. With this insight came a sense of responsibility, and an accepted theory based around the principle that what human beings wrought on earth might, in turn, ultimately affect them.

As with other cultures, when civilization encroached significantly on nature and man's hand began to actually change the landscape, direct access to important natural forms and phenomena diminished. Yet, in China, the yearning for at least a glimpse of nature's balance still remained. When the ideal of a house sited halfway up a gentle hill facing south to the sea proved elusive, the Chinese employed thoughtful, visual references to nature and its perfection, and new feng shui alternatives emerged.

This new harmonization with nature was on a far smaller scale than previously. Using landscape paintings or gardens of various sizes, it was possible to symbolically return to, and reflect on, the ideal balance of nature, in microcosm. By unfurling a landscape painting, the viewer could be transported to a place and time of natural peace and harmony. By glancing through a window or strolling along a winding path in a well-constructed garden, he or she could experience, in miniature, nature's perfection and restful powers.

This chapter will deal with exteriors, proceeding from the Chinese ideal of the landscape and garden to feng shui's effect on modern landscape design and siting. The modern section offers practical ways to position a building, enhance a plot of land or correct unfortunate landscaping.

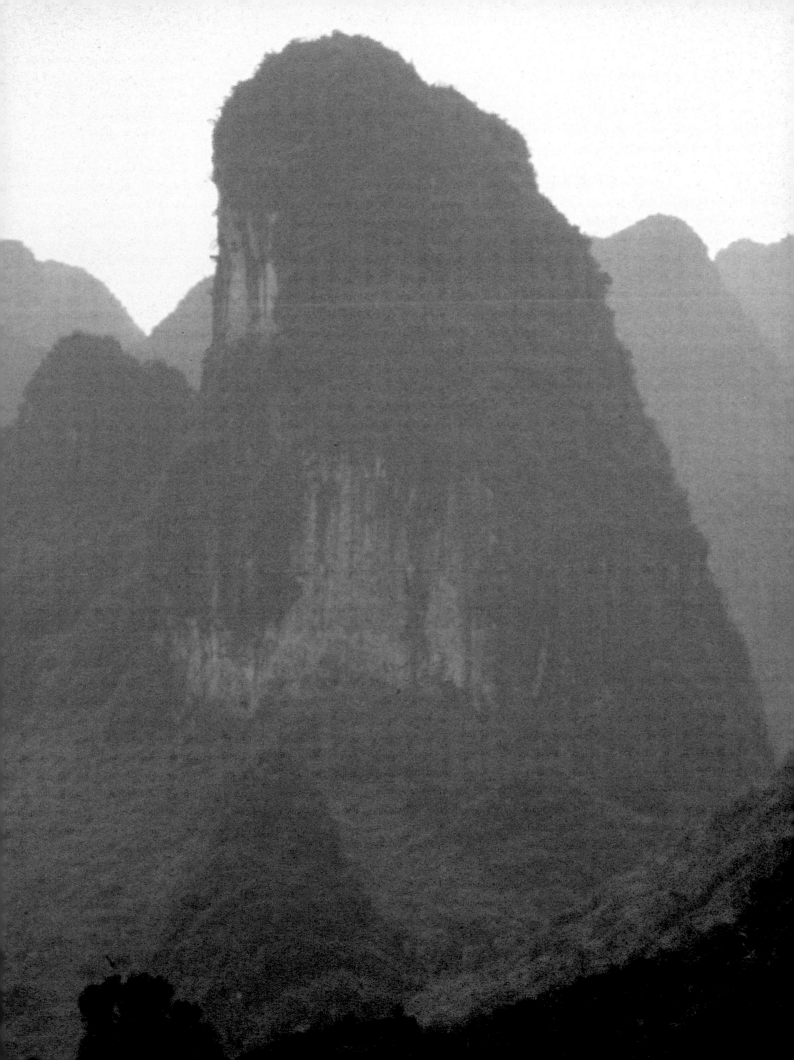

LANDSCAPE PAINTING

If we look through an ancient Chinese painter's eye, we can understand and experience his vision of man, nature and the universe. The aim of the painter was to reproduce the balance and power (ch'i) of nature in miniature. Paintings dramatically underline humans' place in nature: massive mountains, hills and peaks loom over waterfalls that cascade through a void of haze and mist to meander as streams among trees, rocks and, perhaps, past a secluded but auspiciously sited hermit's hut. In these scrolls and albums, nature is shown as monumental and eternal and the role of humans is diminutive and temporary. In Taoist terms, man is but a drop of water in a flowing stream.

Within a single silk scroll exists a symbolic universe reflecting nature's beauty, vastness and magnitude. Monochromatic calligraphic ink strokes and washes form clouds and mists which conspire to create a sense of limitless depths and voids. As the scroll is unfurled or an album opened, new worlds of distant peaks, ravines and streams allow the viewer's eye and mind to roam in a landscape that fuels the imagination, heart and intellect. As an old Chinese saying about landscape painting goes: "Thus may ten thousand miles be illustrated in a foot, and one may wander in a landscape while actually at rest and never have to go any distance."

Together, pools and rocks provide the structure of the garden landscape—the yin and the yang. Here rocks rise like miniature islands out of a pond.

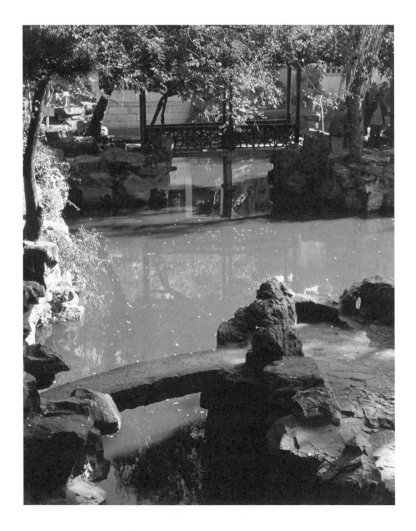

THE CHINESE GARDEN

Another way of reflecting the balance of nature was in the garden. The Chinese developed gardening into an art that captured the essence of their landscape. Their gardens varied in both size and purpose—expansive hunting parks, imperial pleasure gardens and smaller contemplative settings, such as garden courts. Even humble homes cultivated bonsai. Some Chinese, however, prized their gardens more than they were worth. The fall of the Ch'ing dynasty (1644–1912) has been traced by some to the Dowager Empress Tzu Hsi's construction of an enormous pleasure garden to commemorate her sixtieth birthday—with money earmarked for building up the navy.

Nature was present in Chinese urban life in the form of enclosed garden courts. The idea behind them was simple: no matter how far a house lay from a truly pastoral countryside, its residents must never lose touch with the elements of nature. These gardens were versatile: sometimes centers of activity, sometimes spots to seek peace of mind—a place to drink wine or tea, compose poetry or paint. The traditional Chinese home consists of

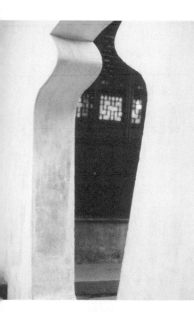

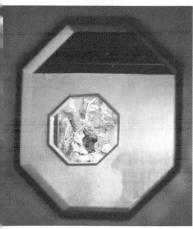

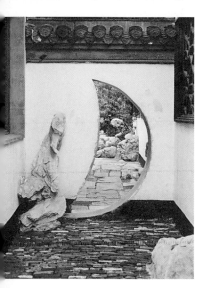

a house and a garden which together represent the harmony of the man-made world with that of nature—within yin there is yang.

The garden was integral to, yet contrasted with, the house. While the home followed formal conventions of symmetry and straight lines, the garden—like nature itself—was asymmetrical, irregular and curvilinear.

Chinese gardens differ widely from their Western counterparts: no fountains, no lawns and no rows of geometric flowerbeds. (Grassy lawns were avoided, as they were reminiscent of the northern steppes, home of barbarian Mongols and Manchus.) Instead, the gardens are irregular, imitating nature in miniature. The concept of mimicking its asymmetrical, haphazard qualities was influenced by Taoist philosophy, which romanticized the return to a simpler life in tune with the rhythms of nature. Following the tradition of poets, painters and scholars retreating to mountains and rivers during political unrest, the garden court was also a place of refuge. In city gardens, people withdrew from the hubbub and stress of the outside world to the quietude of a miniature man-made landscape. Situated at the heart of the home, the garden was a place for imagination and illusion.

Like a Chinese landscape painting, the garden ideal married philosophy and aesthetics. Aesthetically, nature revealed itself in the garden through twists and turns of paths and walkways. Natural vignettes were framed by moon gates and bridges, lattice screens and symbolically shaped windows. Philosophically, the garden design sought to create a universe unto itself, both imitating nature on a small scale and enhancing the balance and ch'i of both garden and house. Feng shui was an important component in informing this philosophy and aesthetic.

Much of a Chinese garden is suggestive. As with the ideals of feng shui siting and landscape painting, mountains and rivers were as essential to the Chinese garden as they were eternal in the Chinese mind. According to Confucius, "The wise find pleasure in water, the virtuous seek mountains." Therefore, rocks and water were crucial features. Water, flowing and shimmering in a fish pool, represents that which is moving, changing and nourishing. Rocks rising at various points like condensed forms of mountains suggest that which is enduring, solid and permanent.

The movements of pools, ponds and miniature streams balance rockery in the ways that rivers balance mountains. Clear water itself evokes positive images and associations. "The highest good is like that of water," wrote Lao-tzu in the *Tao-te Ching*. After all, nurturing water—essential to good harvests born of properly irrigated fields and rice paddies, as well as the source of nourishing fish and seafood—symbolized good fortune for the household or business. In addition, water, with its sounds, constant movement and reflective qualities, provides a positive setting to muse, meditate or create.

Windows and doors provide auspiciously shaped access to a garden. The vase-shaped door in Shanghai (top) creates a restful image—the word for "vase," *ping*, sounds the same as that for "peace." These octagonal windows (middle) symbolize all the elements of the universe as represented by the *I Ching*'s eight trigrams. The moon-shaped gate (bottom) is another soothing image, and an intriguing entryway.

Rocks were strategically placed to provide a variety of inspiring views from all sides and to create a rhythmic flow within the garden. Contorted, oddly shaped Tai-hu rocks, molded by the churning motion of water and sand in Lake Tai, are reminiscent of the limestone peaks in Kueilin. These artificial mountains, potent symbols of ch'i, were objects of appreciation. They were also considered to symbolize immortality, as they resembled the mythic homes of the Taoist immortals in K'un-lun in the far west, which would today be considered the Himalayas, and the islands in the Eastern Sea. However, this appreciation could become obsessive and destructive: in the twelfth century A.D. Emperor Hui-tsung's huge stone collection became a financial drain on the kingdom.

FLOWERS	TREES AND FRUIT
Orchids: culture, nobility	Pine: resilience, integrity, dignity, longevity
Peony: luck, prosperity, honor	Bamboo: fidelity, wisdom, longevity
Narcissus: good fortune	Peach and plum trees: brotherliness
Peach and plum blossoms: beauty, charm	Willow: grace
Chrysanthemum: gentility, longevity	Banana palm: scholarly ambitions
Lotus: purity	Persimmons: joy, luck in business, good start for a new endeavor
Day lily: maternity	Apples: safety
	Oranges: good luck
	Pomegranate: fecundity

Much as the West associates olive branches with peace, red roses with love and laurels with glory, various plants and flowers have their own connotations in the Chinese mind. Flowers and trees were chosen for both innate beauty and symbolism. The white lotus—often a platform for the Buddha in paintings and sculptures—rising out of a muddy pool symbolizes translucent purity; the willow tree with its gently curving boughs represents grace. (However, the Forbidden City reportedly never had trees because wood uproots or destroys earth, the element of the emperor and a symbol of his power.)

Whereas some Westerners romanticize about nature as an uninhabitable wilderness, the ancient Chinese saw man as an integral part of it. Therefore, architecture was also a necessary ingredient to any garden. (So much so, that one Chinese garden expert visiting New York City commented that Central Park would be "more beautiful if pavilions were built on rockeries.") A pavilion might perch on a rock, in an echo of mountainside monasteries and pagodas.

Buildings enhance the experience of a Chinese garden. Pavilions provide resting places and a variety of views; a covered walkway might afford vantage points framed by roof and pillars; symbolically shaped doors or lattice windows of varying designs give tantalizing glimpses of stones, bamboo or pine trees beyond. Doors and windows serve many purposes: they funnel ch'i from garden to garden or garden to room; they serve as artistic frames to capture visual vignettes. They were often talismans, shaped auspiciously to symbolize a good luck object or token. Even plain walls provide a background against which rocks, plants and pavilions can be viewed.

Many plants and flowers symbolize human virtues or aspirations. Bamboo represents fidelity and wisdom, and siphons up positive ch'i. Walls are important features in the garden, separating one room or garden court from another.

A Chinese garden has been likened to a Chinese landscape painting in three dimensions. But, in fact, it is not just one landscape but several, and can reveal new vistas with every step.

While the Chinese garden courts discussed are contained and enclosed creations (yin), their Western counterparts generally exist outside the home structure (yang), with boundaries extending to the limits of the property.

THE MODERN LANDSCAPE

In modern feng shui, nature and the landscape remain important factors affecting our lives. While the landscape generally has changed, the basic concepts and needs remain: if you position yourself in harmony with the elements of the universe, you will enjoy a balanced and fruitful life. So, the exterior application of feng shui examines how to follow or re-create the patterns and flow of nature within a garden plot, both to beautify the property and to enrich your physical, mental and financial well-being.

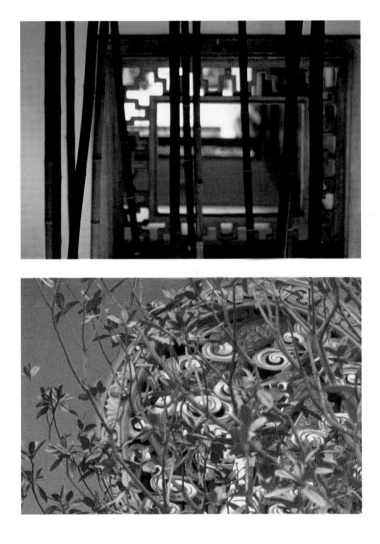

As with the Chinese garden, re-creating and enhancing nature's patterns when siting a building or driveway, planting a tree or bush, or installing a pool or shed, can imbue the occupants of the location with positive and balanced energy—and that energy will usher them along a positive and prosperous life course. If they and their surroundings are poorly arranged— out of flow with the universe—they will struggle, and live unbalanced and difficult lives. It could be said that our needs today for a place or scenery providing visual rest and inspiration are much the same as those of the eighteenth-century emperor Ch'ien Lung. An introduction to the imperial poems goes: "If [an emperor] has a suitable place for [a stroll, look around and relax] it will refresh his mind and regulate his emotions. If not, he will become engrossed in sensual pleasures and lose his will-power."

This ochre wall in a Shanghai garden provides a striking canvas to showcase a blooming magnolia tree.

In modern times, some see feng shui masters as environmentalists. "In Kowloon, on a property formerly owned by a colonial sort, the plot included a magnificent banyan tree, as well as other beautiful landscaping features and views," recounts the architect Bernardo Fort-Brescia. "In my plan for the site, I decided to retain the tree and landscaping, and develop the flat land. The feng shui master then told me that a man had been buried under the tree, and that it radiated energy. I should therefore leave the natural area intact, and build on flat land. He and I had reached the same conclusion, although with different explanations."

SITING: CREATING BALANCED EXTERIORS

Exteriors impact upon us. Whether we are outside or merely gazing out of a window, we respond to the restful and invigorating aspects of nature. The following section will focus on the basic principles of exterior feng shui—how feng shui can enhance the landscape. It will offer ideas on enhancing a plot of land, correcting unfortunate landscaping and positioning a building. While a house situated half-way up a gentle hill facing south to the sea is still ideally positioned, feng shui offers alternatives which will both discern and create a new fortuitous site. This second part of the chapter examines how exterior elements, both natural and man-made, all contribute to the quality and course of our lives.

GOOD CH'I	WEAK CH'I
Lawn: lush, green	Lawn: brown, yellow, bare spots
Trees: healthy, green	Trees: sickly or dead
Flowers: bright, blossoms, fragrant	Flowers: wilted or none
Animals: healthy, pretty (deer symbolize prosperity)	Animals: mangy or sick
Birds: colourful plumage, pleasing song	Birds: squawking
Neighbors: happy, prosperous	Neighbors: miserable, unlucky—bankrupt, ill, newly
General good feeling or impression	divorced, deceased, robbed or hit by fire
	Other bad omens: light bulb explodes when turned on;
	stuck doors; broken windows; dead birds; seeing a hearse

In modern times, earth, plot and building shapes are important, but the first order of business is to assess the suitability of an area for living a good and healthy life. When looking at a property, one must discern the quality of its environment. Is the air fresh, the water pure, the soil fertile? Or is there pollution? Does a plot lie too close to the detrimental effects of high electrical and electromagnetic waves and sounds from a power station or high-tension wires? Is the area overdeveloped, draining the location of its positive attributes?

As in ancient times, the main pursuit of feng shui today is still to identify a location with the best ch'i and then improve on it. Once the ch'i is found and adjusted, its occupants can live or work to their fullest potential. With any dwelling, office, factory or store the feng shui expert first must read the environment to discern the earth's ch'i. A location's features and surroundings provide helpful visual clues to discerning this; plants, animals and humans are beneficiaries and by-products of an area's ch'i. The table above offers some visible tips to discern for yourself whether a place is auspicious. For example, a place with flourishing vegetation, where animals are healthy and beautiful or neighbors are prosperous and successful has good feng shui. Dry, wizened plants, on the other hand, indicate weak ch'i and an area unconducive to growth and furthering possibilities.

While positive facets of a site indicate future good fortune, many negative signs can be adjusted—although generally some emotional and financial price must be paid before this is acknowledged. A feng shui consultant advising a school teacher had reservations about her prospective property, sensing omens and problems with the topography. The front path had been torn up and needed to be replaced, the front gate was stuck and had to be prized open, and the key supplied did not open the door. The back garden was steeply sloped, foretelling money loss.

The consultant advised the teacher to sell her existing home first, before offering for the new one, but she "really liked it," and went ahead and bought it anyway. Six months later her old home had still not sold. She installed spotlights at the foot of the slope, shining back at the house and adjusting the missing marriage area. A week later she had a good offer for her old property—but the delayed sale had cost her $10,000.

Water

While water—its sound, movement and reflection—is both stimulating and calming to the mind, access to and control of water more importantly symbolizes the harvesting of wealth and harnessing the nurturing qualities of positive ch'i in the form of good irrigation. Even for a suburban or city home, where farming, fishing and water transport are not necessities, proximity to or, even better, a view

Built on a former marsh, this home now sits on a man-made berm that both elevates it from tidal floods and provides it with a better vantage point from which to view the neighboring river, and to enjoy good feng shui.

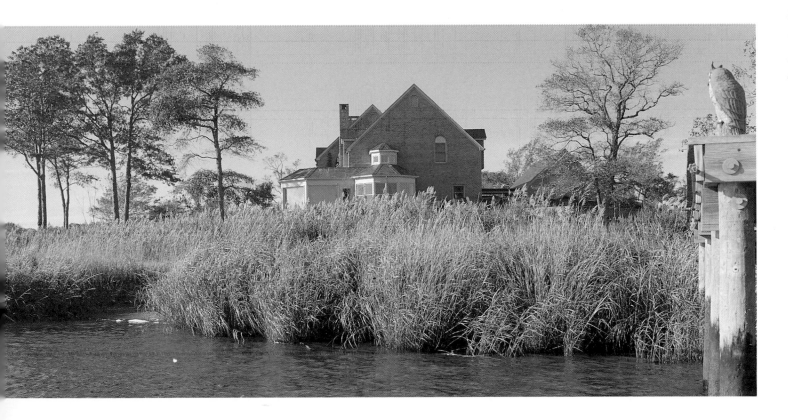

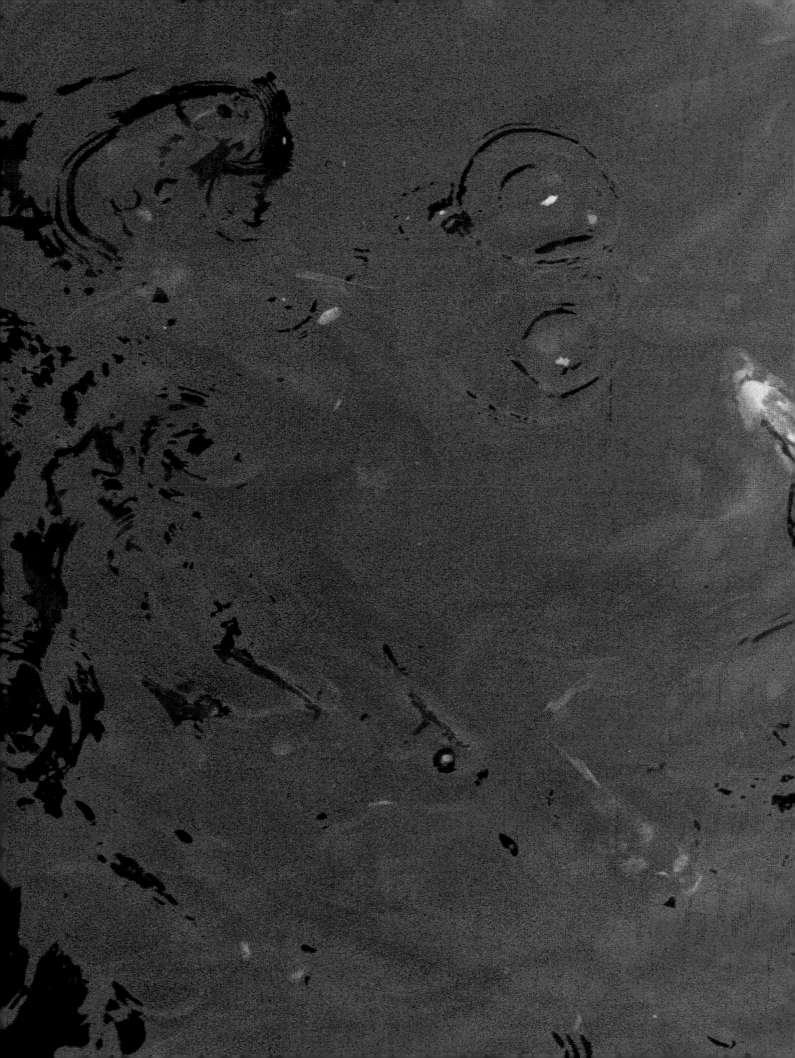

POOLS
AND FISH

Pools are often stocked with fish in traditional Chinese gardens. This creates the artifice that one is but a simple fisherman, and also auspiciously symbolizes abundance and wealth.

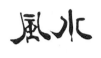

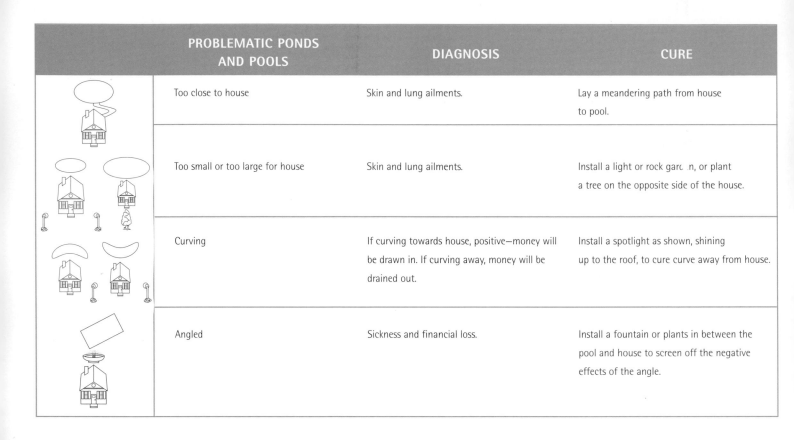

PROBLEMATIC PONDS AND POOLS	DIAGNOSIS	CURE
Too close to house	Skin and lung ailments.	Lay a meandering path from house to pool.
Too small or too large for house	Skin and lung ailments.	Install a light or rock garden, or plant a tree on the opposite side of the house.
Curving	If curving towards house, positive—money will be drawn in. If curving away, money will be drained out.	Install a spotlight as shown, shining up to the roof, to cure curve away from house.
Angled	Sickness and financial loss.	Install a fountain or plants in between the pool and house to screen off the negative effects of the angle.

of water, is important for family finances. Whether a house faces a river, pond, ocean, stream, waterfall or pool, the quality of the water is crucial. It should be pure and moving, signaling good, active ch'i. Stagnant, mucky water means money and ch'i will be tainted.

The main feng shui concept concerning water is to have controlled access to it in order to best grasp positive ch'i as well as opportunity and money. Feng shui even offers methods to improve on a good thing: if a building enjoys any view of water, even in the distance, an interior mirror hung to reflect the scene will draw into the household or business its ch'i and wealth-producing effect. A site without water can be improved by installing a pool, pond or fountain on the property.

However, balancing water—be it a pond or pool—is also an important concern in feng

shui, especially in a suburban neighborhood where individual water features may proliferate. A pond should be accessible to the house and in proportion to the property size, as well as being sited in harmony with the plot's boundaries, buildings and natural features. Curved ponds or swimming pools—such as kidney or crescent shapes—are best. A home with a crescent-shaped pond or pool will be able to grasp money and its inhabitants will enjoy successful careers.

The pond or pool should also be in balance with the house—not too large or so close as to overpower the building, as too much ch'i can threaten the occupants. Too much yin or damp ch'i can also cause lung and skin ailments, and dampen career prospects by sapping residents' ch'i. A positive pond or pool can be anywhere on the property at a safe distance from the house, but must be in balance with the house and size of the plot. When it is in proportion to the house, its siting according to the ba-gua will enhance the corresponding area of the residents' lives.

If a house is partially encircled by a pond for fish or water lilies, then it is good. If a house is surrounded by a man-made swimming pool, however, it is not good, as it increases the risk of drowning and financial loss.

Garden features

Other garden features such as patios, gazebos, jungle gyms, tennis courts and greenhouses can also affect, and hopefully improve, a landscape. All these features enhance the residents' appreciation and enjoyment of nature and life outdoors.

■ Patios and terraces—which buffer the house from the rest of the property—should be wide rather than narrow. A natural, curved shape is better than a square or sharp-angled area. Octagonal sun decks, terraces or patios are also good. One beautiful example is the Szechuan house of T'ang dynasty poet Tu Fu, which has an octagonal court leading to a path.

■ Gazebos—reminiscent of a Chinese garden pavilion—generally enhance a property. They can improve an area of a plot's ba-gua. This all depends on where the gazebo is sited. If, for example, it is in the marriage area, the family will enjoy a happy marriage as well as many friends of the opposite sex. If the gazebo is enclosed, however, a family member will have hidden affairs or a secret life. If it is in the wealth area of a plot, family finances will improve—but if the gazebo is enclosed, money will be stashed away, a family member will have a secret fund.

The position of the gazebo in relation to the house also has an effect. The optimal location is in the back part of a property, allowing privacy so that both visitors and residents can relax. If it is too close to the house, it can be oppressive and create a sense of burden. For example, if a gazebo sited in the children area is too close, children will seem a burden or an imposition.

■ Children's play areas—should be on wide, flat ground, sited far from both pool and pond. It is important to be able to see them from the house. The best sites for jungle gyms are in the marriage, family, and children areas. The best colors are natural wood, light blue or green, the Five Element colors (see page 50), the Six True Colors, or all the rainbow colors (see page 53).

■ Greenhouses—represent a spring-like life force and therefore influence the development of family and ch'i. They should be well stocked with healthy, green plants and accented with red flowers and fruits. Make sure a greenhouse is in good repair, as broken windows represent fractured eyesight and minds as well as broken sleep patterns.

■ Tennis courts—for the most part luxuries. They require considerable space to accommodate them and financial resources for their upkeep; installing or maintaining one should not be a financial burden for the family. Courts are positive if sited as a "wing" of a very large home; if the house itself is small, they can still be assets if used to generate income. The cost of maintenance itself can also determine positivity or negativity: if it exceeds a third of the owner's income, this is negative, unless the court earns the owner money—however, costs should still not exceed half the owner's income. According to the ba-gua, the best positions for a court on a plot of land are in the wealth, marriage and fame areas, and avoid knowledge, career and helpful people. (The family and children areas are both neutral.) The tennis court should also be situated at a good distance from the master bedroom.

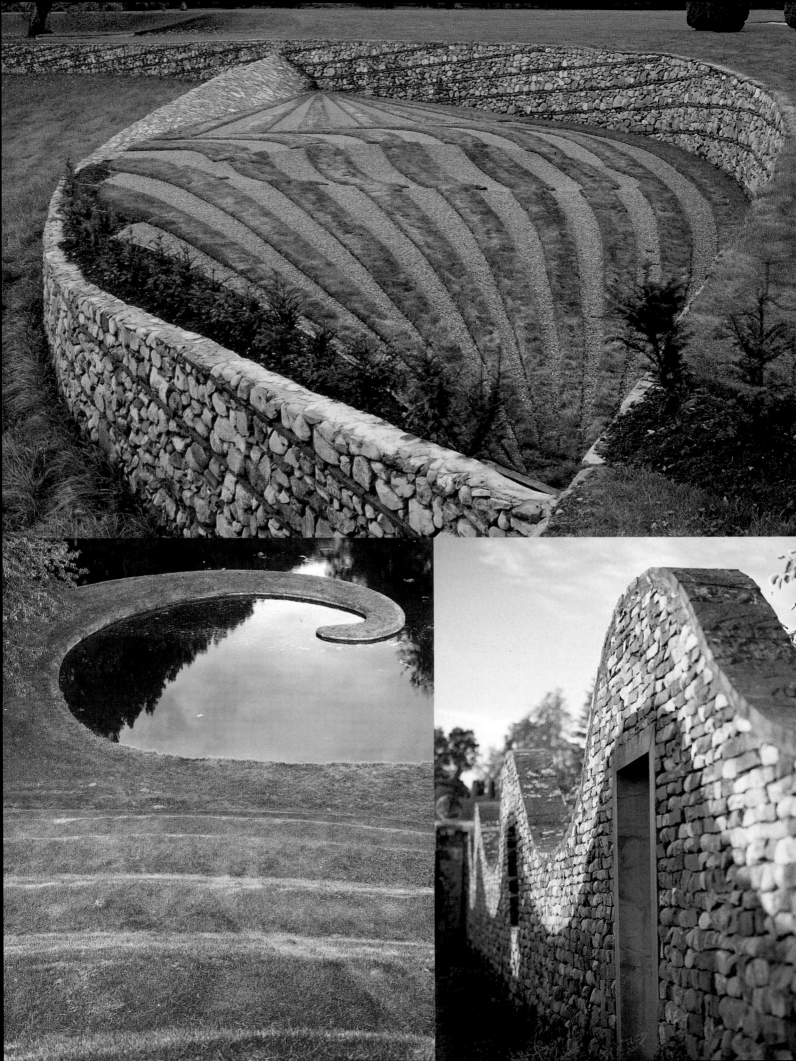

Plots of land

Once a site endowed with positive ch'i has been selected, the next feng shui consideration is the plot of land itself. When analyzing a plot, look at its size and shape as well as the terrain: is it level or sloped? If the land has a gradient, is it gentle or abrupt? Generally, a level plot is the best. However, a gently sloping property is fine, especially if it slopes down to a pleasant body of water.

A house sited on top of a hill will be exposed to strong winds, and thus good ch'i and profits will be blown away. If a property sits on a slope, money, ch'i and opportunity will roll out. With a sloped plot, it is best to position the house on the upper portion, and install a lamp or spotlight at the lowest point to recycle money and ch'i.

As with the various formations of mountains, the shape of a property can also influence the lives of its residents. The best shapes are square or rectangular, giving a sense of stability. However, existing topography and roads, zoning and indiscriminate development of larger plots may create other shapes to be reckoned with. This is where good judgment, a skilled and educated eye and a lucid imagination help the feng shui expert to analyze a shape, and determine how to enhance it or to create balance within its borders. A Chinese painter and poet lived in a house on a hill flanked by two rivers. As a result of the poor siting, it was washed away during a mudslide, and he was killed.

In an art project in New York's Chinatown, artist Mel Chin worked with two feng shui advisers to transform an abandoned area near the Manhattan Bridge into a positive design. While one advised on the orientation, the other commented that the space was shaped like an oyster and that installing something significant, such as a fountain, a statue or a pavilion, where the pearl would lie would revitalize the mini-park and the surrounding area. The project was never executed, and the area remains destitute.

A house should enjoy adequate separation from the street so that ch'i, wealth, opportunity and health can enter in a manageable way. If it is inordinately close to the road—less than half its front-to-back length—the road will overwhelm the residents, who will feel bombarded and will have to struggle in all areas of life. To soften the road's overpowering effect on the house, install a floodlight or fountain in between them, or install a small windmill on the roof. If all else fails, hang a mirror or wind chime on the house, facing towards the road.

When analyzing a plot of land, the expert also considers where the house or building is, or will be, sited. Its position should be in balance with the plot. Ideally, for protection and privacy, the house should be built on the back third of the plot, which is better than the front third. The house should then be balanced with the rest of the property, by planting a tree or installing a lamp post, heavy stone or rock garden in the opposite third of the plot. The diagrams overleaf show plot shapes, house positions and, where relevant, cures.

Trees, shrubs, flowers and plants

One of the Nine Basic Cures of feng shui (see page 40), properly placed plants can resolve a number of siting problems. Trees and bushes can serve as green barriers blocking troublesome views and the malign effects of factories, ugly neighboring houses or power lines and power stations, as well as noise and air pollution. In addition to screening out pollution and negative sights, trees further protect a home by serving as a green fence that can keep children away from a fast or busy thoroughfare shooting by the property. Plants also enhance a site and the residents' luck.

On the Scottish estate of Lady Keswick, her son-in-law Charles Jencks, an architectural theorist, and her late daughter Maggie Keswick, an expert in the Chinese garden, created a landscape in accord with, among other things, the principles of feng shui and Chinese gardens. They sought to re-create the harmony of nature by mounding earth into snail-like hills and snaking walls bordered and balanced by serpentine ponds.

PLOT SHAPE	DIAGNOSIS	HOUSE POSITION	CURE
	Good opportunities to develop and advance.	Build a square house at the center to symbolize an ancient Chinese coin and thus improve finances.	
	Good luck will dwindle.	The existing house is near the front.	Install spotlights as shown, aimed at the top of the roof.
	As above.	As above.	As above.
	Good for career, wealth, and happiness.	Build the house at the center.	
	As above.	As above.	
	Residents' lives have a sense of unfulfillment.	Site the house on an angle and 20 feet or more from the corner.	Plant a tree or install a lamp behind the house. Plant a hedge or vines, as shown.
	Unstable fortunes—suddenly good, then suddenly bad, events.	The existing house is built square with the angle.	1 Place an arrow at the corner of the house pointing at the plot corner. 2 Install a flagpole at the plot corner deflecting ch'i upwards. 3 Place a mirror or reflective object at house corner.
	If properly placed, positive for residents.	Consider the plot shape as that of a shellfish, whose muscle is at one side.	Site house on one side or another, at this point of strength, to grasp money and ch'i.
	Plot narrows to rear; narrowing prospects.	Either consider as above, and position house to one side or another ...	... or place spotlights behind the house to elevate ch'i (see below).
	Narrows at front; diminishing future.	Exisiting house is at the center of the plot, facing the longer side.	Install spotlights in back corners, aiming at either the roof or the corners.
	Financial failure for residents and offspring.	The existing house faces the angle.	Install a flagpole or obscure the corner with plantings.

PLOT SHAPE	DIAGNOSIS	HOUSE POSITION	CURE
	Good for residents.	The house is at the rear of a broadening plot.	Create a flower or brick curve in front to open a "purse"-shaped plot and thus gather money and ch'i, and broaden future prospects.
	Lawsuits, accidents, unexpected disasters and problems.	The house faces the angle of the plot.	Place a flagpole or floodlight, or plant a tree, at the rear of the house.
	Good for career.	House is at center of plot, facing longer side.	
	Residents will suffer in two areas of their lives—if the entrance is on the top of the T, marriage and finances will suffer.	The existing house is parallel with the boundary lines; the entrance to the property lies on a side and not a corner.	Plant vines as shown.
	Strange sexual politics. If the right side is longer females will enjoy greater longevity, business and power. A long left side means male dominance.	The existing house is oriented towards the angle.	Install a tall flagpole, bamboo pole or hollow pole that tapers as it rises, with a spotlight on top at the shorter end.
	If the rounded side is caused by water which brings good, soft ch'i and money, residents will thrive. If it is caused by a road bringing hard ch'i, occupants may feel beset by problems.	Site the house in the front section or in the middle of the plot.	If the rounded side is created by a road, install a fountain, statue or windmill between the house and road. Install flagpoles or spotlights as shown, with spots aimed at the opposite corners.
	Positive for residents—depending on the entrance this creates an addition (see the Feng Shui Tools chapter, page 46).		While this is a good plot shape, flagpoles installed as shown further improve residents' luck.

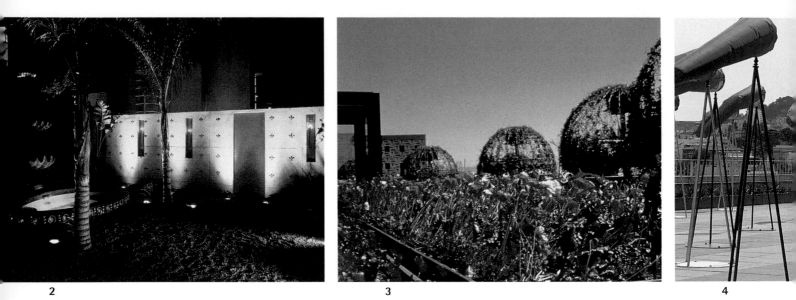

2

3

4

1 This fountain incorporates an auspiciously shaped heavy object, and helps to bring balance to this inner sanctum.

2 Lighting resolves awkard shapes and enhances ch'i. Landscapers Delany & Cochran here up-lit trees and a pool, and dramatically floodlit the back wall.

The Chinese have long conferred symbolism on certain trees and plants, and believed that their location on a property had consequences for its residents. According to a Chinese text, *Yin-Yang Feng-Shui Chiang-i*, specific planting rules include the following. The accompanying photographs show some modern landscape designers' use of feng shui principles not only for planting, but for garden decoration and layout.

◆ *If peach and willow trees are planted to the east, Chinese prune and date trees to the south, gardenia and elm to the west, and apricot and Chinese plum to the north (the house) will be very auspicious and advantageous.*

◆ *If an apricot tree is planted to the east, peach to the west, date to the north and Chinese plum to the south, the planted (trees) will lose their righteousness (in relation to the house), and will be called depraved and lustful ...*

◆ *In general, if the trees are curving and embracing, (the house) will be at leisure and will bring forth good fortune. If peach and apricot trees are planted in front of the gate, (the householder) will be lewd and alcoholic. If weeping willow is growing facing the gate (the occupants of the house) will hang themselves at the beam ...*

◆ *If trees are planted in a line facing the gate, they will protect the prosperity ...*

◆ *If bamboo trees are surrounding the house, the family will have sufficient livelihood.*

◆ *(If a house has) trees growing to the left side of the site, but no trees to the right side, (the house will meet with) many inauspicious matters ...*

1

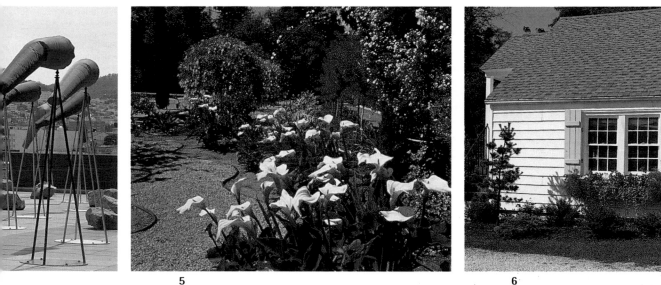

5

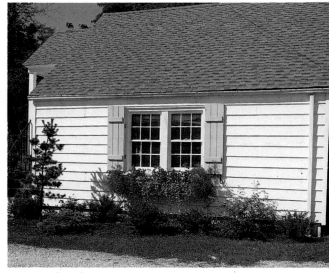

6

◆ If trees are planted on the left side (of the house) and are heavily encircling (the house), the family wealth will be long preserved ...

◆ If a (house) has trees with their lower trunks damaged, the house member will suffer from foot diseases.

◆ If withered trees are hanging over the topmost part of the house, the house will surely produce a widow.

◆ If the Chinese locust tree is growing in front of the gate, the family will be honored and prosperous ...

◆ If trees growing to the side of (the house) are turning and bending, the family will be at leisure and be wealthy ...

◆ If trees growing at the rear of (the house) are dense, family members will be outstanding and will be rich ...

◆ If trees growing on the right side (of the house) are with white flowers, the descendants will be poverty-stricken.

3 On the sheltered side of the roof garden of the Bank of America, large globe-shaped topiaries combine with stimulating floral displays to inspire and energize workers on lunch break.

4 The windward side of the Bank of America roof garden went unused until colorful wind socks were installed, which adjusted the ch'i.

5 The colors in this Delany & Cochran garden guide the eye down a gentle, meandering path and provide visual stimuli.

6 Sited 30 feet from the side entrance to a home, this garage is enhanced by window boxes, evergreen plantings and a bush to attract butterflies. The array of colors suggests the five elements, and so the totality of the universe.

7 At the Marin Cancer Institute, Delany & Cochran enlivened an otherwise "dead" space and visually enlarged it with curving walls, varied perpendicular pavers and lush, colored plantings.

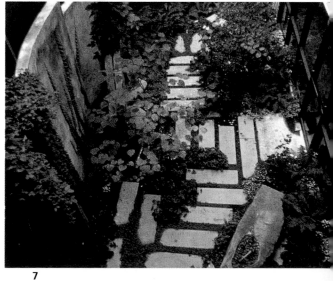

7

Their greenery is a potent symbol of spring, hope and development as well as an indication of life force.

When selecting a tree or bush, be aware of its color and shape and the changes in its appearance as the seasons come and go. Generally, evergreen trees such as spruces, pines, holly trees, boxwoods and rhododendrons, and evergreen bushes like azaleas, junipers and laurels are best, as they symbolize longevity. Unlike deciduous plants, which lose foliage in the autumn, evergreens give a continual sense of life force and contrast with the whites, grays and browns of a winter landscape. Their berries, flowers and cones supply additional visual interest and color, in season.

Fruit-bearing and blossoming trees also enhance a landscape from spring to autumn, as fruit and flowers symbolize abundance and their additional color stimulates the mind and heart. When planting a flower garden, give thought to the color scheme and blooming sequence so that it never lacks a blossom be it spring, summer or autumn.

The shape of a tree can itself influence residents' ch'i. Trees that branch upwards—like cypresses or certain pines—create a more positive upbeat feeling in a property. Trees with downward-sloping branches—such as weeping willows or cherries—while romantic and beautiful can border on creating melancholy or even be depressing. A natural willow is better than one with branches grafted onto it.

While the leaf color and shine of a tree or bush can indicate good ch'i, the shape of a leaf is also a consideration. If it is prickly, like a holly leaf, avoid having it near an entrance. Hollies and shrubs with thorns are good protection when planted on the outskirts of a property, where they serve as a green version of a barbed-wire fence. When sited under a

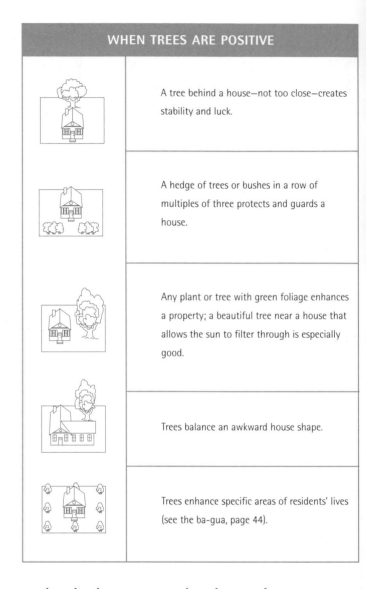

WHEN TREES ARE POSITIVE	
	A tree behind a house—not too close—creates stability and luck.
	A hedge of trees or bushes in a row of multiples of three protects and guards a house.
	Any plant or tree with green foliage enhances a property; a beautiful tree near a house that allows the sun to filter through is especially good.
	Trees balance an awkward house shape.
	Trees enhance specific areas of residents' lives (see the ba-gua, page 44).

window, they become a natural window guard. Prickly plants and trees should be bordered and balanced with softer plants and shrubs.

The colors of flowers and flowering bushes can also be applied to the ba-gua. The choice of a flower's color when planted in a certain area can enhance residents' lives. See page 44 for details of how to use the ba-gua to analyze your plot and identify areas on which to focus. For example, a couple in need of a nanny planted white perennials in the helpful people area, with very successful results.

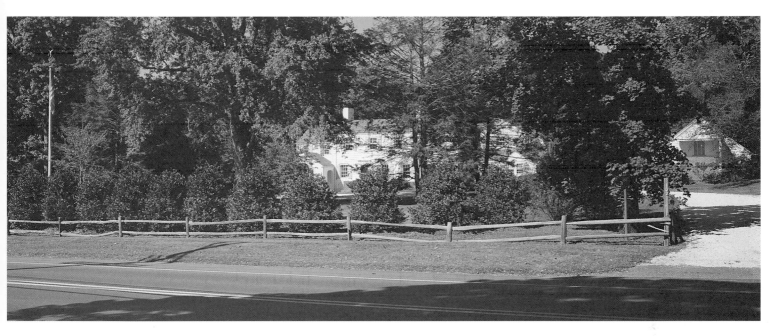

Thirty-nine holly trees (auspicious as a multiple of three) planted along a property bordering a busy road create a green fence that filters out the sound and pollution of car traffic while keeping in any young children. On a smaller scale, the principle of planting in threes could be applied to window boxes at the back of a flat or apartment where protection is needed.

	PROBLEMATIC TREES	DIAGNOSIS	CURE
	Tree too close to the front door	Oppresses ch'i and keeps out money and possibilities.	Hang a ba-gua mirror at eye level on the tree, or a note: "When exiting, receive blessings."
	Tree that stands too close to the window and blocks sunlight and views	Blocks chi and brings in dark—negative—ch'i, resulting in death and misfortune.	Hang five firecrackers, or imitation firecrackers, in the window frame.
	Dead tree on property	Foretells a sad event—accident or death in the family—hardship, decay of plot and occupants' ch'i.	1 When removing a dead tree and roots, sprinkle a mixture of uncooked rice, alcohol/liquor and ju-sha around the tree; visualizing the ch'i of the tree will enable it to become a higher being and not disturb the site. 2 If the trunk is left, place a pot of live plants next to it and sprinkle 3 handfuls of rice, alcohol/liquor and ju-sha over the trunk.

Roads and bridges

Exterior roads impact on a property in much the same way that rivers affect the landscape. As a result, the rules for roads and rivers are similar. As conduits of ch'i, the best roads curve gently with the natural contours of the land. Superhighways and straight roads purvey ch'i too quickly. This is known as "arrow-like" or killing ch'i, and thus can be dangerous for car and pedestrian traffic alike. In addition, homes sited directly at the end of a dead-end street or the center of a T-junction are in the line of fire of both killing ch'i and the headlights of approaching cars. A road directly facing a property can have a negative effect such as car accidents, bankruptcy, injuries or even unexpected death. The occupants of a house that had one pointing directly at its garage door experienced two robberies and a car accident within a year. Such a road's negative effect can be rectified by the placement of a mirror or weather vane with an arrow to deflect its ch'i. If a house is located at an intersection where two roads

converge and point at it, children will be rebellious and eventually leave home. The outcome, if the children are resourceful, will be success, though. Houses that flank a dead-end street are more desirable than those sited at the end of it.

Bridges and overpasses also impact on homes and businesses. It is best to have a house's main door parallel to, but at a safe distance from, them. It is problematic if the structure is too close and parallel to the main door, or if one end of it points directly towards the main door. If a bridge or overpass is close and parallel to a main door, it impedes the progress of residents or businesses, affecting profitability and life force. The greater the velocity of the traffic, the greater the effect. If it points directly towards the door, residents will be insecure and businesses will experience not only cash-flow or personnel problems, but also likely injury, sickness and possible death for its employees.

To cure the negative effects of a bridge or overpass, hang a small mirror outside, on top

This circular driveway is auspicious for residents. Its meandering approach adds to the gracious entry.

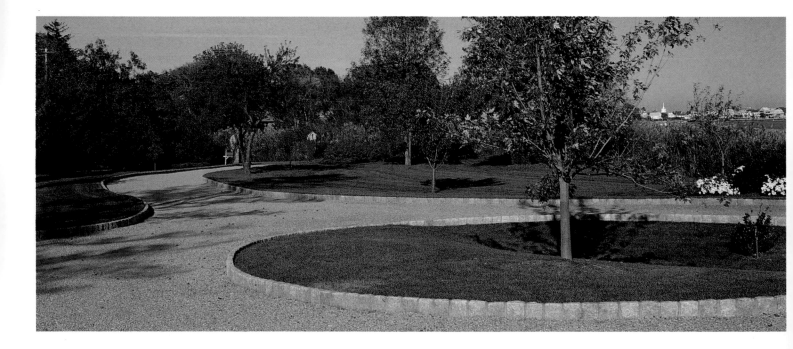

of the door, or point an arrow towards the structure to deflect and break down its malevolent impact. Additionally, place a copper wind chime directly inside the door.

Driveways and paths

The configuration of a driveway or path conducts ch'i and guides residents and visitors alike to a house, thus creating the property's initial impression. The link between the home and the outside world, it should create a gracious entry. As with ancient Chinese sacred sites it should be processional, subtly varying the approach, presenting a number of views of the house, not an abrupt straight line to the front door. A gently curving and level drive or path best filters out negative ch'i as well as providing a smooth, cordial approach. A drive or path should be in balance with the property,

GOOD DRIVEWAY SHAPES	
	Semicircular
	Circular
	Circular with a center island planted with grass or flowers
	Circular with a square center, symbolizing Tao

PROBLEM DRIVEWAYS		DIAGNOSIS	CURE
	Ba-gua/octagonal-shaped	Family discord.	Plant a tree or install a lamp, fountain, flowers or windmill in the center.
	Narrows towards the road	Narrowing of career and business opportunities.	Install a lamppost at the foot of the driveway, spotlighting the door or top of the house.
	Steeply sloping, narrowing towards the foot	Narrowing of career and business opportunities.	Build two brick posts flanking the entrance to the driveway, to recirculate ch'i and opportunity.
	Sloping down to the house	Unexpected problems in finances, marriage, health, career, etc.	1 Create terraces delineated by pavement along the driveway to soften the flow of ch'i aiming at the house. 2 Install a spotlight aimed at the top of the roof to recycle ch'i.
	Narrower than the entrance door	Stifles ch'i and residents' luck.	Widen the driveway.

GOOD PATHWAYS TO HOUSE
An open, spacious path, wider than the door
A path opening out as it progresses away from the house
Round, unobtrusive porch columns flanking, but not crowding, the door
Curved paths
A gently graded downward slope
Healthy plants flanking, but not obstructing, the path
A gradual step leading from a wide landing

not too wide and not too narrow. A drive's exit should always feed into the general traffic flow—towards the more populous district—and its entry should be on the side that heads towards the less populated area.

Entrances and exits

The entrance—or exit—of a home, office or store is poised at the threshold, linking the interior world to the outside. A major consideration in feng shui, the entrance should be welcoming and accessible, and the exit—the first step back into the outside world—should be unobstructed and beckoning. The entrance is the first impression of a building, and determines how we experience the interior; the exit helps us embark on our lives outside our home, office or business. Trees, columns, high walls, utility

POOR PATHWAYS TO HOUSE	DIAGNOSIS	CURE
Narrow, less wide than the entrance door	Limits career and finances.	Widen the path or border it with red bricks or flowerbeds.
Narrowing as it progresses	Prospects narrow.	Widen the path.
Large, round, obstructive columns near the door	Hinders ch'i, health and finances.	Hang a mirror at eye level on a column, or a note: "When exiting, receive blessings."
Square obstructive pillars	Bankruptcy.	Grow vines up the edges of the pillars.
Uphill slope	Residents bring home bad ch'i every day, so careers and finances face uphill battle.	Place convex mirrors on both sides of the house entrance, so when the residents walk home, the mirror will reflect them ascending instead of descending.
Plants with spiky leaves flank the path	Plagued with prickly problems and struggles.	Cut back the plants or replace them with softer-leafed ones.
Narrow steps down	Money will roll out.	Widen the look of the path with red bricks or flower borders or low, fruit-bearing plants.
Narrow steps up	Career faces an uphill battle.	Install a spotlight at the back of the house, aimed at the roof.
Steep slope	Money rolls out.	Install a spotlight in front of the house, aimed at the roof.

poles that are too close to the entrance, can therefore obstruct ch'i flow and keep out health and financial possibilities; clutter and obstacles inside the entrance can block the view and obstruct a smooth passage to the outside. A tree planted at a distance can symbolically function as a protective guard.

The actual path to and from a building also conducts ch'i. It should be gracious, gradual and wide enough to purvey ch'i and human traffic comfortably. It should be as appealing as possible, with attractive stones and colorful plantings that inspire and please.

Neighbors

While residents have control over their own property, there is little—beyond invoking local planning regulations—that they can do to control alterations to surrounding properties that may unbalance the area's ch'i and threaten their home. Residents should be aware of the shapes, sizes and alignment of neighboring buildings. For example, when all the houses in an area are relatively equal sizes and squarely sited on their plots, the residents of each will enjoy peace, stability and security. When the houses differ greatly in size or are sited in conflict with each other—askew—residents may suffer from a range of upsets, from neighborhood discord to career and financial frustrations. While the offending problems are external to the residents' plot, there are small, symbolic cures they can execute within their own borders. For details, see page 105.

The next chapter examines feng shui and modern architecture. It will focus on applying the practice in cities and towns where man-made structures—buildings and their shapes and road-traffic flow—affect residents more than natural features do.

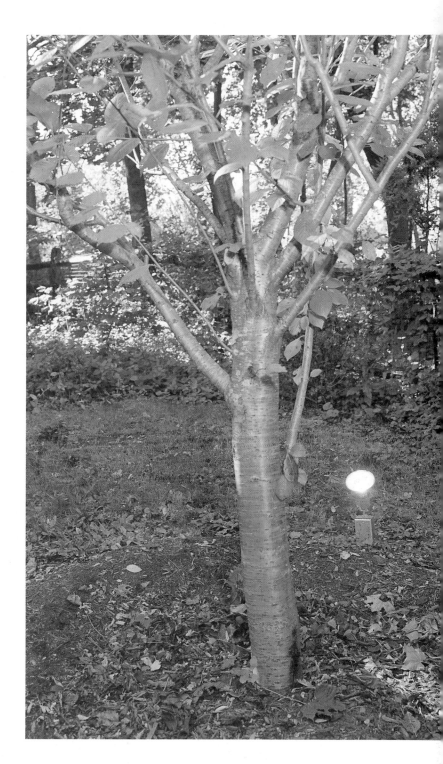

This tree, planted in the wealth area of a property, is further enhanced by back-lighting, thus improving the residents' finances. Trees, plants and lights can also be used to improve feng shui in the vicinity of a problem neighbor.

CHAPTER VI

Modern Architecture and Feng Shui

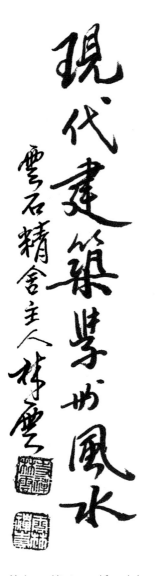

Modern architecture and feng shui

In the modern metropolis, tall buildings, wide avenues and bridges seem to dominate the landscape more than natural features and forces. So, while nature is still important, it becomes less of a consideration in urban feng shui, playing the role more of backdrop and embellishment. Still, city feng shui concerns itself with urban versions of the same basic rules relating to siting, building juxtaposition, neighbors, shapes of buildings and rooms, and access and approach to a home, office or business.

From the Singapore Hyatt to London's Bethnal Green City Challenge, a neighborhood improvement group, and from Donald Trump's $2.5 billion Riverside South in New York to the Vancouver branch of the Hong Kong Bank of Canada, feng shui, in small and large ways, is helping to shape cities around the world. Exactly why it has expanded beyond Asian borders can be traced to a number of reasons. Some clients profess belief. Others express appreciation. Some are motivated by the enormous amount of flight capital leaving Asia. Abe Wallach, vice president for the Trump Organization—which, with Asian investors, is developing the Riverside South project and renovating the Trump International Tower and Hotel in New York—comments, "He who has the dollars will make the decisions on how buildings are oriented and designed." Steven Robinson, an architect based in New York and Santa Fe, New Mexico, who has worked with a feng shui consultant on the Gerald Peters Gallery in Santa Fe, simply comments, "What I know of feng shui makes sense to me." The client, Gerald Peters, echoes his sentiments: "All the feng shui suggestions are being integrated in the gallery—it is a system based on common sense." Mr. Robinson continues, "Feng shui is an aspect inherent in civilization's best architecture over the past two thousand years. It is helpful in reminding us what we as humans are stimulated and moved by."

Feng shui's presence in modern Eastern cities is striking. While it has long been part of the design and building process for Asian firms to call in a feng shui expert, Western companies and architects in Asia must now also grapple with feng shui—either by hiring an expert themselves or by dealing with feng shui stipulations secondhand—before a building is completed or an office opened. "Feng shui is affecting the skyline in the Far East," says Bernardo

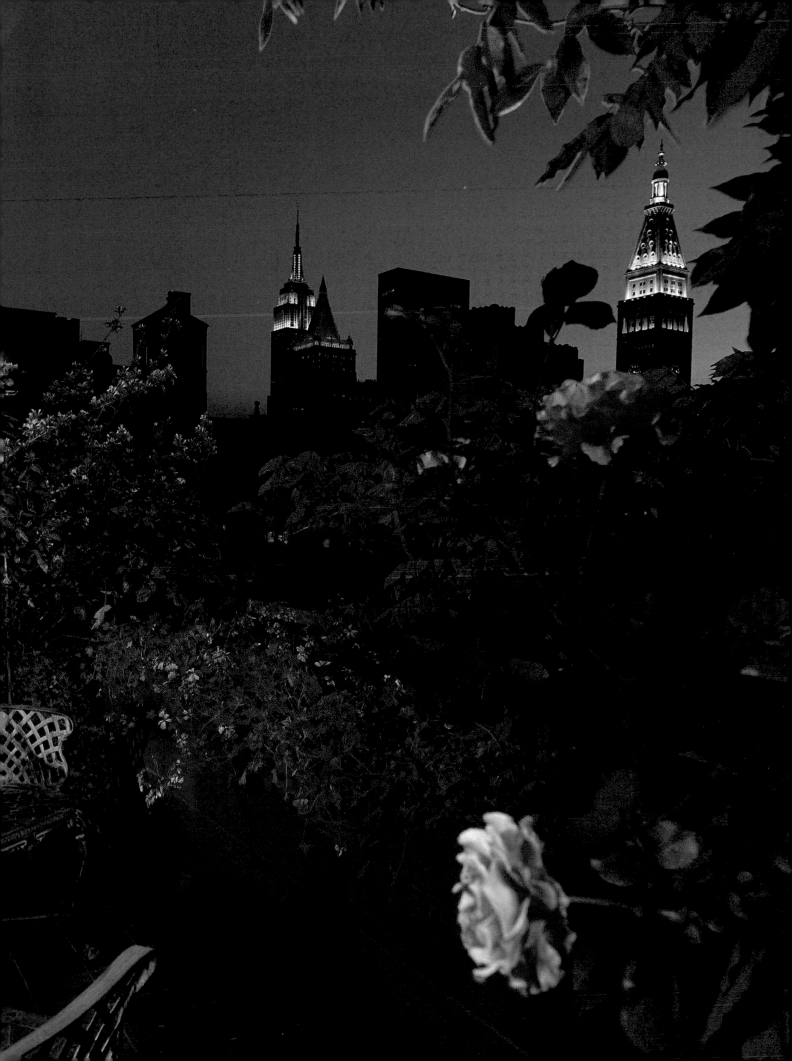

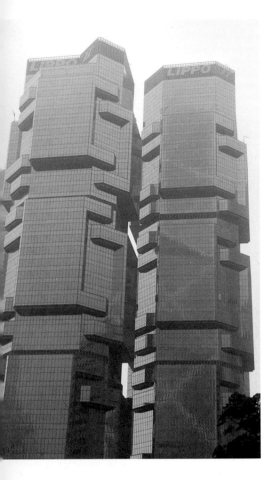

Although its architect integrated a ba-gua shape into its design, some blame the fall of the ill-fated BCCI on the shape of the Bank of China, which neighbored BCCI's Hong Kong headquarters, now the Lippo Centre (above). The next tenants, the Riady family, also allegedly suffered political and financial woes.

Fort-Brescia of Miami-based Arquitectonica, which has offices in Hong Kong and Shanghai. Multinationals such as Citicorp, Morgan Stanley and McKinsey & Co. all routinely hire feng shui experts when choosing and designing office space. Whether a company, property developer or architect embraces the practice or not, most agree it is wise to employ it, if only to please others who do. And in Asia, feng shui fees for some of the larger developments can run anywhere from $20,000 to $200,000.

Urban feng shui is not a new invention. The Chinese imperial cities of antiquity were laid out on a geometric grid with a defined north-south, east-west axis. When Marco Polo visited Peking in the late thirteenth century, he noted its "chequerboard" layout. When siting a town, flat featureless land was avoided, for it was considered too exposed to strong winds and devastating floods. So after the mid-nineteenth century's "opium war," when European "foreign devils" demanded concessions or spoils from China, the emperor and his local governors relinquished the low, flat lands that are now Shanghai, Tientsin and Hankow, which were known as areas riddled with malign spirits and bad feng shui. But to the amazement of the Chinese, the foreigners altered and enhanced the concessions' topography by constructing impressive hill-like buildings.

Protective mountain screens were desirable to the north of a city, but mountainous Hong Kong Island was still considered to have bad feng shui as well as being plagued by pirates. It was ceded to the British much in the way the Greeks bestowed their horse on Troy—and with hopes of a similar outcome. Known as a "barren rock," Hong Kong was deemed devoid of beneficial ch'i and, indeed, the epithet was initially portentous. The Chinese must have smirked to themselves as the British made a bad landscape worse. First, they located their commercial trading center a mile from the port in a low area which they named—without irony—Happy Valley. Then, to link Happy Valley to the port, they built roads that the Chinese said maimed the guardian dragon by severing his feet. Next, they filled in lakes and leveled hills, creating a swamp and wiping out chances for financial success. When the low swamp bred malaria-carrying mosquitoes, and several people died, the Chinese workers boycotted the ill-fated development. However, following the relocation of the trading center in Hong Kong Central, backed auspiciously by the Peak and overlooking the harbor, the colony thrived for a century …

With the rapid growth of Pacific Rim economies, new and old businesses and property developers in Asia are embellishing their corporate images with new buildings that are striking architectural statements of their power and prosperity. Often they hire large Western architectural firms to create their three-dimensional vertical statements. (Generally, a local firm oversees and executes the design.) As a result, East and West are meeting to change the skyline in Asia—sometimes harmoniously, sometimes in conflict. While Western design concepts such as the structure, form and skin of a building are necessary considerations for any high-rise—and the prevailing trend seems to be the taller the better—feng shui still has a strong influence in the design. So while the architect may be creating a space-age symbol of Asian corporate ascendancy in the third millennium, he or she must remain sensitive to feng shui considerations. One principal of a New York architectural firm designing buildings in Asia comments, "Architecture and feng shui go hand-in-hand. The topic inevitably is raised at some point in the course of the project." (As a result, feng shui has increasingly become a factor in property markets around the world. Developers from Singapore to Seattle, Los Angeles to London, are hiring feng shui consultants to advise on designs, thus ensuring rentable and saleable homes and offices, that hopefully guarantee good luck and comfort, for a growing Asian populace. Some developers hold seminars to inform contractors and sales forces of feng shui positive attributes.)

Feng shui arises in a number of ways. Sometimes the client brings in an expert at the outset, and it is integral to the design. Sometimes, feng shui is almost an afterthought, brought in shortly before completion—or later—by an anxious client. Comments one Western architect, "I never know if feng shui is a real concern, a face-saving excuse either for cold feet—to mix metaphors—or for second thoughts to alter the plans late in the project, or if it might be intended as a litmus test of our own understanding and sensitivity to their culture." Sometimes the clients express belief in feng shui; at other times they use it as a way to attract renters and usher in business to retail space. For example, in Malaysia, even though a native Malay who was building a skyscraper did not personally embrace feng shui, he used it to attract Chinese occupants. As Mr. Fort-Brescia explains, "I am always amazed how you stumble into feng shui everywhere in Asia. This is mostly because the Chinese have been successful in business in not just Hong Kong, Singapore and Taiwan, but also in Indonesia, the Philippines and Malaysia, and they tend to be the most important developers and purchasers. So a design must be in compliance with feng shui."

Many Chinese simply will not work in a space that has not received the nod and blessing of a feng shui expert. For example, one British company regularly employs one to advise on its Hong Kong and Singapore offices. When questioned about this, the managing director replied that feng shui "made perfect sense, as the Chinese would not work here" if the office had not received a feng shui visit. He also noted that, after a consultation, business ran smoothly because the employees felt safe and positive: "Who knows, maybe there is something to it?"

On the other hand, it should be noted that there are those who do not embrace feng shui, viewing it as mere superstition. When the Hong Kong subsidiary of an American investment banking firm installed a staircase linking the trading desk on the twenty-third floor to the operations on the twenty-second floor, locals thought it would draw money from its profit center to its cost center. But the Western manager, a self-professed skeptic and good Christian, was uncomfortable "worshipping idols and the spirit world" and did nothing. Profits, in fact, remained strong.

Although many Western architects say that feng shui is not an issue for their Western clients, in London Marks & Spencer and Virgin Atlantic have used it to some degree to improve prosperity and productivity. In New York, Tommy Boy and Elektra Records, as well as the aforementioned Trump Organization, Elizabeth Arden, ABC Carpet & Home and Felissimo, to name but a few, have all employed feng shui. And in Los Angeles, when the Creative Artists Agency broke ground for their new headquarters in 1988, the ceremony was overseen and blessed by a feng shui master.

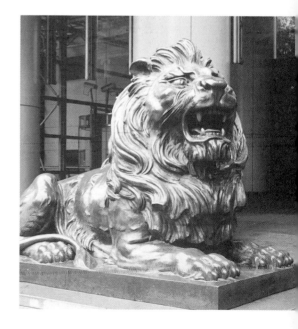

This guardian lion and its mate have long guarded the entrance to the Hongkong & Shanghai Bank. When its new headquarters were under construction, the bank employed a feng shui expert to re-site them.

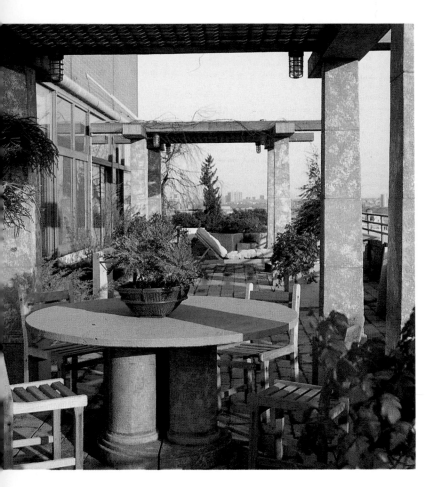

Attractive and strategically positioned plants can improve the general feng shui of an urban home with a terrace, as well as harmonize an imbalanced apartment shape.

SITING

Today, good feng shui often coincides with good city planning and land use. Green spaces ranging from parkland and urban courts to tree-lined streets and terraces help to create good ch'i, benefiting residents. A view of water, be it from a luxury apartment overlooking a bay or river or a pedestrian view of a public fountain, waterfall or reflecting pool, also brings good ch'i and beneficial effects to city dwellers. But in a city, no matter how ideal the location, other factors can alter the feng shui. Proximity to high-tension wires, the corners, colors and heights of neighboring buildings, the direction, speed, noise and curves of roads and overpasses can influence the feng shui of a site.

RESIDENTIAL SITING IN CITIES

While nature is less prevalent in the city, it still plays an important, if smaller, role. Parks and greenery of any size provide a symbolic, if momentary, respite from the city's kinetic ch'i and hard surfaces. The optimal place to live seems to be an urban translation of ancient Chinese precepts. An apartment sited on the mid-level floor of a high-rise overlooking or near water and parkland (or both), with a terrace garden and a southern or eastern exposure, is best.

Garden courts within urban town houses or roof gardens, or terraces adjoining apartments, potentially improve the feng shui of a city home, in much the same way the Chinese garden enhances the traditional Chinese home. They are pleasant buffers from the constant buzz of city life. As places to relax or entertain, these miniature landscapes provide emotional relief from the intense pace and hard surfaces of the cityscape. The sounds of leaves rustling, water falling and birds singing in the garden are all calming and stimulating and also enhance residents' lives. Garden features reminiscent of nature—trees and grass, flowers and potted plants, fountains and fish pools, stones and sculptures—can be used as "cures" to resolve feng shui imbalances such as awkward building shapes, empty air shafts or strangely shaped terraces.

The rules for siting on streets are like geometric interpretations of ancient river rules. For example, an apartment house situated above a confluence of roads is beneficial, but a house sited below it will suffer. If the traffic flows towards the building, residents will fall victim to continuous assault by strong killing ch'i, fierce winds, car lights and horns as well as screeching tires. Urban homes should avoid wide streets if the traffic is generally congested, noisy or fast. A two-way street with a planted center island is preferable. Tree-lined streets are desirable addresses, sites with window-boxes or terraces create a visual reference to the restful powers and beauty of nature. A home on a narrow, but well-lit, quiet street, lined with trees and near the corner of a wider avenue is also desirable.

BUSINESS SITING IN CITIES

When siting any business, the first consideration is the neighborhood. Is it populated with complementary businesses? Are they doing well? In addition to the neighborhood, a business should be aware of the prior tenant's history. Did they move to a larger site because they were successful? Or did they have to shut up shop or go bankrupt? Did the owner die, get divorced or have conflicts with partners? (For cures, see Chapter IX.) There are certain sites where, no matter what business moves in, the owners thrive. There are others where, no matter how good the management, or how brilliant the concept or how appealing the design, businesses fail one after the other.

The location is the first consideration. A store or restaurant should be sited where there is the most pedestrian traffic, or where parking is convenient. One owner of a supermarket chain in Hong Kong is always accompanied by a feng shui master when he is in search of new locations for stores.

Streets

Generally, wide thoroughfares—such as the boulevards of Paris or Fifth Avenue in New York—are good places along which to site businesses and stores. Factories should also be placed on wide roads. Ideally, a business such as a bank, a shop or a restaurant should be on a street corner, with the main access door on a diagonal to catch ch'i pedestrian traffic and money from all directions. As with homes, companies should avoid sites that are aimed at

byroads. Hutchison Whampoa, a company in Bristol, England, with Hong Kong links, has even banned cars parking outside its headquarters, as they represent "hostile tigers" stalking the company. On the other hand, if the traffic is leading away from the business, that is fine. Slants—symbolizing oblique, sudden happenings—are generally avoided, but a slanted entrance is an asset. In pre-communist China, and even in modern-day Macao, casinos employed slanted doors to draw in gamblers and their sometimes ill-gotten gains. In more proper Hong Kong, eyebrows were raised when banks began using slanted entrances. A number of bank doors in New York, such as those of Chemical Bank's Chinatown branch, are also suspiciously slanted. In addition, pedestrian traffic can indicate patterns of the area's ch'i and therefore business prospects. For example, the side of the street that is most crowded and traveled is the most desirable side for a business. A location near a popular cinema or a bank with a money machine would be an ideal spot for a new restaurant or shop.

Accents of nature, be they derived from greenery, water or flowers, further improve the feng shui of a commercial site. The proximity to, or presence of, water is a feng shui asset to business. Fountains, waterfalls and pools help to balance a city's fast energy as well as endowing any commercial location with wealth-producing water. The water, however, must always be kept clean or the money it attracts will be tainted. One pool with fountains outside a popular Chinese restaurant in the United States was not correctly maintained, so business dwindled. After the line of scum had been cleaned from the side of the pool, business picked up.

Proper maintenance is important, particularly in the food industry. Any rubbish, dirt or grime represents careless handling and tainted food.

BUSINESS SITING	DIAGNOSIS	CURE
1 Store at the confluence of roads with one road pointing at it	Business will be either extremely good or very bad.	1 Hang a ba-gua mirror on the door. 2 Install a fountain or windmill in between the road and the entrance. 3 Install an arrow on the roof, pointing at the point in the road.
2 Store with one door on the corner	Well-situated, but the door opens the wrong way to bring in most business.	Change the hinges.
3 Slanted door on corner	Attracts customers, money and ch'i from two directions.	
4 Slanted door with column	Attracts customers, money and ch'i from two directions, but column blocks ch'i; some clients may not return.	Hang a mirror on the store-facing sides of the column.
5 Store with one door on a one-way road	The door opens the correct way so that customers can easily enter.	To improve business, hang a mirror on the wall facing the direction of the traffic, symbolically doubling the store's size and attracting shoppers' ch'i inside.
6 Road where traffic flows away from the store ...	More stable for business.	
7 ... but if an arrow-like road points at the store	Difficult for business, which appears to be better than it actually is; possible bankruptcy.	1 Hang a mirror and wind chime outside to deflect the road's effect. 2 Hang a mirror on an interior wall facing the entrance if the store is wide. If the store is narrow hang mirrors on either side of the entrance.
8 Corner entrance where a column separates two doors	Business will be uneven.	Hang a mirror on the column and hang the door so that it opens inwardly.

City neighbors

As with suburban siting, neighbors and neighboring structures can affect the ch'i of an urban home or business. As property and commercial developments grow, as well as cities themselves, the relationship between buildings and businesses can become acrimonious: formerly good views are blocked, access to sunlight becomes limited and green space is destroyed, creating yet another hard surface that does not absorb noise. What you see as you enter or exit a home or an office, as well as what you see outside the window, all affect your mood, energy level and attitude towards life. Your neighbors and the sights that greet you when you exit your home should be popular, positive and appealing. Negative neighbors can range from an overbearing building to an unsavory business. Common neighbors to avoid are police stations, funeral parlors, factories, churches or synagogues and hospitals. For a retail business or a restaurant, a negative neighbor, such as a funeral parlor or a police station, may be a deterrent to shopping sprees or pleasant dining, and thus thwart financial success. Constant exposure to criminals, victims, hearses, mourners, belching smoke or machine noise is unsettling to residents', employees' and clients' ch'i. The view of a church is also considered bad because it is thought to emit negative or yin ch'i—ch'i of the dead—from funerals and somber services. However, it should be noted that if a church is the site predominantly of weddings and baptisms, then working or living near it is fine, as the ch'i will be positive.

PROBLEM NEIGHBOR	DIAGNOSIS	CURE
Overbearing taller building dwarfing your own	Oppresses ch'i, stunting career, financial and personal growth.	1 Hang an octagonal or convex mirror, inside or outside, aimed at the building to deflect its negative qualities. 2 Place a pool of water or a mirror flat on the roof to raise ch'i; this will deflect the overbearing influence as well as reflecting the building's image horizontally as if it had collapsed. Alternately, use a convex mirror to reflect the neighbor at a disadvantage.
Police station, funeral parlor, church, prison, hospital, courthouse	Too much yin ch'i, the ch'i of the dead and criminals, creates sudden, unforeseen problems and disasters.	1 Plant trees (especially evergreens) along the property line. 2 Seal the door (see Chapter IX); use mirrors.
A sharp knife-like building angle	Threatens luck and success. Leaves residents open to possible blame, violence or surgery.	1 Hang a mirror outside the building. 2 Install a weather vane or arrow-shaped whirligig pointing at the sharp corner.
High-tension wires, power stations	Health problems.	Put nine green plants in the master bedroom to deflect electricity and electromagnetic waves and sounds.
Factories	Oppress ch'i and luck; possible noise and air pollution.	Install lights, trees or plants, or a fountain, along the property line.
The corners of your building and your neighbor's point at each other	Constant bickering, leading, perhaps, to lawsuits.	Each neighbor constructs adjoining sheds, outhouses or garages to create a triangle of buildings.

Residents or businesses who are exposed to too much yin ch'i may suddenly face unforeseen disasters. Some companies in New York City have covered their windows to avoid overlooking St. Patrick's Cathedral. One woman—an ex-Catholic—living and working in an Olympic Tower apartment that directly overlooks it and its spires, found the view disturbing. She experienced the cathedral both as a reminder of lost faith and a sorrowful view. The spires seemed to point in a threatening manner. She felt more comfortable after hanging a small mirror by the window, symbolically deflecting the church's powerful image and ch'i.

The height and shape of neighboring buildings can impact upon residents' lives. Here the ancient concept of mountain symbolism comes into play. The shape of a building is seen to affect the luck and harmony of those living or working near it. For example, in New York City, the knife-like shape of the Citicorp building is thought by some Chinese to threaten the nearby United Nations building, thus thwarting that organization's efforts to establish and maintain world peace.

A more recent controversial structure is the 70-story building for the Bank of China—Beijing's foreign exchange bank—in Hong Kong. Care was taken by the architects, I. M. Pei and Associates, to create good feng shui for the client in spite of the ruling mainland Communists' official polemic against the practice as feudal and superstitious. The building—which broke ground on the auspicious date of 8-8-88—started with good feng shui intentions for the client: it was auspiciously sited on a slope overlooking Hong Kong harbor. Although the building itself was too exposed to active roads, the architects used a series of waterfalls and plantings to screen it from traffic flow. Rumor has it that the Chinese requested the original X-shaped window mullions be altered because of negative symbolism. One architect comments, "In its siting, the building brings in the surroundings. And the diagonal side (of the glass wall) reflects the major open space of the Hong Kong Garden in front."

However, what might be good for the client may be bad for the neighbors. For example, not only did this high-rise dwarf its neighboring buildings, but its angled mirrored glass wall reflects them at a disadvantage, distorting their reflected image. Some trace the downturn in the financial fortunes of former tycoon Australian Alan Bond to the bank's shape. Economists may link his and his company's bankruptcy in the early 1990s to greed and graft, but Hong Kong Chinese insist the blame lies in feng shui—after all, the Bank of China's sharp angles aim towards the Bond Centre, which housed a subsidiary of Bond's BCCI (Bank of Credit and Commerce International) in a threatening, dagger-like manner. While the New York architect Paul Rudolph designed the Bond building in an auspicious octagonal shape, locals feel that even this could not withstand the Bank of China's pointed corners. (Fearing a similar fate, some workers in nearby high-rises have placed mirrors in their windows to deflect the Bank of China's negative ch'i from themselves.) Some say the building, now renamed the Lippo Centre (for an Indonesian conglomerate), is an example of feng shui lightning striking twice. During the 1996 United States presidential campaign, Indonesian principals of the Lippo Group, Mochtar Riady and his son James, were caught allegedly making large foreign (and therefore illegal) donations to President Clinton's campaign.

But Bond and the Riadys were not the Bank of China's only purported casualties. "Some see it as a hostile symbol," explains one American architect, who has designed many Asian projects. "In Hong Kong, it has become a physical embodiment of China's takeover." Indeed, some blame the brief hospitalization (due to a mild case of angina) of the last of the British governors, Chris Patten, as well as his daughter's appendicitis, on the bank's sharp angles which point to Government House. And it is rumored that even Patten's own chauffeur hung a mirror to deflect the bank's ill effect.

Perhaps fearing a similar fate, when the shipping tycoon Tung Chee-hwa, Mr. Patten's successor and Hong Kong's first chief executive under Chinese rule, began his quest for office space in which to organize his new government, he sought feng shui advice. "I've heard that Government House is crowded and the feng shui is not good," Mr. Tung told some reporters, according to the *New York Times*. His feng shui adviser, Choi Pak-lai concurred: "Government House was surrounded by tall buildings, which blocked its spirit." Indeed, who would want to step into the shoes of a governor associated with such a short-lived—by Chinese standards—rule? Mr. Tung settled on two floors in the

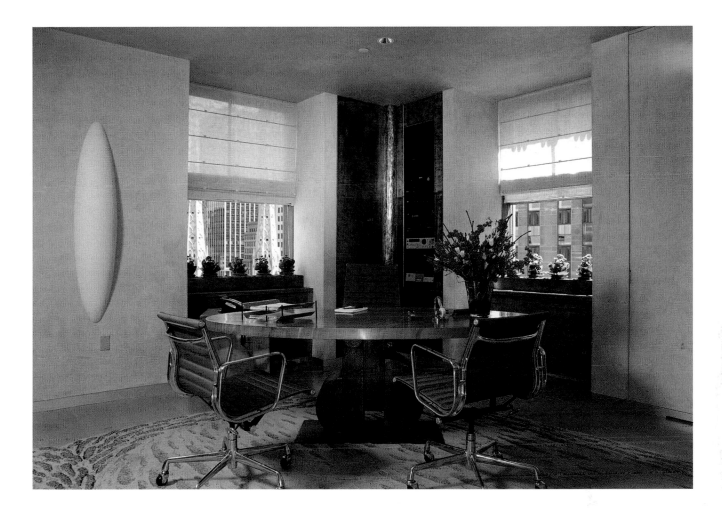

mirrored glass Asia Pacific Finance Centre, a semi-cylinder high-rise a stone's throw from the Bank of China. Stay tuned on the developments, feng shui and otherwise …

BUILDING SHAPES

As well as the regular shapes described in the ba-gua section (see page 46)—squares, rectangles and rounds—which allow occupants to enjoy harmonious, stable lives, other forms can create positive feng shui. For example, a zigzagging lightning-bolt shape is thought to be powerful. Although IBM claims it did not have feng shui in mind, its headquarters in Westchester, New York, seem auspicious anyway. According to Fred McNeese, an IBM spokesman, they were merely trying to flow the building around the contours of the hills and ravines of the site—and so harmonized with nature. But one could say that its architects, Kohn Pedersen Fox, had come up with a lightning-bolt form. Comments Mr. McNeese: "It was a question of topography, not feng shui."

For millennia, feng shui was a major consideration in the shape of Chinese buildings be they palaces, pagodas or farmhouses. However, while these were often a union of regular shapes—mainly rectangles—and were governed by standardized measurements, modern structures present limitless

At Elektra Entertainment in New York, the desk of the chairwoman and CEO is auspiciously placed, seating her on a powerful and controlling diagonal to the door. She is backed and supported by a flat column holding audiovisual equipment, so with one swivel of her chair she controls all entertainment effects in the room, as well as superlative views down the city's avenues. Any negative effects from adjacent buildings and the bustle outside are softened by ch'i-enhancing window box plantings.

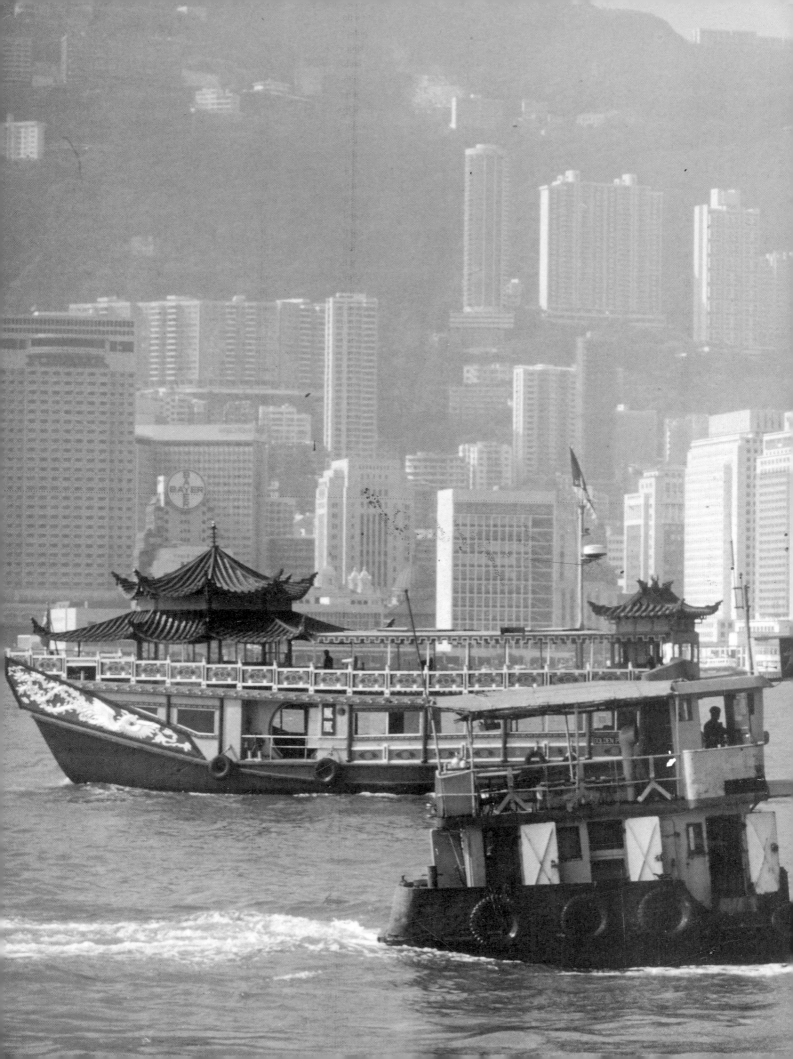

THE FENG SHUI SKYLINE

Hong Kong's ever-changing skyline is widely seen as a *de facto* feng shui battleground. The Connaught Centre dominating this picture is a classic example of this: some see it as tombstone-shaped, worsened still in significance by the incense burner–like tram aligned with it, ascending the backdrop of Victoria Peak.

風水

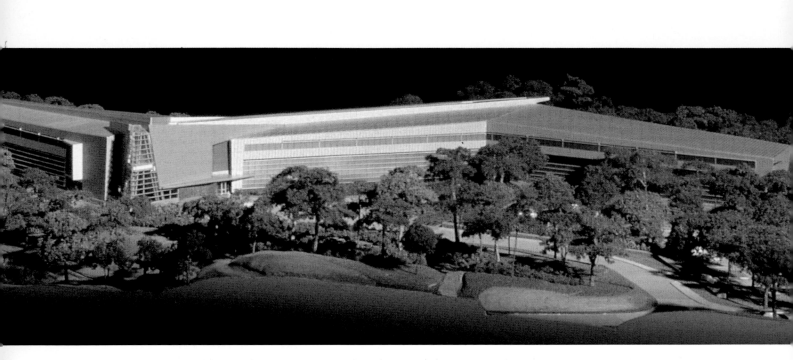

According to feng shui, building shapes can affect a company's fortunes. IBM's new headquarters were designed in a powerful lightning-bolt shape to work with the site's terrain—and, coincidentally, the feng shui.

possibilities for the architect, feng shui consultant and occupant. Today, a building's form—much like the feng shui theory of mountains—can become a metaphor that helps mold its occupants' lives. Indeed, feng shui experts interpret the symbolism of structures in much the same way that they analyze hills. They see the shape of a building as an omen of what might befall the residents. So, obviously, death-oriented symbolism is to be avoided. This can range from tombstone-shaped skyscrapers to coffin-shaped boardrooms.

One classic example of poor feng shui was the Connaught Centre built in Hong Kong in the 1970s. As it was being erected, the Chinese shook their heads in disapproval. They said it had bad feng shui and dubbed it "house of a thousand assholes." It is unclear whether the epithet was for the porthole shape of the windows or for the Western bankers who rented offices there. As expensive tiles dislodged from the exterior wall, lifts plummeted in their shafts and businesses failed, Westerners coined their own nickname for the building: Hancock East, referring to an ill-fated Boston tower which was plagued by structural difficulties. But the blame fell not on poor cement or poor engineering or bad management by the firms involved, but on feng shui. Some people said it was built on the neck of an earth dragon, stifling its luck. Some saw death-oriented symbolism, saying it looked like a Chinese tombstone—the Chinese traditionally paste their ancestors' pictures on circles in the stone—and, further, that the building lined up with the Peak tram, which looked like an incense burner. Others said it looked like a crab cage with water falling out—symbolizing money draining away.

A more recent example of an unfortunately shaped building is a two-tower complex in Manila in the Philippines, designed by an American firm not known for its sensitivity to feng shui. The architects created a floor plan for each tower in the shape of a butterfly, which to the Chinese symbolizes a creature of fleeting mortality. To compound the death-oriented symbolism, the towers were sited near the American cemetery and, worse still, with their pinched design at the center, looked like four towers in total. Not only does the Chinese word "four" sound like their word for "death," but the towers reminded prospective tenants of the incense sticks burned at ancestral altars. As a result, the building is having trouble selling space.

The shape of a building and its meaning for occupants is, however, sometimes a matter of interpretation. And in some situations, good feng shui can be in the eye of the beholder. In one instance, after a design for a 70-story corporate headquarters was completed in Jakarta in Indonesia, its New York architects (working for Kohn Pedersen Fox) were informed that there was one additional step: the plans had to be reviewed by the client's feng shui master. "We were concerned there might be a feng shui problem, because of the jagged edge on top," commented the project architect, James von Klemperer. And the expert did indeed reject the plan. So Mr. von Klemperer asked for a personal audience with the feng shui adept. "It was quite an experience," he remembers. "We went to his temple—which looked like a converted garage—on the outskirts of Jakarta. The place was a strange attempt to create an international headquarters itself. On the wall hung seven inexpensive clocks all showing the same time, but with the name of different international cities above each. When the expert explained that our building's slant angled downwards, portending disaster, we were ready with our reply. We explained that the building in fact was auspiciously shaped: that the top of the building was in fact like a flock of birds ascending, or could be interpreted as being like a stock-index graph foretelling financial success. The feng shui man seemed to approve of our symbolism. Then he retreated to some feng shui details that were easier to correct, such as the angle of the door or the flow of a pool." Another case of negative symbolism was seen in a design for an Asian building that a feng shui expert said looked like a pregnant woman. But instead of seeing fecundity, he saw that occupants would be encumbered, suffer from prolonged and painful labor, and perhaps be in a delicate situation to the point of danger.

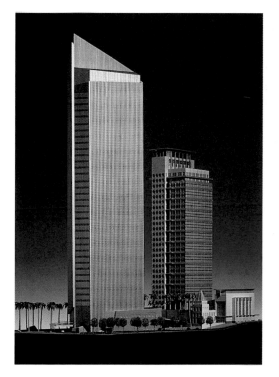
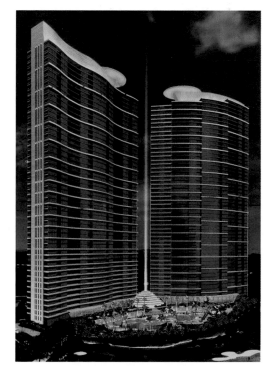

The jagged-edged roof of Niaga Tower II in Jakarta (far left) was initially rejected by a feng shui master, as he saw it as angling downwards towards corporate disaster. The architect, James von Klemperer, achieved resolution with him when he proposed a reinterpretation of the shape as a graph mounting upwards, or a flock of ascending birds.

At the suggestion of a feng shui expert, the entrance to Pacific Plaza Towers in Manila (near left) was slightly moved. "It made sense", said the building's Western architect, Bernardo Fort-Brescia, of the firm Arquitectonica.

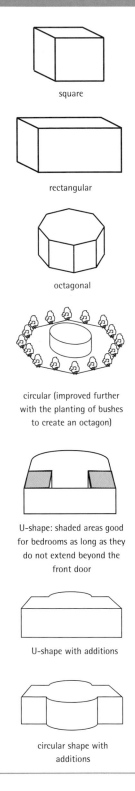

square

rectangular

octagonal

circular (improved further
with the planting of bushes
to create an octagon)

U-shape: shaded areas good
for bedrooms as long as they
do not extend beyond the
front door

U-shape with additions

circular shape with
additions

L- and U-shaped buildings

Many houses and high-rises feature L-, T- or U-shaped ground plans, which are in feng shui terms incomplete and unbalanced. In addition, some buildings form a vertical or horizontal L shape, which can be construed as being death-oriented or accident-prone. For example, a building shaped like a meat cleaver may augur that residents will be sleeping, eating or working "on the edge." In this case, it is advisable to live or work in the tower—the cleaver handle, and therefore the source of control. Avoid having a bed, desk or stove positioned against the "blade" wall, too, although this can be cured by hanging a mirror on the wall opposite the blade, to symbolically bring the occupant safely away from the edge. These rules also apply horizontally, where a home, office or room has an L-shaped floor plan.

Another L shape to avoid is the "boot." If faced with a boot-shaped floor plan, occupants should not install a stove, a desk or a bed in the "toe" area or they will "trip up" in life and thus hurt their finances, perhaps to the point of bankruptcy. The

"ankle" area is a more advantageous site since, being a joint, it wields more power and energy.

Particularly problematic for any L- or U-shaped apartment, home or office is the wing or wings extending beyond the front door. Great thought should be given to how this space is used. In a home, if the wing houses the master bedroom, dining room or kitchen, then the family may have marital problems: one spouse will eat or sleep away from home and eventually stay away altogether. A two-career couple changed the main entrance of their large Victorian house from the front to the side, so that access to the house was easier from the car park. However, the living room and the master bedroom above it jutted out from the new entrance. Shortly afterwards the husband took a job some distance away, at first coming home for weekends but eventually not returning at all. The next family changed the front door back to its original location and has lived in the house happily.

In the case of an office, if a wing juts beyond the front door employees working in it will rarely stay put and

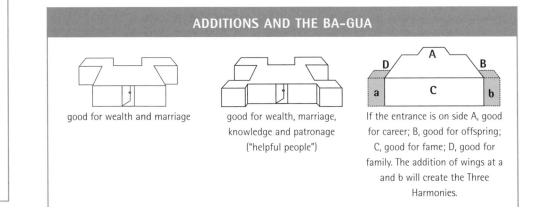

good for wealth and marriage

good for wealth, marriage,
knowledge and patronage
("helpful people")

If the entrance is on side A, good
for career; B, good for offspring;
C, good for fame; D, good for
family. The addition of wings at a
and b will create the Three
Harmonies.

staff turnover will be high. A designer was warned of this during a feng shui consultation, and was advised to hang a mirror to draw the wing symbolically into the main part of her office. Only after a number of prized employees had moved on to other jobs did she call in a mirror and glass company.

Along with jutting wings, slants should be avoided, as they symbolize both something missing and something oblique or unforeseen happening—sometimes good, but generally bad to the point of disastrous. The Chinese also avoid modern architecture that appears dangerous or gravity-defying, preferring a more balanced and stable-seeming building shape and structure.

The diagrams on the left show good shapes for rooms, homes or offices, and some methods for enhancing them further with additions according to the ba-gua.

BUILDING FACADES

In urban feng shui, the exterior of a building has impact. So feng shui experts pay attention to its colors, entrances and exits, landscaping and design details.

URBAN COLORS

Historically, color was an important element in feng shui, and colors remain important in cities. In general, hues should not be monotonous: a city should be embellished with a variety of colors and lights. Lights—neon for exterior commercial use, incandescent for homes—as well as colored entry awnings and brightly colored plantings can all enhance the ch'i of an area.

As in ancient times, when yellow—the colur of the center and earth—was employed in the Forbidden City to reinforce the emperor's strength, power and righteousness over the empire, modern use of colored building material is also symbolic. For example, one Western architect reports that a feng shui expert rejected his plan for a high-rise with a green glass wall, explaining that, according to his calculations, after the year 2004 the green glass would not be harmonious with nature. He suggested using a more earthy bronze-colored glass instead. And in New York City, a feng shui master suggested that the Trump International Tower and Hotel—formerly the Gulf and Western building—be sheathed in earth-toned glass.

In San Francisco, a Western architect designing an apartment for a Chinese client fully expected some feng shui requests. But he was still a bit surprised when these included a demand that the exterior wall be painted fire-engine red to attract Chinese home-buyers. Mr. Fort-Brescia comments: "In Asia, there are less requests for black and more for red granite or gold."

Colors for business exteriors

The best external colors to ground a large building such as a tall skyscraper are those associated with the earth element: gold or yellow, bronze or coffee brown.

There are specific colors which will enhance certain types of business—for instance, a furniture store should use green, pink, sky blue, beige or cream as its primary exterior tone. A bank should offer a "safe" aspect to reassure its customers, and so should employ beige, black and red combinations, and earth tones—all "serious" colors. Earth tones will also give police stations a sense of trustworthiness, for the benefit of the population. Expensive clothing boutiques

FENG SHUI COLORS FOR BUSINESS EXTERIORS

Agent (e.g., literary, dramatic)	Pink, red, white
Art gallery	Pink, red, white
Artist's studio	Dark green, black, purple
Bakery	White, multicolored
Bank	Beige, earth tones, red-and-black combination
Beauty salon	A combination of white and blue
Bookshop	"Serious" colors if more academic—black, white, purple, dark green—otherwise multicolors
Car park	Light blue, light green, white, black, gray
Car wash	Black, beige, yellow
Clothing boutiques	Simple color schemes—e.g., white and black, or red and green; colorful if inexpensive boutique
Computer company	Dark green, black, gray, beige, yellow
Construction firm	Green, white
Estate agent	Dark or light green, white, yellow or brown, multicolored
Executive office in creative fields	Light or dark green, red/purple, white; avoid black, gray or dark browns
Film, television or recording studio	Light blue, dark green, red/purple, multicolored
Funeral parlor	All-blue, all-white, all-black
Gourmet food shop	Dark green, dark brown (coffee color) and "serious" tones
Grocer	Light blue, light green, beige, yellow
Library	Green, red, black, gray, dark brown, purple
Lighting shop	Red, purple
Music shop	Green, all-black, all-gray, all dark brown
Pharmacy	Light blue, light green, pink, white
Police station	Earth tones
Psychic's salon	Dark green, red, black, all-purple
Psychologist	Dark green, red, black, purple
Restaurant	Light, simple, monochromatic or two-color scheme
Stationery shop	White, yellow, beige, multicolored with pink; avoid black
Supermarket	Light blue, green, purple
Toy shop	White, multicolored
Video shop	Multicolored
Wine shop	Green, pink, white, black, gray, beige, yellow; avoid red or purple

should have classy monochromatic color schemes, but more down-market ones much more color. See above for further specific examples. But, in general, a store's exterior should be appealing and unique, to stand out and impress the shopper.

Colors that create a literal metaphor can also make a positive visual statement. For example, to symbolize development, growth and prosperity, a large building might be constructed with colors suggesting a fruit-bearing tree. Its base and lower levels might be brown or deep red to symbolize the trunk, and its upper floors might be green with red accents, symbolizing the leaves and fruit.

In Asia, death-oriented colors are avoided. A facade that is white, symbolizing mourning, must be tempered with positive accent colors. For example, without its rose garden, yellow flowerbeds on the lawn and other plantings, the color of the White House would portend greater problems for the United States. Blue, a secondary mourning color to the Chinese, is also generally avoided in projects in Hong

Kong. Color symbolism goes so far that a seafood restaurant in Taiwan was advised to change its exterior from red—the color of cooked (and therefore dead) shellfish—to green, the color of living shrimps and lobsters.

Lively colors associated with productivity—green for spring and growth, yellow for autumn and harvest, and red for summer and fruition—are best for street-level establishments such as schools, stores and businesses. However, black, dark brown and charcoal gray, colors associated with winter and hibernation, might augur dormant intellect and sluggish business.

NUMBERS AND DATES

As in other cultures, numbers possess a special and sacred meaning for the Chinese. After all, it is recognized that Western Renaissance poets organized their lyrics and syllables according to numerological schemes to create a subtle, if subconscious, sense of harmony for the reader. The number three recurs in Western cultures as a powerful triad: the magical three wishes in fairy tales, the Holy Trinity in Christianity, and the sacred and restorative powers of pyramids—composed of four triangles.

So, too, in Chinese civilization do certain numbers carry a sacred and important symbolism, and auspicious numbers are traditionally employed in architecture. In the *Rites of Chou*, a text on the ritual practices of the Chou dynasty, the capital city repeatedly employed the number nine: it was built as a square walled city of nine *li* (Chinese miles) on a grid of nine north-south streets bisected by nine east-west roads. Further, the north-south streets were to be wide enough to accommodate nine chariots. There were purported to have been exactly 99,999 rooms in the Forbidden City. And south of the Forbidden City, the Temple of Heaven is approached by a series of three tiers of nine steps.

Because it is homophonic, the Chinese language is full of puns, symbolism and multiple meanings. This is particularly evident in numbers, which regularly evoke omens and symbols foretelling the future. For example, the Chinese word for nine

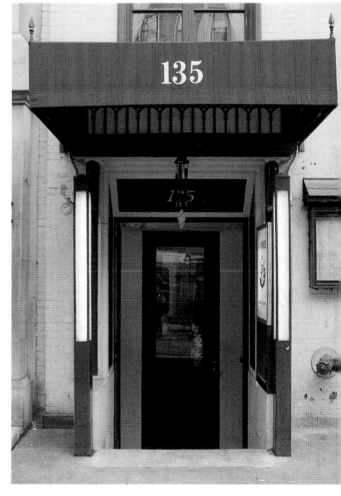

is *chou*, which sounds similar to the word for a long time or longevity. The number four, on the other hand, sounds like the word "death" and so is avoided by many Chinese. The Hong Kong developer of a large office complex had problems selling any space that contained the number four. And some buildings in Asia are missing the fourth floor, in much the same way that Westerners avoid the thirteenth one. "We are careful not to have four-sided buildings," notes one architect. "Sometimes, we slice corners to create a more auspicious eight-sided form."

The number eight is deemed to be auspicious because it sounds similar to the Cantonese word for prosperity. It is also desirable because it evokes the eight trigrams of the *I Ching* ba-gua, and therefore

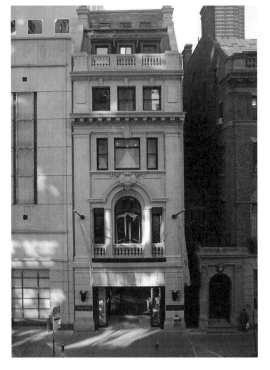

The Beaux-Arts facade of the nineteenth-century townhouse now housing the department store Felissimo creates a pleasant contrast to its high-rise neighbors, attracting the potential customer's eye. A spacious entryway, colourful banners and attractive displays draw customers in; curves in the pillars and window shapes soften the stony streetscape, hinting at the echoes of nature within.

the power and perfection of the universe. The number one is lucky because it signifies the beginning and birth, as well as being the leader. In the San Francisco area, a Chinese client of Skidmore, Owings and Merrill insisted they add four floors to a 54-story building, because he felt that the number 58 had a luckier ring to it. Even dates for ceremonies are chosen for their auspicious numbers as well as their astrological harmony.

The best numbers for a house or office are one, two, three (and its multiples, six and nine) and eight. The worst are four (see above) and seven—in Chinese ritual, memorial services are held every seven days for seven weeks after a death.

THE ENTRANCE

The importance of procession to an entrance has long been important in Chinese culture. The access routes to tombs, palaces and temples were carefully planned to create a new

view of the structures from each stage of the approach. Stone animals lined alleys leading to important tombs. Gates of varied shapes framed access to cities and traditional urban homes. And *fu* dogs and stone lions historically served as sentries symbolically guarding palaces, pagodas and large businesses. In the late 1980s, when the Hongkong & Shanghai Banking Corporation was having its new headquarters built—designed by the British architect Norman Foster—they shelled out $500 U.S. to divine when, where and in what direction they should temporarily relocate their stone lions. The statues were placed in a park opposite the construction site "to keep an eye on things." Indeed, correct placement of these guardians is crucial. For example, at the Four Seasons Hotel in Toronto, Canada, according to bell captain Tommy Huen, the guardian lions were brought into the lobby for decoration. "It was like they were in jail, and everyone was sick," explained Mr. Huen. On his and some foreign visitors' advice, the lions were "released" outside to guard the entrance. All recovered shortly afterwards.

The approach to a building should ideally be processional and should engender a welcoming sense of arrival. What you see as you walk in or towards a building will influence your feelings and interior experience of the space—whether it is a home, office or business. There should be a harmony of perspective. Harking back to ancient Chinese approaches to important sites using the concept of *guo-bai*, symbolic gateways, guardians and even modern versions of spirit screens are still sought in urban feng shui. Columns, arches and plantings are used to flank entrances like sentries and lend visual importance and direction to the entrance.

Columns can be either positive or problematic depending on where they stand. Ones that stand at a distance, but flank the entrance to a store or business, act as symbolic sentries and create a sense of arrival and procession. Columns that obscure the door, be it slanted or flush with the wall, obstruct business and profits. Round columns are best, as the angles of square pillars can point at customers and workers to create a blocked and threatening feeling, discouraging return business and thwarting sales. A feng shui expert, brought in by Donald Trump and his partners to analyze the Gulf and Western building in New York, commented that the columns there were positive, as they symbolized the three partners and therefore harmony between them in the project.

Interior fountains and exterior sculptures, stationary or kinetic, are placed in front of doors where they act as modern versions of spirit screens in their function of adjusting the flow of ch'i to and from a building. In a 30-story design in Kuala Lumpur, Malaysia, the feng shui expert—concerned that a garden outside the building would draw out money—suggested installing something that moved, such as a revolving door, to moderate the flow of ch'i and money. In another design a feng shui expert asked that an exterior fountain in which the water flowed away from the entrance be removed or wealth would flow out. A fountain or waterfall *towards* the building was fine, as it would steer prosperity towards the structure.

When the landscape architect for a 35-story building in Jakarta designed a driveway that approached it on a diagonal so that the initial view of the structure was its knife-like corner, the feng shui expert complained. So the approach was altered to lead frontally to the flat side of the building. The building's architect, Mr. Fort-Brescia, commented that in any case, "in the history of architecture, there is an order. It is important to go through a threshold to give a sense of arrival. With the diagonal approach leading to the point, there was no sense of welcome." He adds, "Most of the time—a good 90 percent—the feng shui doctor is right and often improves the design. The comments are constructive as a lot is common sense, and often feng shui is sensitive both to natural forces and a symbolic vernacular on and in buildings."

Exterior ornamentation can improve business. Lights, topiary or plantings or mirrors flanking the entrance doors create visual interest and attract pedestrian ch'i. The appealing sounds of bells or wind chimes for a small business, or fountains for any business, attract the attention of nearby patrons. The sounds should be pleasant, but not overpowered by city noise. If they are too loud or clanging, they will thwart business. Subtle, pleasant smells of flowers or pines also create interest, especially for a beauty salon or cosmetic shop. Make sure the scents are slight and suggestive and not pungent and overpowering.

What you see when you leave a home or a business also has an impact. An exit onto a spacious park or city square is ideal, giving you a positive sense of the outside world. If, however, you find yourself facing a dark street or the back of a large building, your ch'i will be lowered. When a major United States company was designing a new retail entertainment complex close to its existing hotels, its in-house design expert—who happened to be Chinese—invoked feng shui to amend the original plans. In these, a new 30-foot-tall cinema had been located with its back to a hotel. He pointed out that in terms of feng shui, this would be bad for the hotel. "It made sense," commented an architect attending the meeting. "It just didn't feel right." As of this writing, they are working to reposition the cinema to avoid blocking the path of people exiting the hotel. Stay tuned …

Feng Shui Interiors

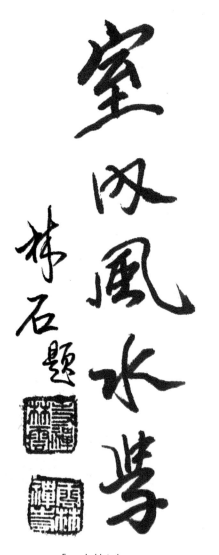

Feng shui interiors

In modern homes and offices, interior feng shui seems to affect people more than exterior feng shui, and while the practice is crucial to all design in Asia, its appeal in the West seems to be primarily in its interior application. Through feng shui, patterns of behavior and life courses, as well as business fortunes, can be determined simply by the structure and furniture arrangement in homes and offices. Following the same precepts as those of ancient feng shui—that the earth possesses veins that bring beneficial ch'i to those who positively tap into its pulse—the modern feng shui expert looks on a home or a business as a body, with similar patterns of metabolism. This ch'i, entering through a building's mouth (doors) and eyes (windows), courses through corridors and hallways that conduct it from room to room. Furniture, walls, interior doors, plants, lights and fountains moderate and channel ch'i flow within a room. So, in an interior space, harmony is sought so that its occupants can draw strength from their surroundings and use them to live balanced, positive and prosperous lives.

The next two chapters take the reader visually through first businesses and then homes, to see what a feng shui expert sees and envisions. Most of the illustrations are of the creations and interpretations of architects and designers who have incorporated feng shui advice into their projects. The expert works as "extra" eyes for the client and architect, analyzing how the angle of a corner, or a corner jutting into a hallway, or the alignment of doors, will affect the occupants' lives. You may find that many of the feng shui suggestions are common sense. Indeed, more than one architect has noted, on reviewing feng shui–amended plans, "We should have caught that."

Most of the photographs are of interiors by Clodagh, a minimalist designer who "designs for all the senses." She also believes in "bringing in all the elements" and feels feng shui is one way to accomplish this. "I bring in my feng shui consultant much in the way I bring in a lighting consultant or structural engineer. It is as important to my design."

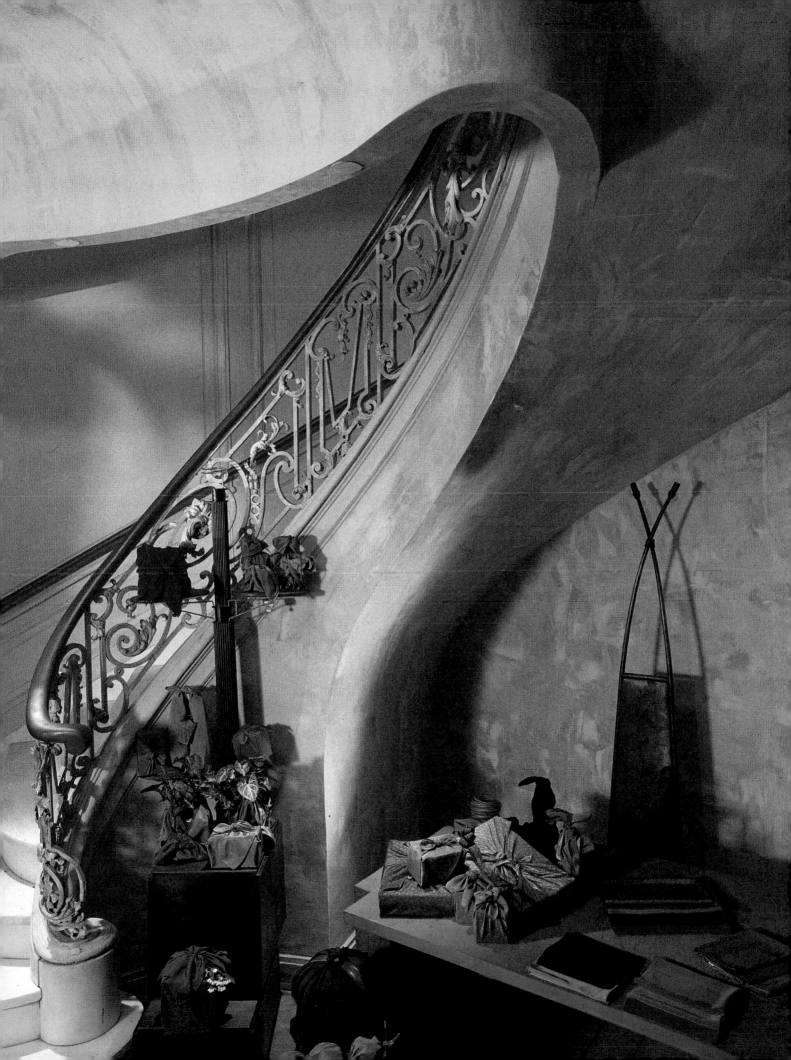

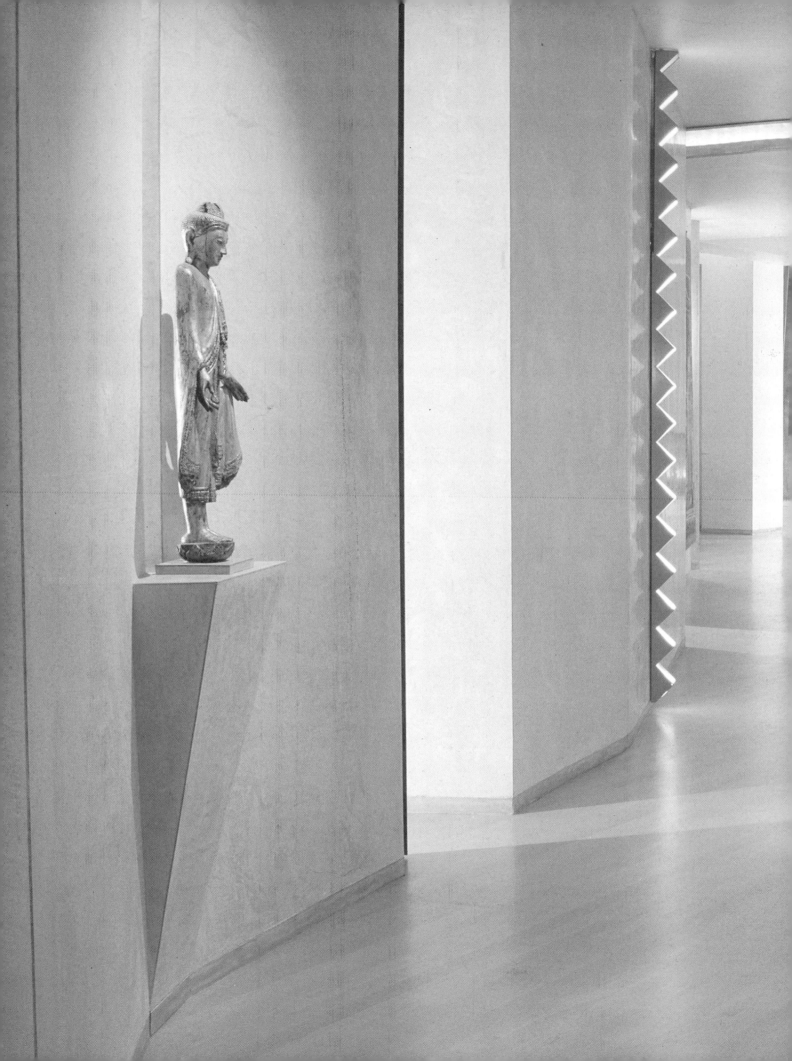

Ch'i, money and opportunity can escape too quickly when a hallway corridor ends in a wall of windows. But the designer of this penthouse created a meandering gallery of light with wall niches for artworks, creating both points of visual interest and balancing the uneven view. The corridor was anchored with a fireplace at the living room end, to stop the eye and ch'i from flowing out of the apartment.

風水

CHAPTER VII

Feng Shui for Business Interiors

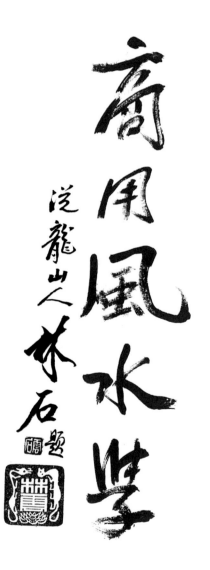

Business feng shui

Feng shui can be particularly effective in work and business. Indeed, to the Chinese, it has long been an essential part of business management. As one Citibank officer comments—and many other executives echo this: "We always have someone call in a feng shui expert in Asia—if we didn't, our Chinese staff would probably quit."

Today, more and more Western companies, businesses and individuals are incorporating the elements of feng shui, both to appease Asian employees and in the hopes of using it to attain a financial edge. For example, in 1988 Sir Richard Greenbury of Marks & Spencer called on a feng shui expert to apply feng shui principles in the company's Hong Kong store. After sales rose significantly, Marks & Spencer employed feng shui in the layout of Asian and British stores, as well as the London offices of its chief executive officer and its financial controller. Along with strategically sited carp-filled fish tanks, the stores in Hong Kong and Britain all contained "lucky" gold coins, buried in auspicious spots.

While Marks & Spencer's Asian presence can explain feng shui's emigration to its London properties, the use of feng shui is now arising in the designs of Western companies. These range from hedge funds and merger and acquisitions firms to advertising agencies of all sizes, from retail stores to beauty spas, and even to hotels and recording companies. Carlos Caballero, the head of Colombia's Stock Exchange, had his office rearranged according to feng shui, to steady and improve the performance of that institution. One hedge fund has employed a feng shui consultant for each of its four moves to larger offices as it grew from a small three-person operation to a 100-plus-person billion-dollar company within ten years.

While profit is generally the primary motive for using feng shui in Asia, it is used for a number of other reasons in the West: to energize an office or a business, to take some stress out of a business environment, to improve productivity, to encourage employee harmony and to create a comfortable yet stimulating space in which to work. Yet in addition to profit, certain givens are good for business. Feng shui also emphasizes values: be honest, compassionate, respectful, hard-working, trustworthy, diligent and thrifty. Strive to provide

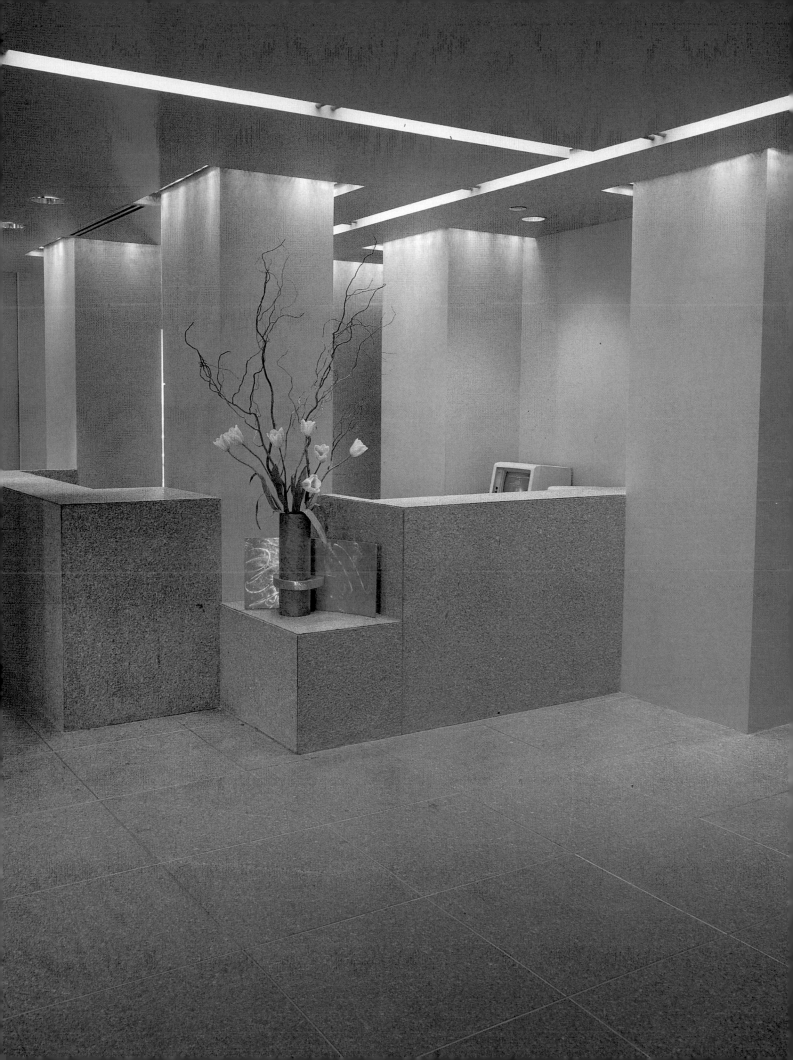

better and more sales services. Avoid being greedy or opportunistic just to make a quick sale. Never belittle others or attempt to raise your own reputation or importance at someone else's expense.

For those in public service, wisdom, power and cooperation from others are feng shui goals. In Bogota, Rosso Jose Serrano, the highly respected three-star general and head of the Colombian National Police Force, had his office redecorated in accordance with feng shui principles. Not only were the walls and windows taken into consideration, but so was the crucifix hanging behind his desk, which was relocated to help generate an atmosphere conducive to proper fulfillment of his duties.

THE IMPORTANCE OF HISTORY

Place defines destiny. In Asia, the sense of a place that bestows good or bad luck on occupants remains strong. Certain successful entrepreneurs maintain the original site of their earliest business triumphs—no matter how unchic the address—much as a Westerner might keep a lucky rabbit's paw. The Chinese pay attention to the history of a place because they feel that moving into a site is like stepping into the former owner's shoes. So always investigate the previous company's reason for leaving a site: was it the need for larger quarters as a result of healthy growth, or was it due to failure? One example of an abandoned site tainted with a history of bad luck is a Shearson Lehman office in Hong Kong. The firm lured some bankers away from Morgan Stanley but the formerly successful bankers' personalities, as well as their performance, proved a liability. They were dismissed, leaving Shearson burdened with hefty severance packages and also encumbered with a large, empty office space that none of their other employees would agree to occupy, fearing they would suffer a similar fate.

GOOD AND BAD OFFICE FENG SHUI

THE ENTRANCE

The first consideration in a business interior is its entrance: the doorway—or *ch'i kou*—and the lobby. The entrance should be comfortable, large and welcoming. The lobby of a building, or the foyer of an office space, should be bright and open. In a public lobby, there should be a sense of arrival, clearly directing employees' and visitors' eyes, bodies and ch'i to the reception area, escalators and elevators. The progress from the entrance to the elevator or escalator should be processional, clean and balanced. When the Miami-based architectural practice Arquitectonica was designing the 52-story Pacific Plaza Towers in Manila, the feng shui expert modified the entrance. "Most of the time, the feng shui doctor is right," comments Bernardo Fort-Brescia. As the design developed, "The columns in the lobby became off-center. Using his own mystical reasons and calculations, the feng shui doctor said to move the entrance to an angle. But," continues Fort-Brescia, "in fact, it made sense—design-wise and financially." The new angle of the entrance harmonized with the columns, creating a positive first impression of the lobby.

The placement and direction of lobby escalators can also become a feng shui issue. At one point panic overtook some clients of the Hongkong & Shanghai Bank when its new headquarters was deemed to have too many down escalators, seen to conduct ch'i, and their savings, on a descent. And recently in Shanghai, designs for a towering office complex were delayed when much concern was given to escalators that angled upwards towards each other as they rose. The client was concerned that this design looked similar to chopsticks, and gave the lobby a "pinched" feeling.

In addition to a lobby's structure and shape, other elements can enhance—or diminish—the feng shui. Generally, interior fountains and plants improve feng shui and profits, as water symbolizes money and greenery brings a life force to an interior. While the Chinese owner of 40 Wall Street, in New York's financial district, is a professed non-believer in feng shui, he nonetheless commissioned a $300,000 pool in the building's lobby on the advice of a feng shui expert, for aesthetic reasons and to attract Chinese tenants. And at the $15 million China Trust Bank, also in New York City, the automated teller machine area was rearranged—in mid-design. On the advice of a feng shui expert, the architects relocated the elevator shafts and installed a two-foot-high water fountain near the machine.

Office buildings and suites

The entrance door to an office building or suite should not be too heavy, but should open with ease to help usher in good luck, prospects and profits. It should be larger than interior doors to other office rooms, to allow people, ch'i and opportunity to enter easily. It should be welcoming, enticing workers and clients into its interior space. One example is the front door of the Tokyo presentation center of Dentsu, the world's largest advertising agency. Designed by Clodagh, it is located in a basement. "When you reached the building, you got into an elevator and pressed a button marked 'basement,'" remembers Clodagh. "You came out into a fairly dark corridor leading to an

interior space with no natural light or windows. Since I was designing the space to be powerful, I wanted to make some extremely important doors—which I designed in bronze—to greet you as you came out of the elevator. My feng shui consultant said bronzed frames were fine, but there should be etched glass with light behind them to pull people into the space, and to create the promise of something happening beyond the doors. I immediately switched my design to do so."

What you see when entering helps to create both a mood and an impression of the entire business. A logo or a symbol of the company should be visible from the entrance, giving a clear sense of arrival. Other positive sights and sounds are something mobile or with life force, such as fountains, aquariums, healthy plants, appealing chimes. These "cures" can improve the profitability and productivity of a firm. And also note that generally, when you first enter an office, you should not be able to see the toilet areas or profit may be flushed away.

The reception area

An important facet of an office is the reception area—and the receptionist. Too often not enough importance and thought are given to this employee, who both welcomes visitors and guards access from the outside world. The receptionist is often in the line of fire—exposed to visitors and placed at a disadvantage to the rest of the office—an unnerving position. As a result, in many companies, turnover is high in this position.

Ideally, the receptionist is at the front and hub of office activity, helping to make the process of entering and exiting the office a positive experience. Sitting in the controlling position of the reception area to see everyone coming in and leaving, receptionists themselves should be visible from the entrance, and yet not too close to it—especially if they are

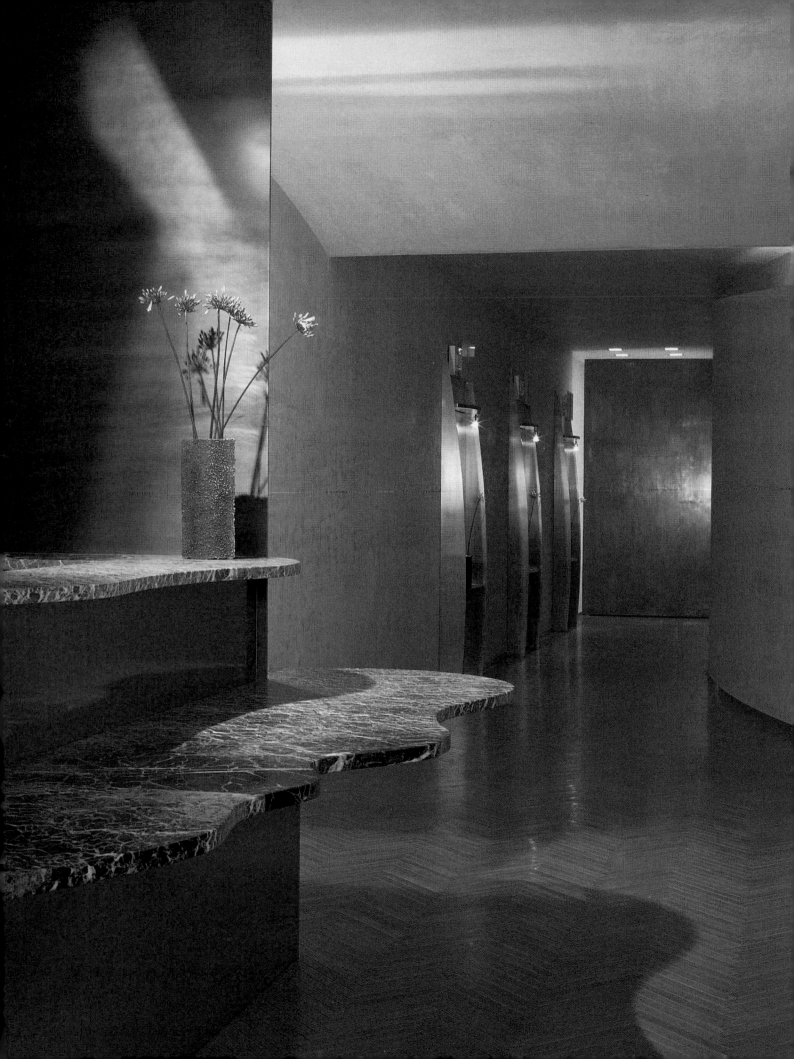

directly in front of the door—as they will feel assaulted by entering ch'i and impatient visitors. But the receptionist should also be able to monitor people leaving the office or placing a package for pick-up. At the same time he or she should sit where they are protected from the onslaught and anxiety of the internal office buzz. If positively placed, the receptionist will feel an integral part of the company. On the other hand, one who is seated at a disadvantage, and is approachable from behind, will be constantly startled, and so jumpy, irascible, unpleasant and forgetful.

Sometimes, a particular office's spatial logistics mean that the receptionist cannot be placed in an advantageous position. In the plan for one floor of Elizabeth Arden's newly renovated New York salon the reception area had to be placed behind the elevators. Entering clients were not able to see it, and did not have a sense of arrival and direction when coming out of an elevator. However, the siting of a mirror on a structural pillar facing the elevators served to reflect the reception area to clients.

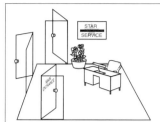

The receptionist should always sit at a vantage point where all who enter and exit can be seen.

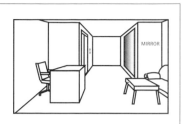

In this plan for a second-floor beauty salon, mirrors were placed opposite the opening elevator doors, so that the receptionist could see visitors arriving, despite the positioning of the reception desk.

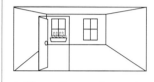

In this reception area of a record company's offices, a window box was installed to recirculate ch'i, money and opportunity within the office, and stop it from flowing out.

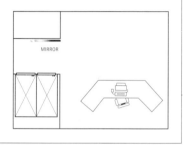

Part of the reception area of Dentsu's Tokyo presentation center, left. It uses welcoming curves and undulating surfaces, which also offset the possibly negative effect of its basement location, as well as the positive natural finishes of stone and wood. The wavy shapes suggest fluidity and flexibility in the professional area—and the reception area itself is fluid in its uses, sometimes doubling as a party area. To stimulate ideas and feelings, a sitting area in an office at Elektra, decorated in neutral tones is accented by red pillows (below).

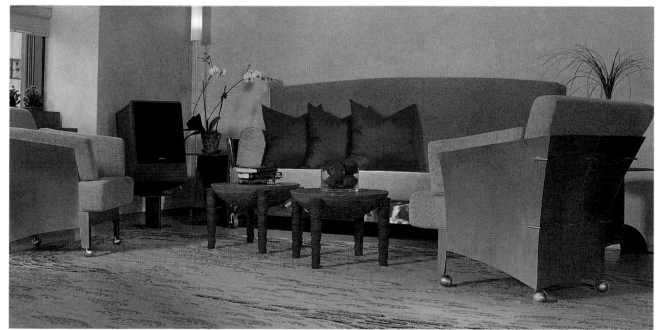

OFFICE LAYOUT

In certain businesses, privacy is important. In one office in midtown Manhattan, a glass wall behind the receptionist revealed the corridor leading to the CEO's office. A feng shui consultant suggested blocking off the wall to create a sense of privacy and to channel and filter outside ch'i into the work space in a more balanced way. An open-plan office arrangement and individual offices are both acceptable in feng shui if they give a feeling of security and comfort as opposed to creating one of claustrophobia and uneasiness. However, if the office has an open plan, the general staff should occupy the open area, while the individuals who make the decisions and shoulder the most responsibility—general managers and controllers—should have their own individual offices. If the corporation occupies an entire building, the office of the president should be situated at its hub, at mid-level in the front part of the building or at mid-level in the back of the building—the wealth, fame or marriage areas of the ba-gua. This allows power to emanate from the center. If the company only occupies several floors, the office of the president should be situated on the middle floor. (However, it can also be situated on the highest one if it is located in the wealth corner—the far left corner of the floor, see page 44.)

The corner office is considered a position of power: it has the most access to light and views, and is generally the farthest point from the entrance so that unnecessary facts, people and problems can be filtered before they arrive at the president's door. Access to natural light and inspiring views has a positive impact on any office worker; an office with no windows can inhibit creativity. To open new avenues of inspiration, either install fake windows or hang mirrors or landscape paintings, to give a more expansive impression of spaciousness and nature's nurturing properties.

In this New York foreign trade facilitator's office, designed by architect David Van Buren, the president chose to face the window in order to enjoy and be inspired by the fine view. However, this left her with her back to the door, a position of potential vulnerability. A strategically placed Ch'ing dynasty mirror corrects her disadvantaged position, augmented by a crystal paperweight placed on the desk.

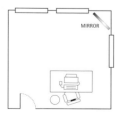

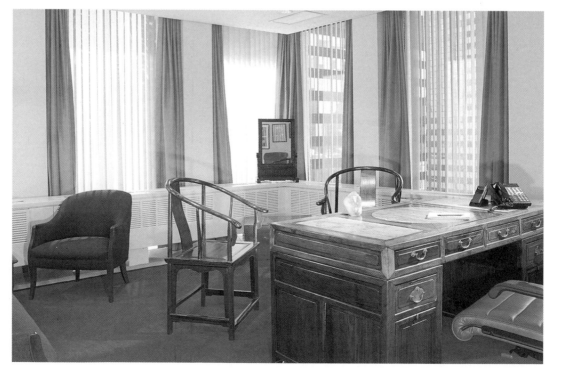

DOOR AND WINDOW ALIGNMENT

The correct alignment of doors and windows is important for office profits, opportunities and employee health, harmony and efficiency. Ideally, an entry to a business or an individual office should not face a window or an exit door—although profits, business prospects and positive ch'i will enter the space, they will quickly leave it again before circulating within. In addition, this flow of ch'i carrying away potential prosperity can be divisive for the business, and create an invisible barrier between one sector and another. A screen, plant, chandelier, crystal or mobile placed between the entrance and the exit or window will symbolically help possibilities and prosperity to circulate throughout the business—a concept that harks back to ancient Chinese building practice and folklore, and the spirit screens that were placed inside doorways both to shield a family or business against demons, and to redirect and modify the ch'i, or draft, of the world outside, in order to create a more comfortable place in which to work and generally exist.

Such was the case with the entrance to the corner office suite of a record company executive. Her predecessor had been removed for over-spending on office renovations and business entertaining. On the advice of a feng shui consultant, her designer installed a box of living plants on the windowsill directly opposite the entrance. The box worked both to circulate prospects and prosperity and to add an extra sense of life force that nurtured positive ch'i in the corporate environment. The executive is not only thriving but has been given increased responsibilities.

Another situation to avoid is an office where the window is off-center with the door, so that when someone enters it one eye can see out of the window while the other sees only the interior wall. This is uncomfortable and unbalancing. To remedy this, hang a mirror or a landscape painting on the wall facing the door to create a sense of depth that balances with the view outside the window.

INTERIOR STRUCTURE

Within an office building or suite, or a store, the structure—its columns, corners, walls, long corridors, overhead beams, staircase—can all create patterns in employees' work habits, productivity and lives. Structural columns can block ch'i flow and unbalance that of its occupants' ch'i. One that is poorly placed can create an unbalanced vista, where a person's one eye has a long-sighted view while the other is arrested by the column. Rounded columns are preferable to square pillars, as they allow ch'i to circulate better. In addition, square columns have sharp corners that can point at occupants in a threatening manner.

In feng shui, corners that jut into a room have sharp edges that can threaten its occupant. A television producer who sat with his back to a corner was unfairly criticized behind his back, and was eventually fired. Long straight corridors are also problematic. Reminiscent of ancient Chinese rules for rivers, they conduct ch'i too swiftly within a business, affecting the health and inter-office relationships of employees. A drafty fast flow of ch'i can act as an invisible barrier between offices on either side of the corridor. While a long corridor is not long enough to channel killing ch'i, the velocity is strong enough to cause internal distress along the central meridian of occupants' bodies. The feng shui expert should always be aware of a strong axis. In Santa Fe, the designs for the new Gerald Peters Gallery included some long hallways and axes. The feng shui consultant recommended that something such as a sculptural mobile be suspended from the ceiling, to help ch'i circulate better throughout the art gallery.

When a corridor is not only long but narrow, this generates a constricted feeling; luck and prospects may also be choked, and office harmony affected. In feng shui terms, a narrow corridor is one where the width is less than the height of the owner or head of the corporation. But a corridor is also considered narrow when people instinctively feel confined. Install mirrors on both sides of the corridor to remedy this, or decorate the walls with paintings, calligraphy, artwork or plants. Or hang a crystal ball or a wind chime along the central line of the corridor.

Back-lit tenting playfully stretching over a long corridor softens the strong flow of ch'i, and the hard hallway surfaces, at Noelle The Day Spa, but this cure can also be applied in an office corridor situation.

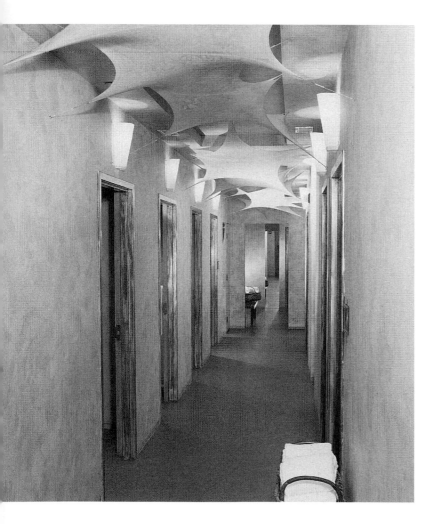

In addition, beware of long hallways with slight jogs—corners or other shapes jutting into the main shape. The slightly blocked sight lines increase office stress, as they are visually unbalancing, allowing one eye a long-sighted view while blacking out the other's. In such a case, installing a mirror or a landscape painting at the point where the hallway bends will balance the view.

If an office covers several floors and is linked by stairs, the position of the stairway is important. Stairs funnel people, ch'i and money from floor to floor. Ideally, they should curve gracefully upward—and steps should be fully connected using risers, so that ch'i and finances don't escape. Spiral staircases tend to be dangerous. Avoid having a stairway that aims at the entrance or ch'i and money will flow out of the door.

Stairways should generally be sited in the front area of an office, to avoid disturbing employees' concentration and work. However, in certain situations, a staircase at the back of an office can enhance morale and business. If a company utilizes and is involved with fame and publicity—a talent agency, for example—the stairs should be situated at the back of the office so that the actor, actress or producer client with an appointment will walk through the general staff area and be recognized, thus adding to their fame as well as the morale, reputation and ch'i of the agency.

INDIVIDUAL OFFICE LAYOUT

Within an individual office, there is much that can be done to encourage productivity, profits and promotions. The first consideration is the desk position. Ideally, this should be in the opposite corner to the entrance—the power

STRUCTURAL PROBLEMS	DIAGNOSIS	CURE
Square columns	1 Block ch'i flow. 2 Have sharp, threatening angles.	1 Hang mirrors running edge-to-edge on all sides. 2 Train vines to grow up the edges, softening their effect.
Corners	Knife-like corners point into a room threatening and accusing occupants, increasing chances of violence or unfair blame.	1 Hang a mirror on one or both sides. 2 Grow a vine up the corner. 3 Hang a crystal in front of the corner.
Long corridors	1 Funnel ch'i too quickly. 2 Are divisive in an office. 3 Can cause health problems along the central meridian.	Hang crystals, mobiles, wind chimes or hanging lights along the path of the hallway or corridor.
Overhead beams	Are oppressive to those sitting underneath them. Can cause headaches and interfere with efficiency and profitability.	1 Obscure with back-lit shoji-screen-style false ceiling. 2 Create a ba-gua shape with flutes.
Staircases	Funnel ch'i from floor to floor. Spiral staircases choke ch'i.	If a stairway faces an entrance, hang a crystal, chandelier or mobile between the last stair and the entrance to hold in the ch'i; wrap something green around the banisters of a spiral staircase.

VINE   MIRRORS

CRYSTALS, CHIMES OR MOBILES

OVERHEAD LIGHTING

position—so that the occupant can exert and enjoy maximum authority, concentration and control while working. This position is good for expanding business. Besides being able to enjoy the greatest scope of vision—and thus have a healthy and positive perspective—the person sitting there will feel in command of the environment, be able to take on more responsibility, and be less likely to be startled, or distracted from a task, when a visitor—be it boss or underling—drops by. If people are startled, their ch'i can be unbalanced and they can lose their train of thought and be jumpy, easily rattled, distracted and upset.

However, when the surroundings outside a building are compelling, some opt to enjoy this view over a view of the door. In this case, hang a mirror where it will reflect the door back to you. The alternative way to enjoy both a good position and a good view is to sit facing the door and hang a mirror to reflect the outside scenery. When the view is of water, a mirror can even symbolically draw the money-endowing view over the desk. Sometimes, because of lack of space and the pre-existing office setup, a built-in desk will face immovably away from the door. In this case a mirror, once again hung to reflect the door, is a good cure. A further variation may be that the occupants face a door, but one wall behind them is an interior glass wall and they feel that things are going on behind their back. Again, a mirror reflecting what is behind them will correct this problem.

Balance is important when positioning the desk. It should not be so close to the door that the approach is ungracious and sudden, and anyone entering might seem to topple over the occupant. But it should be removed enough from the back wall for him or her to sit in comfort. A desk too close to the rear wall creates a pinched or trapped feeling, and narrows business prospects. Each of these desk situations can also unbalance the occupant's ch'i, creating a feeling that life and work are a struggle. Balance should also be achieved in the selection of the size of furniture, to ensure it harmonizes with the office. A small office will be overwhelmed by a large desk, while a spacious office will diminish someone sitting at a small desk. While floor-to-ceiling book-

shelves and filing cabinets are fine in a large office, they can be overbearing in a small one. If the shelves are for miscellaneous use, desk-high ones are preferable.

If a small office is over-populated with employees, this will affect harmony. Install mirrors—the bigger the better—on all four sides. Also, decorate the office with nine plants, or hang a brass wind chime in the center of the room.

Other positioning concerns include where the occupant sits in relation to the entrance. For example, someone sitting too close to the entrance will habitually leave early, as they are constantly aware of the door. And just as in an individual office, the manager in a small open-plan one should sit in the opposite corner to the door and the chain of command should radiate from there. Anyone who sits closer to the door than his or her subordinates will be bossed around by underlings, who will hold all the cards and treat that person with disrespect. If the office is arranged like a classroom, with

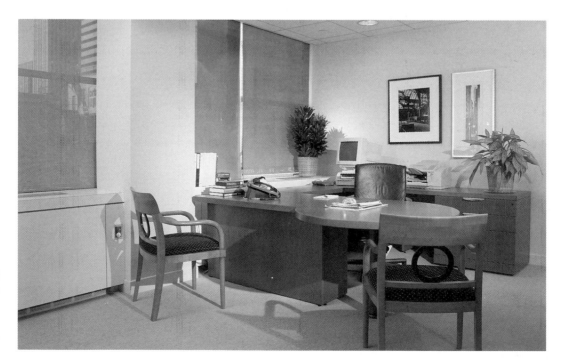

A well-placed desk, sited in the commanding position of a financier's office. The desk also has a positive, curving shape, and the visitors' chairs incorporate such forms, too.

the boss sitting closest to the door, productivity and morale will be low, as employees will feel monitored and distorted, and shirk responsibility like schoolchildren. Bosses in this position may easily oversee the other workers but, with their back to the door, their ch'i will be made jumpy, excitable and irascible.

A bright flower installed between the door and a nearby boss will attract his or her attention, so they will be more aware of comings and goings in the office, and less likely to be startled.

While proximity to the boss is good, a desk that is too close will create the feeling that the boss is breathing down the employee's neck. The stress of this situation can be lessened by placing a crystal or a bowl of water—with or without fish—on the desk. And if two people share an office, site the desks on a diagonal to form part of an octagon; this can create an auspicious and non-confrontational arrangement.

With an open-plan office, desk or cubicle, location is also important. A desk or cubicle in the wealth area is very good, as is one in the center of the room, the ming t'ang position in ba-gua terms. It is not only at the hub of things, but also connotes physical and mental health, strength and stability. A two-person cubicle sited in the ming t'ang area can be further enhanced if one desk is black and one white, representing the yin-yang symbol of the Tai-chi. This auspiciousness can be further improved if the black (yin) desk is occupied by a man (yang), and a woman (yin) sits at the white (yang) desk—within yin exists yang and within yang exists yin—thus symbolizing the harmony of Tao. No

matter where you are sited, however, you can apply the ba-gua to your own desk, cubicle or office area.

SHAPES AND SYMBOLS

Within the most corporate of interiors there exists the ancient feng shui theme of shapes and symbolism. As with mountain formations, river courses and the layout and forms of traditional Chinese homes, palaces and pagodas, the shapes of a floor plan, the individual offices and the furniture within them can help to determine the future of an enterprise. Whole, balanced shapes such as squares and rectangles are best.

A conference room in a New York advertising agency happened to be hexagonal, in a shape resembling a coffin, and nearly all the agency's advertising pitches died there. Knife-like shapes are unfortunate because they are missing a gua—see the Feng Shui Tools chapter.

The best shapes for desks are rectangles, U shapes, fan shapes or a rectangle with sides that curve slightly toward the occupant. The best ones for conference tables are round, oval or U shapes. In the Dentsu advertising agency conference area in Tokyo, Clodagh was designing a conference table. She was hoping to have a slab of wood sitting on steel supports that ran in a wave-like pattern lengthways along the table, protruding into the wood. On the suggestion of a feng shui expert, who said the steel line would be divisive for meetings, she deleted the line and the shape became oval.

Color can improve chances of success and increase mental and physical

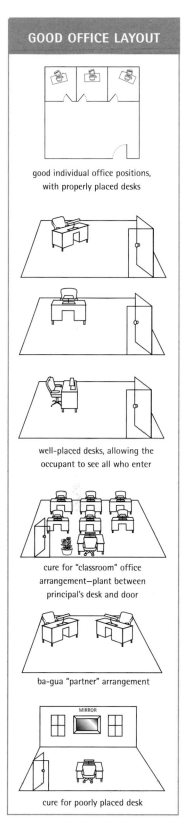

GOOD OFFICE LAYOUT

good individual office positions, with properly placed desks

well-placed desks, allowing the occupant to see all who enter

cure for "classroom" office arrangement—plant between principal's desk and door

ba-gua "partner" arrangement

cure for poorly placed desk

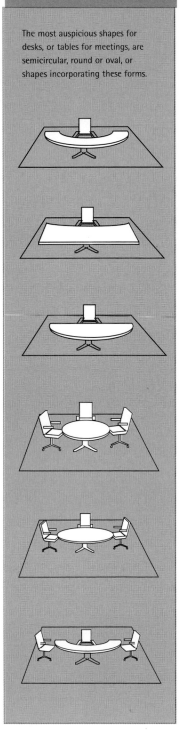

GOOD DESK SHAPES

The most auspicious shapes for desks, or tables for meetings, are semicircular, round or oval, or shapes incorporating these forms.

activity. While the choice of color and tone is highly personal, bear in mind that as green stands for growth, development and career potential it is good for new business. Black stands for water, which traditionally symbolizes money. Red means happiness. The color scheme should reflect the activities of the business. For instance, an advertising agency should combine "serious" and "light" colors, echoing the many functions of those who work there, and a public relations company should have "serious" colors in areas such as the reception and the conference room, where client meetings take place, rather than unusual ones which could clash with the mood of the encounter.

The chart opposite offers particularly advantageous colors for various types of business. For instance, a bank was decorated in autumnal yellow and brown. This created a heavy, dull feeling and both staff and customers tended to be confrontational and irrational. After painting one wall green, business, and staff and client relations, improved.

Beyond its structure and furniture layout, the accoutrements of an office are not only symbols that affect the occupant's life and performance. They also give visitors clues to the occupant's personality and talents. What is on a desk and walls may indicate more to others than is verbally told to them. While every type of business relies on a variety of attributes—financial prowess, "people" skills, creativity, intelligence, humanitarianism, humor—certain feng shui rules can be followed to magnify assets. Mementos of past successes —such as photographs, awards or inspirational books—can subtly spur

additional coups. Professional awards, for example, remind occupants of their achievements as well as enhancing their image to clients and higher-ups. Ideally, a display should be limited to one spot. To be discreet, use the career area, or to be more obvious, the fame area.

Plants and aquariums, two of the Nine Basic Cures (see page 40), are calming and aesthetically pleasing reminders of nature's perfection and peace. They can enhance any area of the ba-gua as well as curing structural problems. As they symbolize respectively growth and wealth, they should be fastidiously maintained and placed in areas of an office where they will thrive, such as those that are naturally lit. Sickly plants and murky aquariums not only forebode withering prospects for the occupant, but also indicate to others that the occupant may be careless and not oversee projects properly. Fish, moreover, often require great care: in Hong Kong, a successful major merchant bank had a large exotic-fish tank whose rare and expensive residents went belly up when its filtration system overloaded one weekend. Wary that employees might take their demise as an ominous symbol, the manager secretly acquired new look-alike specimens to restock the tank before Monday morning. Some bankers and lawyers in Asia opt for fake plants and metal fish rather than struggle with the upkeep of the real thing.

One interior designer found that three commissions materialized after she installed an electrically powered fountain in the wealth corner of her office. "However," she commented, "while my luck has improved, the sound

FENG SHUI COLORS FOR BUSINESS INTERIORS

Academic's office	Dark tones, green, blue, maroon, brown
Accountancy firm	White, yellow
Advertising agency	Mix "serious" colors (e.g., dark green, coffee) with light colors
Agent (e.g., literary, dramatic)	Dark green, red, white, black, gray
Appliance/hardware store	White, multicolored
Architect or designer	Blue, green, all Five Element colors
Art gallery	Pink, red, white, light yellow
Artist's studio	All-white, all-black, multicolored
Bakery	All-white, multicolored
Banks and investment firms	Blue, green, white, yellow/beige
Bar	Green, white, black/gray; avoid red
Beauty salon	Black and white, multicolored
Bookshop	Blue, light green, yellow, pastel shades; if academic, dark colors—green, blue, maroon, brown
Car park	Light blue, light green, white, light yellow, bright colors
Computer company	Blue, green
Computer store	Light green, red, multicolored
Construction firm	Green, white, black/gray
Doctor	Blue, green, pink, white, purple
Estate agent	Light green, white, beige/yellow
Executive office in creative fields	Sky blue, green, red, multicolored
Film, television or recording studio	Blue, light green, pink, white, black/gray
Funeral parlor	Light blue, red, all-white
Furniture shop	Blue, green, red accents
Gourmet shop/delicatessen	Bright colors, pastel green, sky blue
Jeweller	Blue, red, white; avoid yellow
Lawyer	Blue, green, white, black/gray, yellow, beige
Library	Blue, green, red, white, black/gray
Lighting shop	Light blue, light green, pink, white
Men's clothing shop	One or two colors in a simple or monochromatic color scheme, e.g., black and white or red and green
Music shop	All-blue, all-green, all-red, all-white, all-black
Pharmacy	Light blue, pink
Police station	White, all Five Element colors, multicolored
Psychic's salon	All-white, all-black, multicolored
Psychologist	White, all Five Element colors, multicolored
Publisher	Blue, green, purple
Restaurant	Blue, green, multicolored; avoid red for seafood restaurant
Shoe shop	Red, white, gray, brown; avoid black with white
Software company	White, black/gray, beige/yellow
Stationery shop	Light blue, light green, pink, white
Supermarket	White, gray, light yellow, mutlicolored
Toy shop	Light green, pink, white, light yellow, multicolored
Trading company	Green
Video shop	Light blue, light green, light pink, all-white, light yellow
Wine shop	Light blue, light green, pink
Women's clothing shop	Blue, green, bright colors

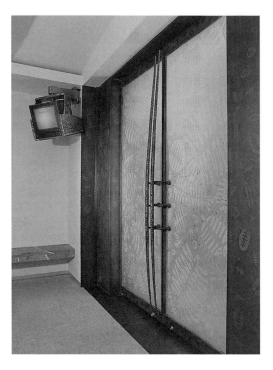

Back-lit etched glass doors to Dentsu's presentation center in Tokyo, right, serve to draw employees and clients into the space, their motif reflecting an image drawn from nature.
For Dentsu's conference room, opposite, Clodagh modified her table design, removing the steel line a feng shui expert advised her would be divisive, and softening the corners to create a positive oval shape.

of the flowing water increases my need to go to the bathroom during the day. But I'm afraid to unplug it!"

Photographs, drawings and paintings are good for any office, especially windowless ones, as they afford an extra view and inspiration for the occupant. Make sure that their content is positive as well as arty, for they speak visually to both occupant and visitor. Another message-giver is the computer screen-saver. It allows visitors to peek into the occupant's mind. Choose a message with some originality and wit to entertain and attract attention.

For computers, fax machines and other office machinery, the best places are the family, wealth or fame areas. The helpful people, knowledge and career areas are also acceptable, but avoid siting this equipment in the marriage and children areas. If the computer faces away from the door, place a small mirror (or mirrored frame) on top of the monitor, to reflect anyone behind the worker.

LIGHTING

Lighting in an office where computers are used on a daily basis should be bright, but not so bright as to cause reflections on screens. While it should be soothing, too dim a light will induce a somber feeling. In an office where a lot of people work, it is better to err on the side of being bright. In individual offices the lighting should mainly be soft, with good light sources available for brighter visibility when this is needed.

EXITS

What you see when you leave your office is as important as the entrance. Since you leave it numerous times in a day, the exit has a frequent impact upon you, physically and mentally. In feng shui terms, if you exit onto a corridor hall you will experience very slow progress. Your career will be ignored or hardly noticed by others. Always keep the door of your office closed and hang a ba-gua mirror—or a wok mounted so that the shiny inside faces outwards to act as a shield—behind where you sit at your desk. If you leave and immediately face a corridor wall, this will inhibit career development. To open new prospects, hang a landscape picture or a mirror on the wall to draw you out and to create a sense of depth. If you enter or exit and see another door to an office, hang something—a wind chime, a crystal, a mobile or a light—in the space or hallway between the facing doors, to disperse the ch'i flow. And if you see part wall and part doorway, or a corridor or a column, when you leave your office, hang a mirror or picture on the near surface to create a more harmonious and healthful exit.

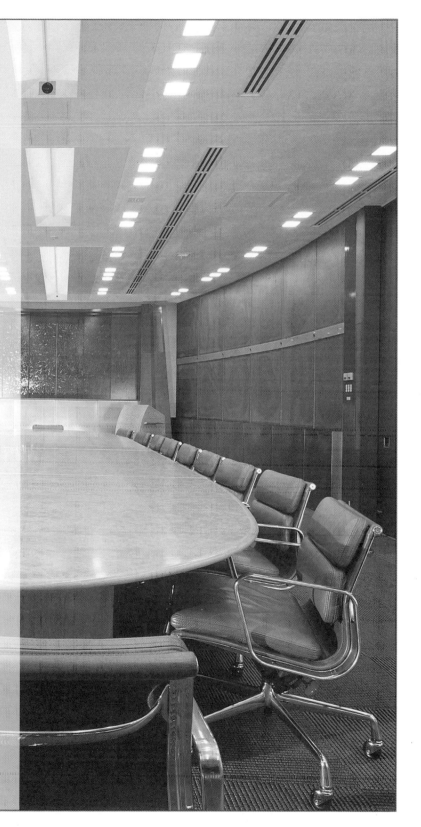

SEVEN FENG SHUI POINTS FOR CHIEF EXECUTIVE OFFICERS

1 To maintain mental clarity, be sure that the route from your car to the office is pleasant and free of obstacles and sharp angles. Avoid large columns, which can be oppressive. The route should be as smooth as possible, but not necessarily a straight line.

2 When you open the door to your office, you should get a pleasant feeling from the quality of light and the colors of walls, carpets and furniture as well as the arrangement of furniture.

3 Pick the colors of your office according to your own taste. Bear in mind that light colors can invigorate you while darker tones can make you feel oppressed. Too much dark wood may create a heavy, ponderous feeling. Use lively colors as accents to stimulate creativity and productivity.

4 In the office, avoid sharp angles that appear to point in a threatening manner, and protruding columns that make you feel pressured. Size must be in balance. If the office is too large, a person can feel lost. The best-sized office is one that makes you feel comfortable, as if you have control over all parts of the room.

5 If you are suffering from low ch'i, a crystal to refract light, hung from the ceiling in front of the desk, will stimulate the brain and energy. Mobiles and wind chimes are energizing. And green plants and aquariums bring life force into the room, thus improving your ch'i and financial prospects. Avoid taxidermy, which symbolizes death.

6 Mirrors will calm your mind and create a relaxed atmosphere—this is important when you are feeling stressed.

7 Mirrors also promote material success. If you have a view of water outside your office, hang a mirror to reflect that view.

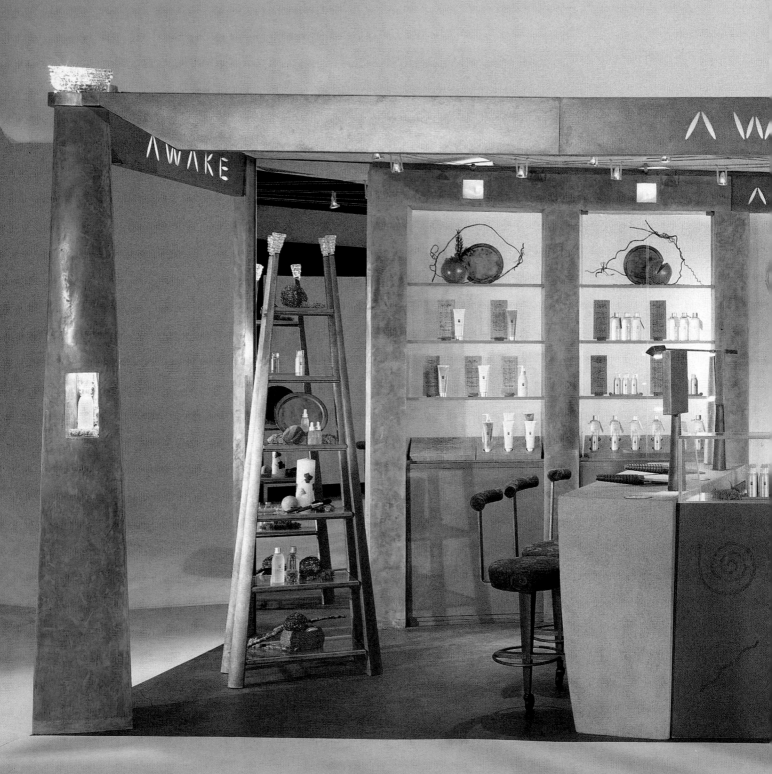

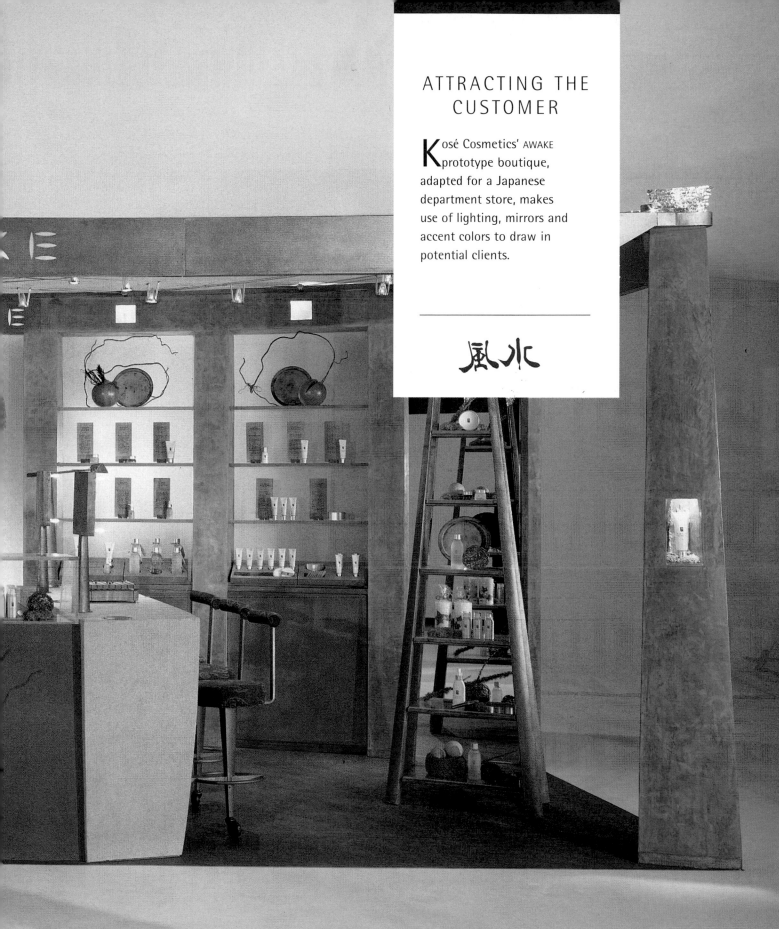

ATTRACTING THE CUSTOMER

Kosé Cosmetics' AWAKE prototype boutique, adapted for a Japanese department store, makes use of lighting, mirrors and accent colors to draw in potential clients.

風水

FENG SHUI FOR RETAIL ENVIRONMENTS

In the United States and Britain, more and more stores, shops and restaurants are employing feng shui to improve business and to create a positive environment for shoppers and sales force alike. In New York, stores ranging from ABC Carpet & Home to Jamson Whyte for housewares and furnishings, and from Tahari and Dana Buchman for fashion to Elizabeth Arden and the environmentally conscious department store Felissimo, have applied feng shui to their spaces with felicitous results. In Tokyo, as well as at their Henri Bendel boutique in New York, Kosé Cosmetics' AWAKE department store display was designed with feng shui to help merchandise products. In London, not only has the venerable department store Marks & Spencer used feng shui, but couture shoe designer Jimmy Choo flew a consultant in from Malaysia to bless his new shop, and the salon of the holistic hair stylist Paul Edmonds incorporates feng shui in its styling and layout.

Jamson Whyte is a home furnishing store in New York's SoHo and Miami's South Beach, imported from Singapore. While the venue and design are Western, the furnishings, goods for sale and ambience draw on its Eastern roots. To create real-life vignettes, the New York store includes a drawing room, dining room, library, conservatory, master bedroom and guest bedroom. There is even a stocked bar in the corner, where customers are welcome to mix themselves a drink. Within these rooms, the furniture is placed according to feng shui, and the decor reflects a palette of earth tones, ranging from golden bamboo to faded cinnabar, to green bamboo, thus helping to preserve a sense of balance of the natural elements. Further, there are no sharp edges; rather, there are smooth organic lines to encourage positive forces of ch'i. Smell and sound are used in addition to sight to heighten the experience, wafting the fragrances of clove, cinnamon and sandalwood. Music drawing on Indonesian and Indian traditions can be heard, as well as sounds of nature.

Feng shui also showed up in the display mounted by Trevira, the fabric and yarn company, at a Brussels trade fair (see pages 22–23). When asked to design a pavilion to market Trevira's product and the use of fabric in design, Clodagh opted to create an "oasis." She comments: "I've been to trade fairs and I've seen people's misery—sore feet and harassed faces—and I wanted to create a moment in time where one could stop and experience an interactive healing space. And it worked. People walking around would go in and sink on the pillows and listen to the water and the soundtrack of sounds ranging from Tibetan and Indonesian music to traffic noise. Feng shui touched all aspects, from the choice of color to the use of up-and-down lights to the movement and sound." There was wind, water, light, metal—water flowed over shimmering metal into a pool. Fabric, back-lit by a lamp that suggested moving, dappled leaf patterns, slowly billowed to a false summer breeze. The kinetic, non-static aspects were balanced by uplit receding columns embossed with Clodagh's emblem, much as hieroglyphs adorn Egyptian temples. The result aroused so much interest for Trevira and was so successful that Clodagh has been asked to reproduce it.

Lighting on top of the display systems at Felissimo helps to draw customers' attention up above eye level, to a wider array of goods.

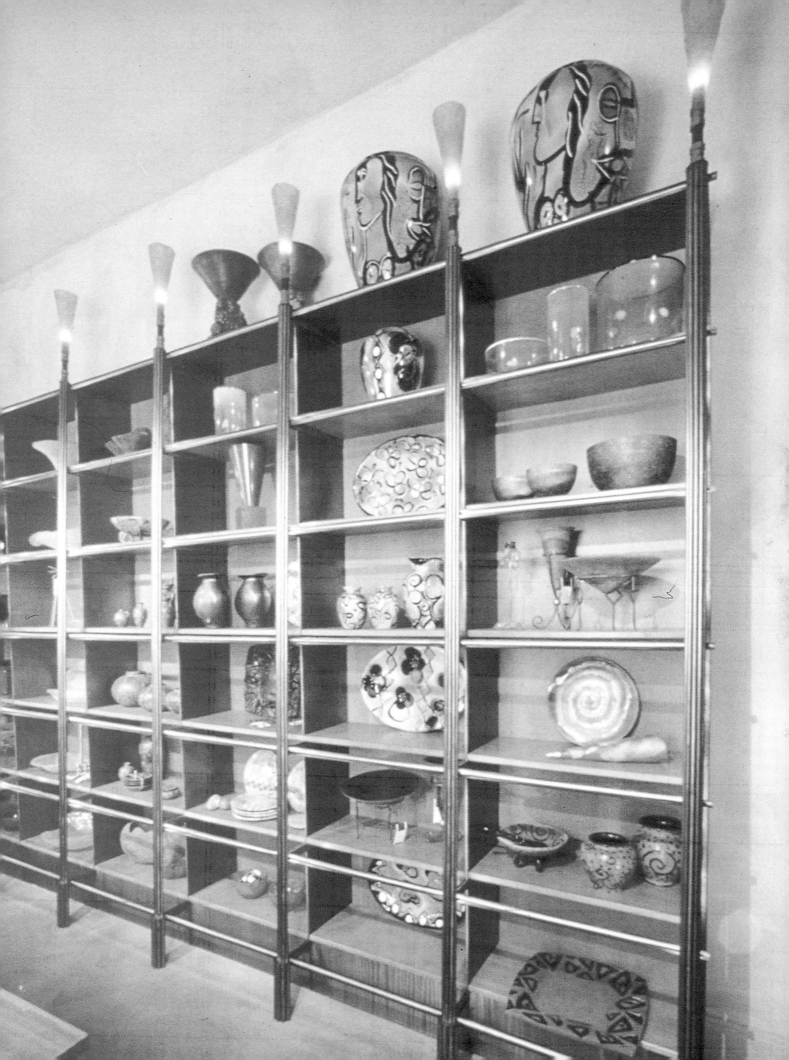

SHOPS AND STORES

It is important in retail stores to appeal to all the senses. Therefore, colors, sound and smells are essential, as they can stimulate business and help create harmony for employees. When customers enter and hear delightful sounds, or smell fragrant flowers, or when colors are cheery, this creates an atmosphere more conducive to spending. For example, colors drawn from nature—green, for example—and others with a sense of vibrancy and life force can affect customers. When they enter a shop, these will greet their eyes, and what they see will send messages to their brains, which will affect their impression of the store positively. A further by-product of a pleasant environment is that employees will also be in a good mood and provide better service, always an attraction for customers.

A person enters a shop or department store led by their ch'i and the hope of finding what they are looking for. Lighting in stores should therefore be as bright as possible, although not over-stimulating, as this can make customers uncomfortable and prompt them to leave again.

Window displays are another obvious lure to prospective customers. Placing "active" decorations in a shop window will attract the attention of passers-by. The classic rotating red-and-white barber's pole is one example, and shops that sell watches often display large, see-through, working models of their timepieces. Water-resistant watches are often in aerated tanks to stimulate interest and ch'i. Angled mirrors near a store's entrance will also attract passers-by. Although they may initially stop to admire their own reflections, their eyes and interest will eventually be caught by the merchandise, and this will lead them in to examine the goods in further detail.

Product, atmosphere and service all conspire to whet a customer's purchasing appetite. Quality and affordable bargains, as

Mirrors and lighting can draw shoppers' eyes to the rear of a shop, as shown here at Felissimo. They bring attention to the goods on display there, and help to make that area a destination.

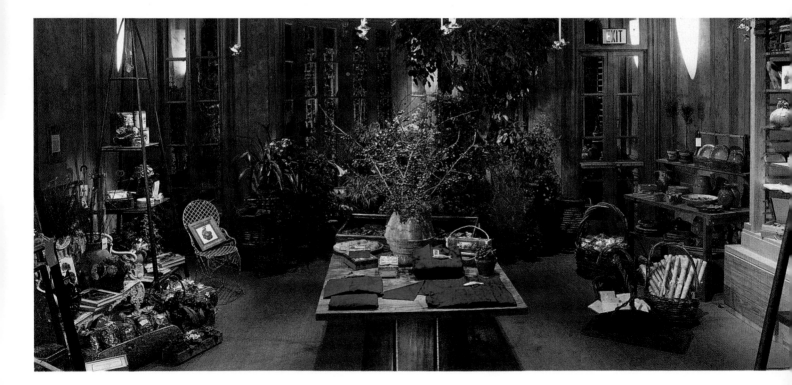

well as unique and original products which are well showcased with props such as fresh and fragrant flowers, will enhance a customer's desire to buy.

The purchasing atmosphere can be further encouraged by energetic or soothing music, or an amiable and helpful sales force.

Naturally, the placement of merchandise and cash registers is important in any retail space. As a rule, the best position for the cash register or money-collecting area(s) is in the wealth area or the helpful people position—the back left or the front right of the store when looking in from the entrance—or in the rear of the store for a commanding view of shoppers. If the store is deep and long, however, the register should not be in the back area, as this will be too far away from the front. The register should be a bright, lively color that has life force—green, red or a golden wheat tone of beige or tan.

Felissimo

While each space has its own feng shui challenges, Felissimo provides an interesting example of its uses in a retail space. (Of course, with any store the quality of the merchandise has to be good and available at moderate and reasonable prices, as well as being durable, of the latest design and worth its value.) Generally, classically designed stores are better than ultra-modern ones, as their design tends to attract a wider range of customers, and ones with more discerning tastes. At Felissimo a feng shui expert was brought in before the abandoned 1901 town house was renovated. While pigeons roosted on interior windowsills, the consultant advised on everything from methods of attracting street traffic and conducting shoppers through the store, to ways of creating effective displays and the placement of cash registers and individual objects for sale. While many of the store's

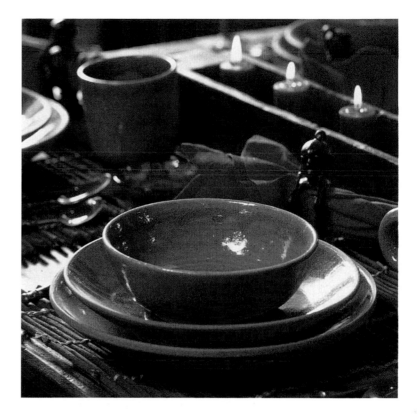

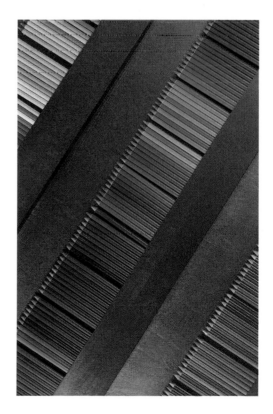

This table setting is one of the many display vignettes at Jamson Whyte that employ color and layout to encourage customers to buy—in this case, dining furniture and tableware.

Colors juxtaposed or arranged to create an auspicious rainbow spectrum help items to appeal to a broad range of clients. These pencils are on display at Felissimo.

classical features—gracefully curving stairwells, crown molding, Beaux Arts facade—were retained, the store is today a subtle study in the effects of feng shui as lights, mirrors, fountains, plants, organic colors, graceful curves and natural design motifs all conspire to create an inviting, comfortable yet stimulating space to showcase and sell merchandise. Much like the garden courts in ancient Chinese cities (see page 76), Felissimo provides a stylish and stylized contrast to New York's hard surfaces and lines with references to faraway nature. For example, ultra-modern but complementary fountains provide a soothing auditory and visual break from the urban landscape as well as the task of shopping. Moreover, the presence of water hopefully will keep business and profits flowing. In addition, furniture is placed according to feng shui rules for homes in order to create a sense of comfort, and help shoppers envisage how the items displayed might best fit into their own houses.

Noelle Spa aims to beautify both mind and body, offering a wide range of treatments. In one of its hydrotherapy rooms, where water is a calming yet stimulating focus, a natural and neutral palette of natural tones and finishes is given a starry sparkle with crystal-like lights even though there are no natural light sources in this room. A mirror heightens this, and also reassuringly enables the bather to see anyone entering.

OTHER BUSINESSES
Noelle Spa

Feng shui can enhance any retail space ranging from a store to a service-oriented business. Noelle Spa for Beauty and Wellness, which offers beauty treatments for both mind and body, uses feng shui to generate a sense of well-being. While working with a pre-existing space, the designer followed feng shui advice to cure some structural problems and to enhance the overall environment. Besides the soothing fountains and ch'i-dispersing crystals and mirrors that are strategically placed around the spa to redirect energy, plants and small gardens crop up to emphasize the relationship between beauty, happiness and the restorative and calming properties of nature. To correct unavoidable internal and windowless treatment rooms, the designer hung lights, mirrors and photographs in the rooms and added crystals to invigorate their ch'i. Interest was added to the stark ceilings of long narrow hallways by light, billowing, back-lit tenting. And accent colors were added to the bare palette of warm earth tones employed throughout the space, to create visual interest and to help the salon appeal to a variety of client tastes.

Health centers

Health care facilities and healing centers should be designed to put patients at ease. Soothing music will also affect them favorably, as the body heals faster when the mind is calm. Visually, the facility should be accented with either the Five Element colors (white, blue or green, black, red, and yellow or brown) or a whole spectrum of colors. In specific situations, specific colors can reinforce the healing process.

For example, in a heart specialist's office or heart unit, red can aid patients with "weak" hearts. It is associated with the heart and fire.

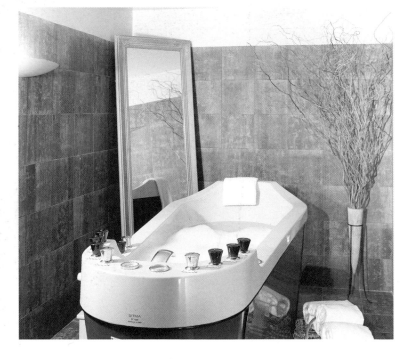

However, if the heart is too "strong" (and this can also apply to stroke patients), black or yellow should be used. Black, the color of the water element, puts out fire; yellow, associated with earth which is produced by fire, symbolizes the dispersal of excess fire ch'i, and will enable the patient to move on in life.

Black can aid patients with weak kidneys; these organs are associated with the water element, and its color will strengthen them. An over-active kidney can be remedied by earth, which moderates water, or the element water creates, wood—in other words yellow, or blue or green. White, the color of metal (which creates water), can also strengthen weak kidneys.

Restaurants

Whether feng shui was ever used in imperial banquet halls, teahouses or floating restaurants where sing-song girls entertained between courses is unclear. What is clear today is that feng shui is used in many restaurants, particularly Chinese ones. For example, San Francisco's Flower Lounge and Hong Fu restaurants both requested feng shui help when business was slow. Both noted marked results after installing fountains near their entrances. A fish tank could be used in this position. Another restaurant has a black marble waterfall in this area, which serves as a spirit screen. For the Hong Fu, the feng shui expert also provided his own blessing in the form of calligraphy inscribed in red cinnabar ink so the walls are festooned with his mantra, benefiting host and guest. In New York, a Japanese restaurant, Four Winds, employed a feng shui expert while design work was being completed, with very positive results. Further, many restaurants employ feng shui symbolism to reinforce good ch'i.

The location of the chef's station is an important consideration in any restaurant. The

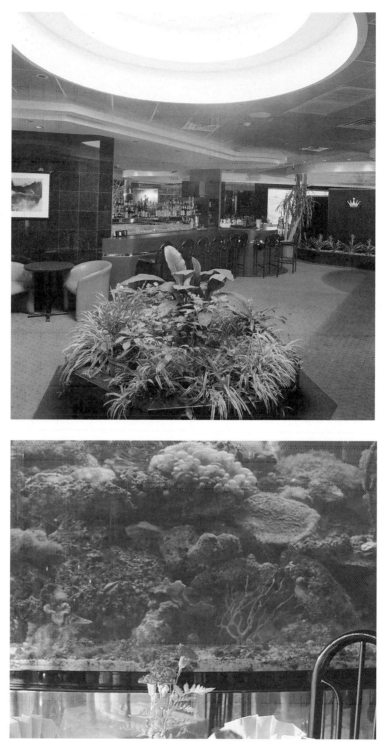

Feng shui tools in a Chinese restaurant: one is greeted with a ba-gua-shaped planter, lit by a three-tiered skylight; the bar is mirrored to bring in business; there is a spirit screen with a wealth-inducing waterfall; all topped off by a large, circular, well-lit aquarium.

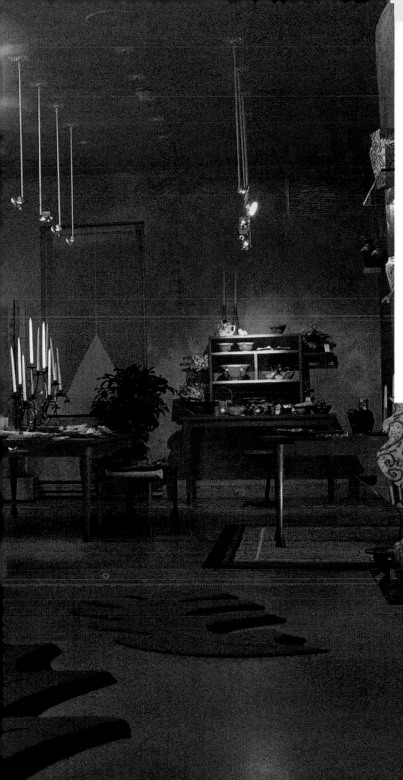

ECHOES OF NATURE

In contrast to the hard, cold surfaces of New York City, structural curves in walls and stairwells of this department store, with plants and leaf motifs in rugs and on the walls, evoke a sense of hope and development as well as symbolizing natural life force. Flowers and plants also balance internal energy, improving weak ch'i flow and dispersing fast ch'i.

風水

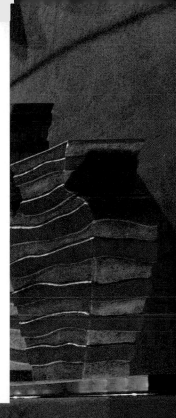

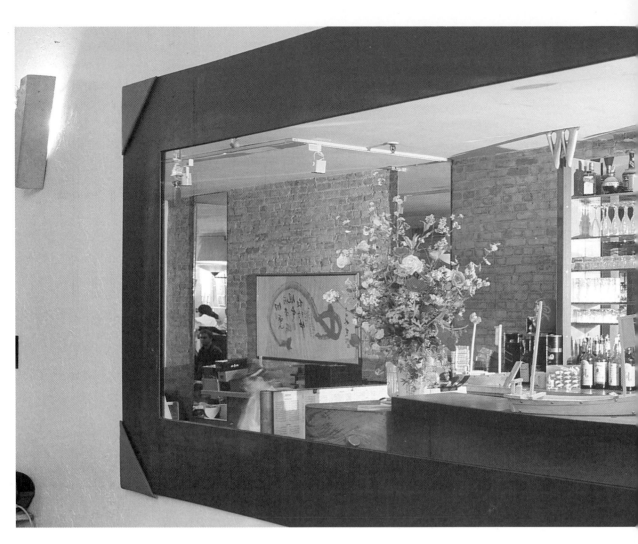

To draw in more business, bars should be mirrored, as shown here at Four Winds Japanese restaurant, where another mirror facing the bar both reflects it again and offers the bartender a view of the full length of the restaurant. Mirrors should be placed behind cash registers, in order to symbolically double takings.

worst position for a stove is in the wealth area, as the intensity of its fire will symbolically burn wealth up; or the center area, as this increases the risk of fire. The career position is also bad, as this is associated with water, which does not coexist well with fire. The best place is the fame area—fire is associated with this, so the chef will be working up more and more wealth. Also, this position will generate good publicity for the restaurant food.

As at home (see pages 173–176), the chef should not cook with his or her back to the door, or any place where he or she cannot be aware of who is entering. If the chef is surprised, this will set off a nervous chain reaction affecting everything from the food to the waiters' and, ultimately, the customers' satisfaction. A mirror or reflective aluminum panel behind the stove will allow the chef to be aware of all who enter. A restaurant in New York hung a wind chime behind the chef's station to wake up her culinary subconscious and draw publicity to the food. A light above it would also put the restaurant in the spotlight and improve its dishes and income. In a restaurant where the kitchen is in the central area, making for a fire hazard, mirrors should be placed on all four walls.

Lighting depends on the nature of the business. For example, a fast-food outlet or one

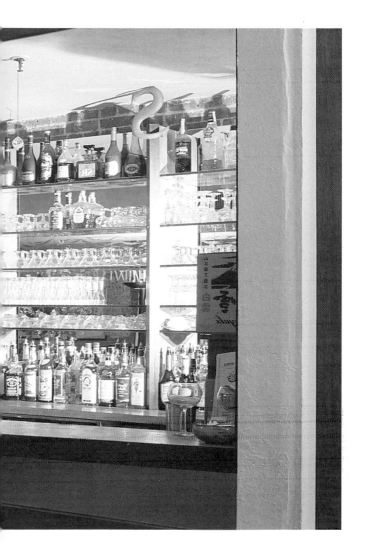

create a new and energizing dynamic.

As in a store or shop, the cash register's position is very important. If properly placed, it attracts money. Ideally, the money-taker should face the door. The register should generally be in full view so as to absorb the guests' money, but if the restaurant is in a more dangerous area it should be obscured for safety and to protect business and profits. For added security, a bamboo flute can be hung behind the register to serve as a symbolic sword, protecting profits and patrons, and as a conduit of ch'i, making business better and better.

A mirror behind a money-making area such as the cash register or bar (frequently the most lucrative area of a restaurant's activities), will symbolically double profits. Of course, the cashier or barman will also be able to see anyone approaching from behind, making for greater till security, and better customer service.

Tables should be graciously spaced and far enough apart to allow customers and waiters to move freely and protect privacy, without creating a sense of isolation. Avoid columns that obstruct ch'i. Mirror these from the shoulder of a seated diner to at least seven feet so that the diner's face is not cut off when seated, or a major part of the diner's body is not cut off when standing.

serving late-night snacks should be brightly lit for quick turnover. In a more upmarket restaurant, where people go to celebrate special occasions or merely to enjoy the scene and ambience, the lighting should be mellow. A soft glow will provide an aesthetically pleasing and gentle atmosphere. This can be achieved with dimmed lights, or appropriately secured candles. To create a fun spot for a young clientele—to discuss work or meet friends, perhaps near a school or university— the lighting should be varied. Some areas should be bright and others more subdued, to make it a destination for all. One area should perhaps have a revolving lighting system to

In Felissimo's tea room, the sight and sound of water trickling down a fountain contrasts with the harsh buzz of city life. The fountain helps to create a calm atmosphere, attracting shoppers to rest weary feet and take a quick bite. Graceful, curved walls and espaliered and fruit-bearing plants add to a pleasant and comforting experience.

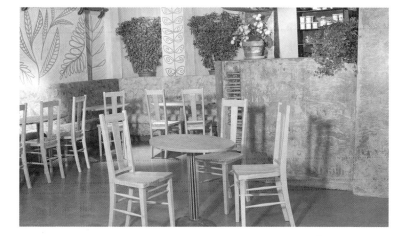

CHAPTER VIII

Feng Shui at Home

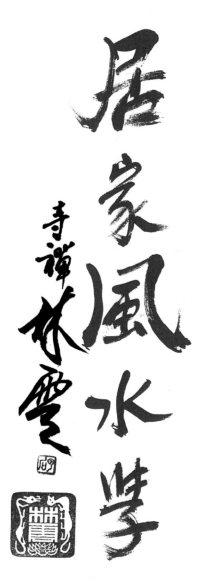

Feng shui at home

A home is not just a shelter or an empty shell of plaster, wood or brick into which we move our furniture, appliances, personal belongings and selves. It is a major influence on our minds, bodies, feelings, habits and lives. It provides many things: protection and shelter, nourishment of mind and body, inspiration, security, comfort, regeneration, entertainment. As a result, our home affects our ch'i.

In analyzing a home, a feng shui expert works as a "house doctor," examining the interior as if it were a human body with its own metabolism, taking the pulse of the place, seeing if the circulation of ch'i is healthy and balanced—not too fast and not too slow. Aware of all aspects of the home, he will be able to see and intuit the germs of problems that only an eye trained in feng shui can recognize.

To arrange living quarters, the expert will seek to harmonize the environment by channeling the currents of ch'i. And so, he considers room placement, house structure, hall length and width, door alignment, shapes and sizes of rooms, colors, the placing of beds, desks and stoves. Certain homes feel comfortable when we enter them, while others give us a sense of dread or oppression. The relative size of a house or apartment is also a consideration. It should be appropriate for the size of the household. A large family living in cramped quarters will find their own ch'i and prospects cramped, while a single person living in spacious quarters will feel a need for companionship—the company of roommates, cats, dogs or birds. This chapter will explain why, and offer ways to improve, resolve and enhance a home and therefore its residents' fortunes.

There are many considerations in approaching a home and a person's life. There may not be one possible cause for a problem. For example, if a couple is having marital difficulties, the expert will examine a number of imbalances in the structure and layout of a house or apartment that might affect family harmony. He or she will inspect the placement of the couple's bedroom within the home, making sure that it is not located outside the "entrance door line." Within the bedroom, the expert will see whether the couple's bed is in fact two twin-sized beds placed together, which is divisive, or a solid king-sized one—

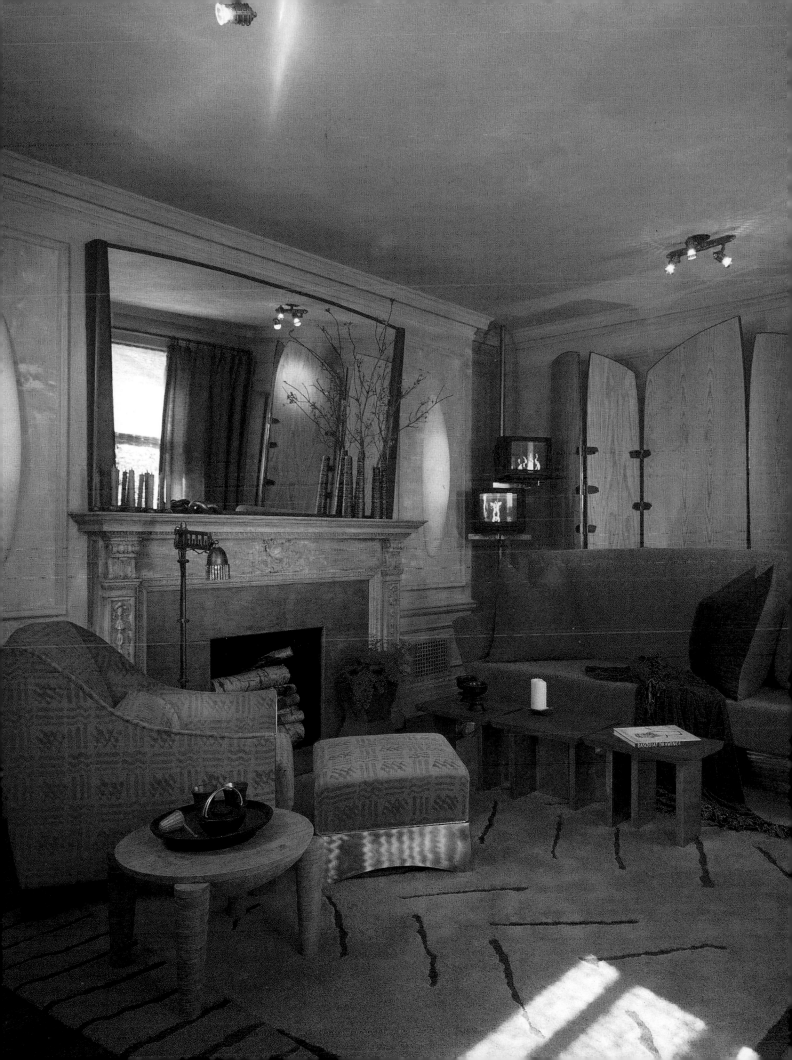

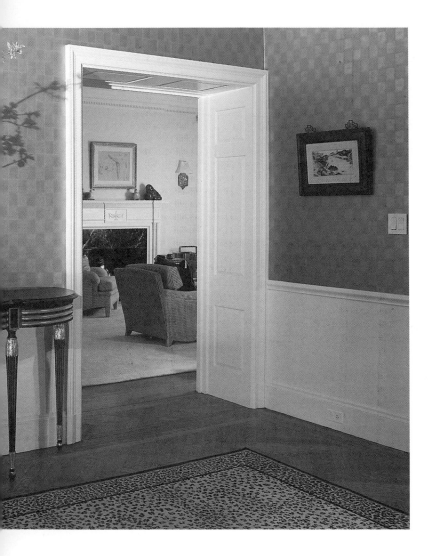

After entering the foyer or hallway, both resident and visitor will be affected by the first room they see beyond. The sight of this living room will encourage the occupant to relax when returning home.

a daily basis, what unbalances ch'i and what enhances it; what, within the structure, layout and symbolism of a home, is determining the habits, behavior and moods that affect its residents' lives.

THE ENTRANCE

The entrance is the threshold of your home experience. As you pass over it, there should be a sense of wholeness, harmony and welcome, and a sense of arrival. Light wall colors are best, especially blue or green, pink or white. Avoid brown, gray or black. Ideally, the door should open easily to view the widest area of a light, airy foyer, in order to elevate ch'i and mood. The view should be balanced and inviting. A dark, narrow entry, on the other hand, can choke and oppress luck and ch'i, as well as causing constrictive health problems, ranging from respiratory distress to difficult and dangerous childbirth, along body canals. Psychologically, a dark, narrow entrance can depress residents. Similarly, returning to an entrance door that opens directly onto a close wall inside a home can inhibit ch'i and, at worst, cause failure within three years. Residents will find that they are constantly coming up against a brick wall in their lives, that possibilities are thwarted, and physically and mentally they will look and feel oppressed and defeated. Life will seem a struggle. One such example is a young family whose entrance door opened into a dark area, with a wall directly in front lined with bookshelves. The husband had been out of work for three and a half years—every job prospect proved disappointing. At a feng shui consultant's suggestion, they replaced the book shelves with a large mirror. Four months later, the husband landed the job of his dreams. "Feng shui made me feel better about my surroundings and myself. It helped me get

a better, more resolved option. Is the headboard loose? If so, fix it immediately. Are there any obstructions when entering the bedroom, such as clutter behind the door or a wall that may cause an imbalance in emotions and thoughts? Are there "argumentative doors" that constantly knock against each other in the house (see page 161)?

With its many considerations, a feng shui analysis of a home starts with the beginning—the entrance, the residents' first experience and the opening of ch'i—and proceeds throughout the interior. The expert is alert to see and feel what the occupants encounter on

	ENTRANCE	DIAGNOSIS	CURE
MIRROR	Open, light foyer	Gives hope and conducts ch'i and opportunity into the home.	
MIRROR	Narrow, dark foyer	Chokes ch'i and luck. Can cause respiratory problems or endanger delivery in childbirth.	Install a bright ceiling light and hang a mirror on the wall you see as you open the door, to create a sense of greater depth.
MIRROR	The entrance to a foyer faces a wall that is too close	Depresses and inhibits ch'i. Life will seem a struggle. Residents may suffer failure within three years.	Hang a mirror on the wall to create a greater sense of depth and allow better ch'i flow.
	Front door faces back door or window	Money, opportunity and ch'i enter the home, but leave too quickly to enrich residents.	Hang a wind chime, mobile, plant or crystal ball to disperse ch'i flow allowing it—and good fortune—to circulate better through the house.
MIRROR	Entry with an unbalanced view	Unbalances the mind and body, leading to quarrels and violence.	Hang a picture, mirror or something attractive on the near wall to balance the view and the residents' ch'i.
	Entry door faces staircase	Money and ch'i escape.	Hang a crystal ball or wind chime from the ceiling at a point between the bottom stair and the entrance.

over what I assume are inner barriers to achieving what I wanted."

If the entrance door is directly opposite the back door or a window, ch'i, money and opportunity may enter, but will exit too quickly to circulate. Occupants, therefore, will not be able to grasp or enjoy any opportunities that come their way. (The closer the door or window, the worse the situation. The farther apart they are, the greater the chance for ch'i to circulate.)

Another entrance to avoid is one that is unbalanced, where the door opens to both a partial, long-distance view and a shorter one created by a close wall. This configuration can unbalance the occupants' optic nerves and immediate vision, and thus their ch'i, language and movement, and ultimately affect both work and marriage. If the long-distance view is on the left, the "movement" side of the brain will develop, while the "speech" side will be stunted, causing residents to act more and think and discuss less, leading first to quarrels and later to violence. If the long-distance view is on the right side, the "speech" side of the brain will overdevelop, leading to arguments, disputes, migraine headaches and perhaps nervous breakdowns within three to five years. The couple's health and marriage will be adversely affected.

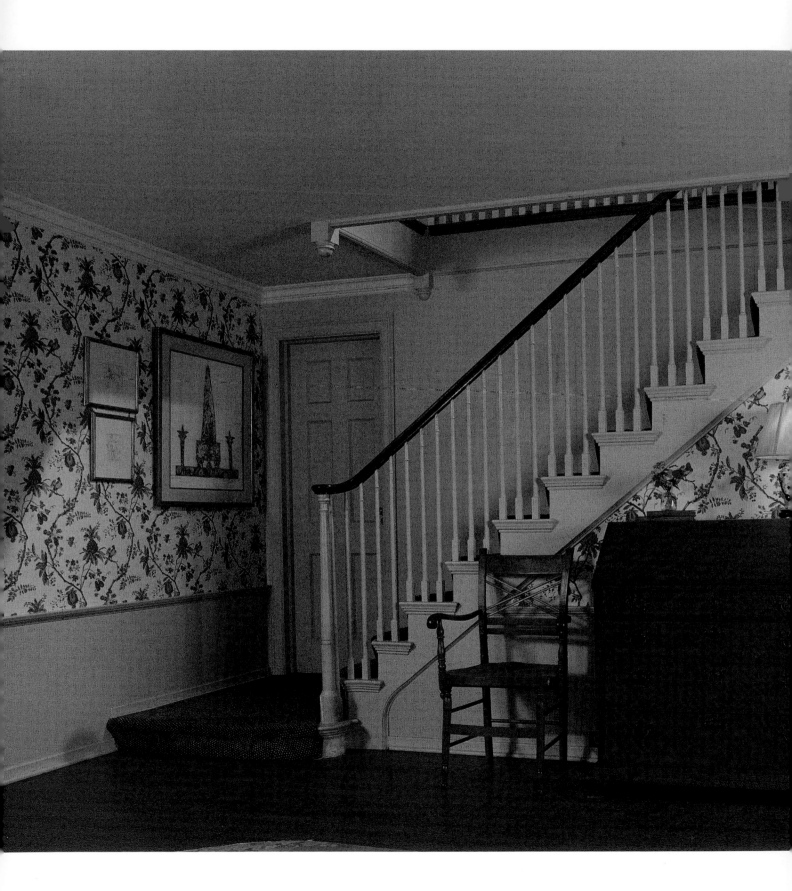

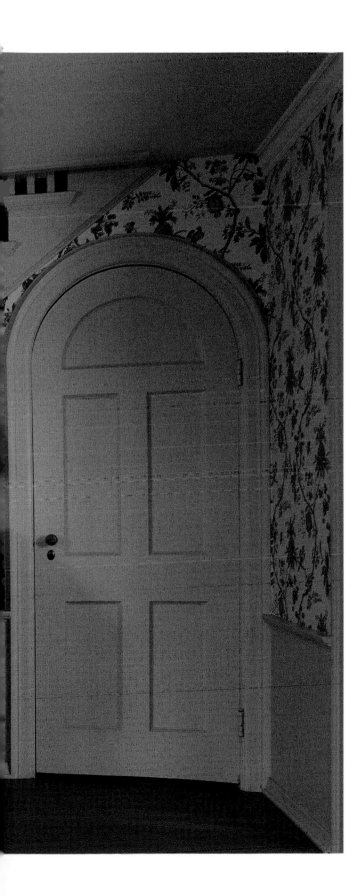

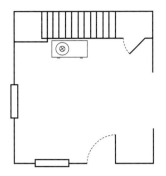

This entrance hall to a home decorated in the American colonial style is well appointed. Spacious and well lit, the stairway graciously enters the space. This spaciousness elevates ch'i and the moods of the inhabitants.

Lastly, avoid an entrance that directly faces an oncoming stairway, as money and opportunity will roll out of the front door. In Indonesia, the design by Western architects for a 2,000-unit residential development ran into problems when the front doors of all the maisonettes faced the stairway that led directly up to the master bedroom. "When the feng shui rule of entrances and stairways was mentioned," comments the principal architect, "it made sense, and helped create order. Our original layout lacked privacy and allowed the wind to blow right through. We modified it and the maisonettes immediately became marketable."

THE NEXT ROOM

Proceeding from the foyer—or entrance if a home has no foyer—the first room that is seen after entering can influence residents' ch'i, setting their mood, focus and pattern of activity. The closer it is to the entrance, the greater its influence on their behavior and lifestyle. For example, if the first room is the kitchen, the household and their guests will be food-oriented. The moment they return home, residents will gravitate towards the kitchen and refrigerator. This will result in compulsive eating habits. Children in particular will suffer, tending to be overweight and underachieving, focusing on ingesting

ROOM SEEN ON ENTERING	DIAGNOSIS	CURE
Study or library	Bookishness.	
Living room	Helps residents relax and feel at home.	
Kitchen	Residents are food-oriented, overeating compulsively; children tend to be obese.	Hang a mirror in the foyer or on the entrance side of the room's door. If there is no door, hang a wind chime or curtain in the doorway.
Bedroom	Residents feel fatigued.	As above.
Games room	Time and money are wasted on games.	As above.
Bathroom	Causes digestive and financial problems.	As above.

food rather than digesting books. And friends will visit only to eat and run. On the other hand, studies, libraries or living rooms seen from the entrance have a more positive influence. A library or study may not encourage residents to unwind, but will bring out their bookishness, so that they focus on work, studies and correspondence. The sight of a living room will help them relax and feel at home.

If the bedroom is seen from the entrance, residents will constantly experience fatigue and need to rest after returning home. A games room will encourage them to spend their time and money playing.

But the worst room to see directly after returning home is the bathroom. This situation can harm residents' health and wealth—with money being flushed away. Their activities will be focused on the bathroom: constantly primping, or relieving bladder and bowel problems. Its influence when it is seen from the entrance can be so strong that residents may constantly feel the urge to go to the bathroom even before they have entered the house.

COLOR AND LIGHTING

Color and lighting are further influences affecting a home's atmosphere and feng shui. Two of the Nine Basic Cures of feng shui (see page 40), they are powerful influences on our personalities, moods and ch'i, and can depress, stimulate or relax as well as helping us to adjust our moods. Home colors and lighting should be restful and relaxing, to help residents shift from work stresses and outside stimuli to a more calm and nurturing environment.

While color selection and preference are highly personal, color can be employed in a number of ways. One, as described in the Feng Shui Tools chapter, is to enhance a desired area of residents' lives by adding a specific color to an area of a home or a room. Black, for example, in the career area of a room, will improve professional prospects. A general rule is to choose the colors that please you aesthetically, making you feel comfortable and happy. However, a knowledgeable use of color can help to create a desired response.

By understanding that certain colors are particularly effective, experts can employ them on walls, furniture and upholstery to adjust the outlook, fortunes and ch'i of a family and home. They know that, with a range of appropriate colors, every room, with its assigned uses, can be enhanced to improve residents' lives. For more specific information, see the Movable Parts section of this chapter (page 169) and the ba-gua (page 44).

The use and moderation of light, be it natural or artificial, is important in feng shui. For example, a west-facing window may produce too much stress—and headaches—by allowing strong and oppressive sunlight to glare into a room. On the other hand, the gentle and warming light of an eastern-facing bedroom window will awaken its occupants pleasantly. Poorly lit halls and rooms can be depressing and cause eyestrain. Soothing, moderated light is relaxing and comfortable and in tune with a home's function as a refuge for its occupants.

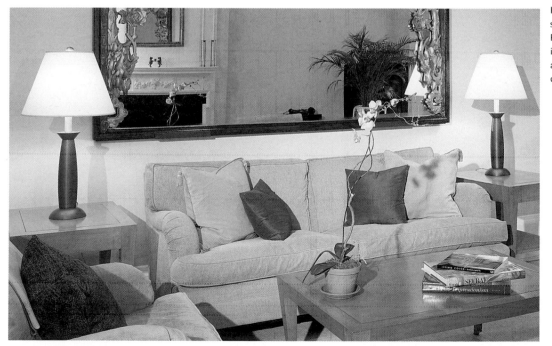

In a living room, the best seat is facing the door. Pillows and scatter cushions in different hues serve as accents to enliven conversation and ch'i.

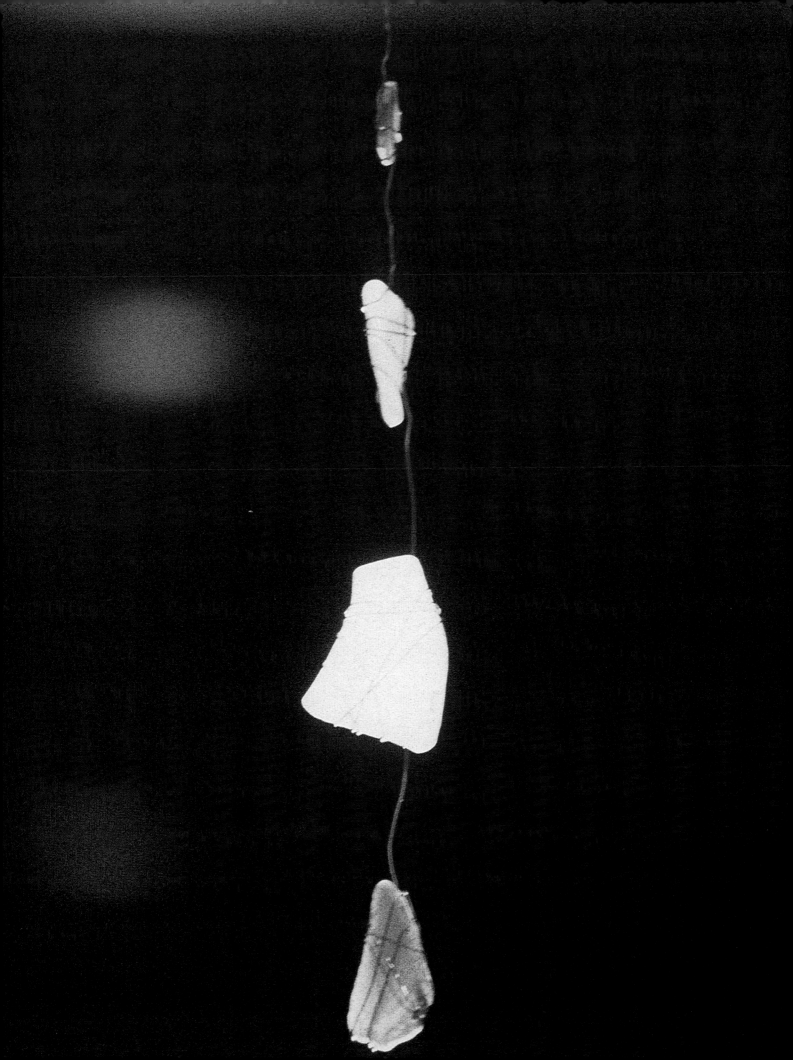

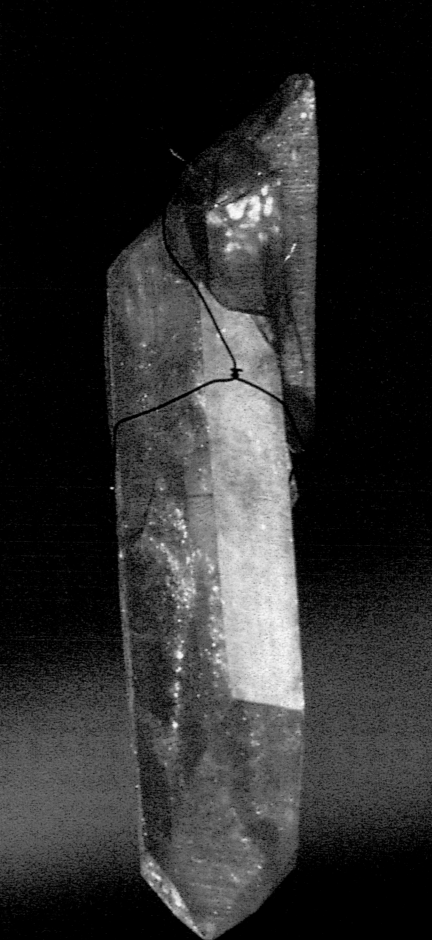

CRYSTALS

As bright objects, crystals are one of the Nine Basic Cures of feng shui. Whether in the form of a prismatic crystal ball, cut-glass chandelier pendant, natural quartz or another stone or mineral (right), or even sea glass (left), they diffuse excess or negative ch'i, which bounces off their many facets. They also refract oppressive light, and can create positive rainbow spectrums.

風水

STRUCTURAL ELEMENTS OF A HOME

HALLWAYS AND CORRIDORS

Hallways and corridors conduct ch'i and residents from room to room. By being aware of the way they funnel ch'i, you can adjust the flow and harmony within a home. One example is a slightly lovelorn, footloose bank executive who had not found the right woman in his life. His bedroom was down a long hallway from the living room. On the suggestion of a feng shui consultant, the executive installed a series of crystal balls in the corridor—and today he is happily married.

A long, narrow corridor leading to a room inhibits residents and ch'i from entering. Besides being divisive, it funnels ch'i too quickly and can cause internal distress along the central meridian of residents' bodies. If it is particularly narrow, it can also cause breathing problems. Clutter in hallways is a stumbling block to residents' ch'i and future.

DOORS

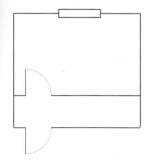

good door alignment

Whether they lead off a hallway, link one room to another or merely close off a closet, doors can affect residents in a number of ways. A general rule is that a door should open up easily to the widest area of a room. (One that opens to the smallest area will cramp residents' ch'i and luck.) It should not be obstructed or knock against other doors.

While the entrance is the most crucial door, the back door, which symbolizes indirect opportunities, is also important. It should open out onto a wide path, symbolizing greater potential for financial growth.

WINDOWS

Like doors, windows regulate ch'i flow. When a window, a door and a further window beyond are aligned, the effect is less strong than the effect of three doors in a row, but they still funnel ch'i too quickly and can be divisive in a space. Crystal balls, wind chimes, mobiles or plants hung from the ceiling (or plants on the windowsill) will help disperse ch'i.

Windows are symbolic. They represent the eyes of a home. So broken or dusty panes can augur lack of clarity in vision and thought. Make sure that all windows are clean and in good repair.

Windows also represent the voice of the children in a household and should not outnumber the doors (the parents) by a ratio of three to one, or children will argue with their parents and be rude and insubordinate. Family dynamics will also be out of whack if windows tend to be larger than doors, symbolizing the children overpowering their parents and thus being unheeding of parental guidance, discipline and love. (This rule doesn't apply if the larger windows have small panes.)

The way windows actually open can affect residents and ch'i flow. Ideally they should open completely outwards to best conduct ch'i into and through a home, thus enhancing the residents' ch'i and career prospects. The outward motion of opening them helps to develop positive, harmonious ch'i for residents. Inward opening windows are good, too, but the opening action inhibits ch'i, making residents less outgoing.

Windows that slide up or down let in only half as much ch'i as their size as they never open up more than halfway. So residents tend to give others a false impression.

The top of a window should be at least as high as the tallest resident. If it is lower it will

PROBLEMATIC DOORS	DIAGNOSIS	CURE
Door opening to the wall of a room or corridor	Inhibits ch'i. If the door is often used, residents will struggle.	Hang a mirror on the wall.
Door opening to the narrowest area of a room, or to a wall	Cramps residents' ch'i and luck, eventually creating physical problems and emotional anxiety.	1 Change the door's hinges so that it opens to view the widest area. 2 Install a mirror on the near wall, to reflect the rest of the room's space. 3 Install a bell that rings, or a light that goes on automatically, when the door is opened.
Two aligned bathroom doors	Causes sickness along the central meridian of the body, physical and financial diarrhea.	Hang a mirror on the outside of each door to stem health and money running out.
Opposite doors that seem aligned but are askew—"bad bite" doors	Unbalance residents' ch'i, mind and body, resulting in health problems and affecting effectiveness in personal and professional relationships.	Hang an ornament, mirror or picture at eye level to create greater depth and resolve the edge that is disrupting and unbalancing the view.
Unaligned doors	Inhibit residents' ch'i.	As above.
Hard to open, or stuck, doors	Life will be a struggle.	Fix the door so that it opens easily.
Door at the end of a long hallway	The hallway's fast ch'i is dangerous for residents' health, causing anxiety, intestinal problems. Limits career advancement.	Hang a mirror on the hall side of the door to deflect strong ch'i and create a vista symbolizing prospects in career development.
Unused or boarded-up door	Residents' opportunities are lessened.	Install a mirror on the would-be door to open up new possibilities and outlets.
One parallel, aligned door is larger than another	1 Good if the larger door leads to a bedroom or a living room, and the small door to a bathroom or closet. 2 Negative if the larger door opens to kitchen, bathroom or closet, and the smaller to bedroom, leading to poor priorities, wasted time.	To cure the negative door situation, hang a mirror on the larger door to reflect the bedroom so that both doors seem to lead to bedrooms.
"Argumentative" doors that knock together when they open	Cause family friction and marital conflict.	Tie a red ribbon the length of a multiple of nine inches on the knocking door knobs, then cut it in the middle.
Three or more doors or windows in a row (windows create less of a problem than doors)	Funnels ch'i too quickly; inhibits occupants' ch'i.	Hang crystal balls, wind chimes, mobiles or lights from the ceiling to disperse ch'i flow.

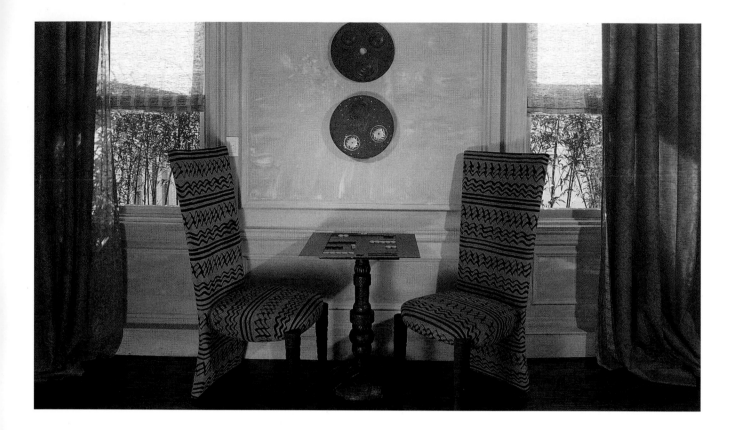

In this show house, an interior designer was presented with a room looking on to an air shaft. At the suggestion of a feng shui consultant, she installed window boxes with bamboo grasses, thus creating privacy and pleasantly shielding the drab view.

depress his or her ch'i. Windows should also be comfortably wide. If they are small and slit-like, they choke ch'i flow, narrowing occupants' prospects and perspectives.

As before, be aware of western-facing windows. In the afternoon, the hot glare of the setting sun can cause headaches and interfere with work. This can be remedied by hanging a cut-glass crystal in the window to symbolically disperse the sun's strong glare, changing it into an inspiring rainbow.

STAIRS

In a two-story or split-level home, stairs conduct ch'i from floor to floor. Ideally, a stairwell should be wide, graceful, well-lit and not constrained by a low ceiling. A confined, narrow or dark stairway can choke ch'i flow. The style of the staircase is also a concern.

While space is often at a premium, it is important to have a safe and graceful ascent and descent. Steep stairs can conduct ch'i too quickly. The stairs should have proper risers between them or ch'i will escape and not circulate adequately upstairs.

While gracefully curved stairwells are desirable, a spiral staircase can be dangerous, as it bores through a house like a sharp drill, creating holes in the home's body. A spiral staircase that is located at the center of the home is particularly lethal. Residents may suffer heart or other medical distress within a few years.

Split-level houses or apartments can also be problematic, as their residents will experience many ups and downs in business, emotions and life. Make sure the stairs are wide and well-lit to give a more stable feeling to a home.

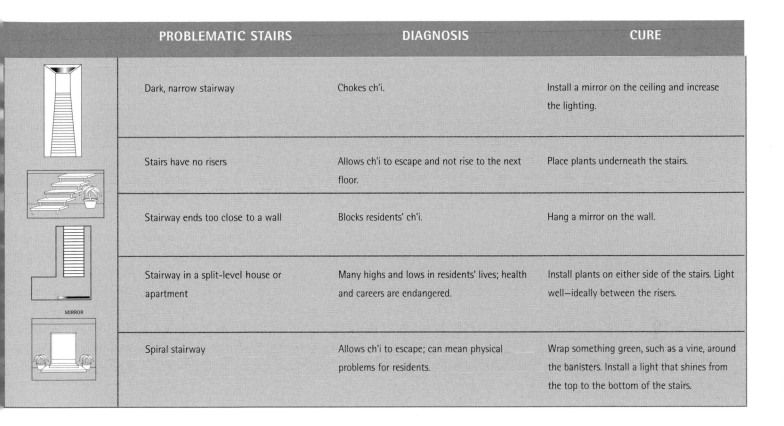

PROBLEMATIC STAIRS	DIAGNOSIS	CURE
Dark, narrow stairway	Chokes ch'i.	Install a mirror on the ceiling and increase the lighting.
Stairs have no risers	Allows ch'i to escape and not rise to the next floor.	Place plants underneath the stairs.
Stairway ends too close to a wall	Blocks residents' ch'i.	Hang a mirror on the wall.
Stairway in a split-level house or apartment	Many highs and lows in residents' lives; health and careers are endangered.	Install plants on either side of the stairs. Light well—ideally between the risers.
Spiral stairway	Allows ch'i to escape; can mean physical problems for residents.	Wrap something green, such as a vine, around the banisters. Install a light that shines from the top to the bottom of the stairs.

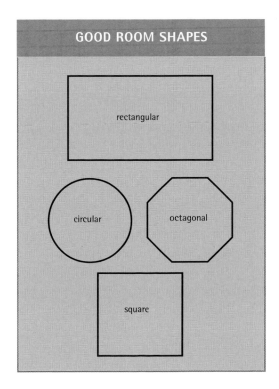

GOOD ROOM SHAPES

rectangular

circular

octagonal

square

ROOM SHAPE, SIZE AND STRUCTURE

Generally, room shapes follow the rules of building shapes (see page 107). Ideally, use regular, resolved shapes such as squares, circles, rectangles and even octagons, as they create a feeling of something complete. Unresolved shapes can present problems (see the ba-gua, page 44). Particularly problematic are boot and cleaver shapes (see page 112). A mother who was worried about her teenage daughter, who had suffered from health and occasional adolescent emotional problems, consulted a feng shui expert, who remarked that the daughter's bedroom was shaped like a cleaver, and the bed rested against the edge of the blade. After a mirror had been hung on the wall opposite the bed to draw the daughter away from danger, her health and mood improved.

BEAM LOCATION	SITUATION	DIAGNOSIS
Bedroom	Over the head of the bed	Causes headaches or migraines.
	Over the middle of the bed	Causes stomachaches, ulcers, intestinal problems.
	Over the foot of the bed	Hampers mobility in travel and life.
	Down the center of the bed	Makes occupants feel as though something is going on over their heads; divisive to relationships. Can cause uneven, disturbed moods in a solitary person.
Kitchen	Over the stove or a table	Causes financial loss; loans are not paid back.
Dining room	Over the table	As above.
Study or office	Over the desk	Blocks creativity and thought processes.
Hallway	The more confined the space, the worse the situation	Impedes ch'i flow; chokes residents' luck.

CURES FOR BEAMS

The cures for beams can be applied to any of the above problems.

1   Move furniture away from the beam. If this is not possible:
2   Hang two bamboo flutes with red ribbons wrapped around them on the beam, to create the beginning of the auspicious ba-gua octagon of the *I Ching*.
3   Attach a red fringe to the length of the beam.
4   Camouflage the beam with tenting.
5   Install bright lights overhead and then mask the beam with a translucent glass or plastic shoji-screen-style cover, making a false ceiling. This is particularly uplifting and effective in hallways, but also works in larger spaces.

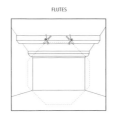

FLUTES

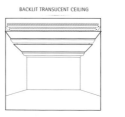

BACKLIT TRANSLUCENT CEILING

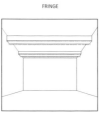

FRINGE

The size and structure of rooms have an effect. For instance, joining two small adjoining rooms to create one may open up the space, which is good for family or living rooms, but may be problematic for a bedroom. One example is the luxurious Hong Kong home of an attractive, successful woman who had a string of wealthy admirers, but no long-term suitors. She had linked two rooms, a sitting room and a bedroom, with an arch-shaped entry; on examination, a feng shui expert informed her that the rooms were too exposed, or had an "empty door." In Chinese literature, "empty door" is a euphemism for a nun or priest, a person fleeing the material life to enter a spiritual world. As the woman had no intention of becoming a nun, she followed the expert's advice to cure the problem, namely to drape the arch to re-create the sense of two rooms. Shortly after she had hung up a transparent curtain, she met the man she has now married.

COLUMNS, CORNERS, BEAMS AND SLANTS

Columns, corners, beams and slants can all create problems in room shapes. These structural elements can be obstructive to ch'i flow, and create an incomplete shape signaling that something is missing in occupants' lives (see the ba-gua, page 44).

Columns and corners

Just as in office spaces, columns and corners can create menacing physical and emotional problems at home. Rounded corners and columns are best, allowing smoother ch'i flow. When sharp-edged they can seem knife-like, threatening the residents, who may find that they have to confront violence. The edges even resemble an accusing finger falsely blaming or criticizing occupants. (See page 131 for cures.)

Beams

While beams affect the topography of a ceiling, they also affect the people living beneath them. Even when they are attractive and decorative, they can harm ch'i flow in a room and the residents' ch'i and luck. Load-bearing beams, in particular, create compression, oppressing and wreaking physical and emotional havoc on those eating, sleeping and working beneath them. The effect of a beam depends on its placement; see opposite for effects and cures.

Slants

A room with a strange angle can be problematic, causing a visual imbalance and a disquieting experience for its occupants. For instance, an acute angle is visually awkward and can trap ch'i flow, creating a dead end for residents' luck and business. Any slanted wall, furthermore, connotes an unforeseen or oblique event—usually bad, like a freak accident or unexpected failure. Awkward shapes can be remedied in a number of ways. If the slanted wall is perfectly flat, a mirror will symbolically straighten it by visually creating the illusion of resolution. If the angle in the room is acute, or the wall uneven, install a tree or a flowering plant in the corner; this will allow ch'i to flow through the plant and thus enliven and circulate otherwise dead energy. Back-lighting the plant will further resolve and enhance this disturbing shape (see left).

Problematic slants can be cured with appropriate use of some of the Nine Cures.

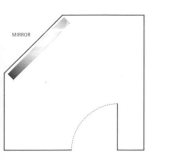

MIRROR

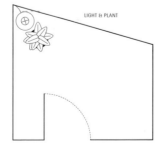

LIGHT & PLANT

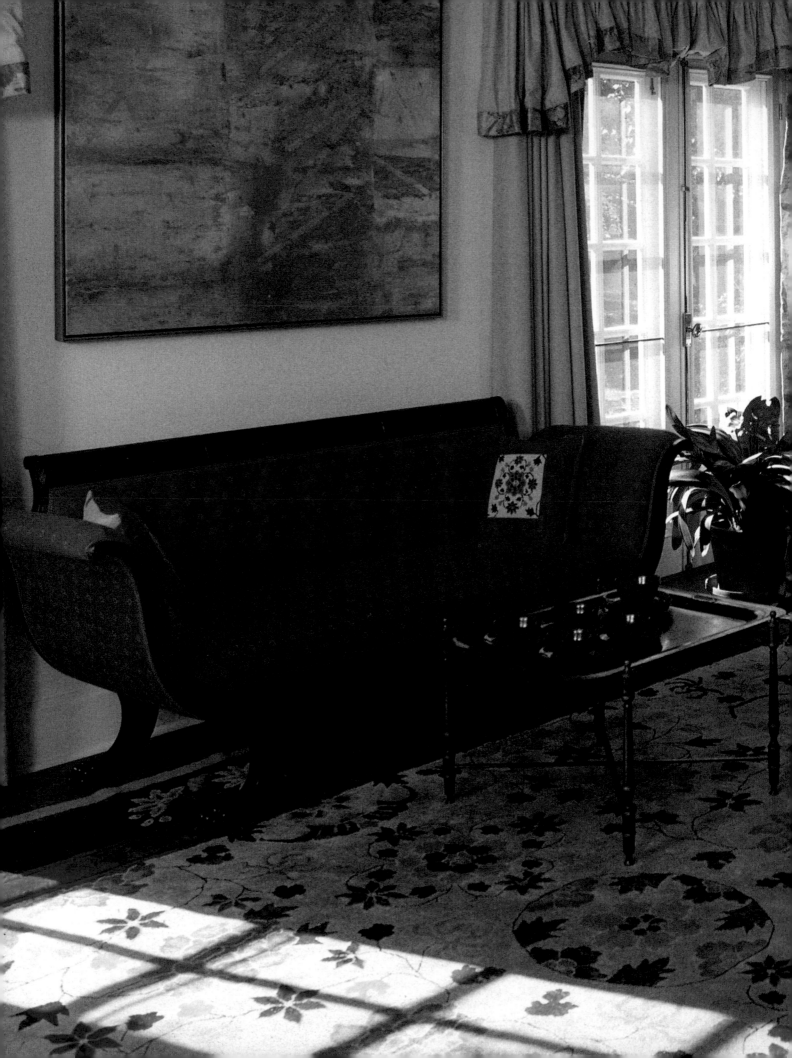

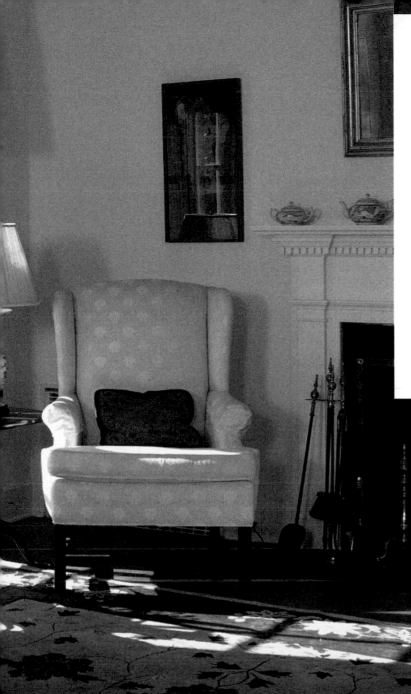

FURNITURE ARRANGEMENT

In this classically styled drawing room, great care has been taken to arrange the furniture auspiciously and in the use of colours in certain areas. The mirror above the fireplace balances that opening and draws in views; flowers and plants enhance ch'i. Overall, there is a feeling of spaciousness and light.

風水

	ROOM	POSITION	DIAGNOSIS	CURE
	Master bedroom	Opposite corner to main front door	Best controlling position.	Not necessary.
		Behind the central meridian	Good, secure, peaceful.	Not necessary.
		In the front half of the home	Insecure, unsettling.	Hang a mirror behind the front-door line, reflecting the room into the main part of the home.
		In a wing that juts in front of the entrance	A family member eats out most of the time; divorce.	As above.
	Dining room	In a wing that juts in front of the entrance	A family member eats out most of the time; divorce.	As above.
	Kitchen	In a wing that juts in front of the entrance	As above.	As above.
		Close to the dining room	Good.	
		At the center of the home	Bad for family fortunes.	1 Hang mirrors outside doors leading to the kitchen. 2 If the kitchen is narrow, mirror the stove splashback, install a crystal ball above the cook's station.
	Bathroom	At the center of the home	Money and health are flushed away.	If the toilet is in the center, mirror all four walls. Hang a full-length mirror on the outside of the door.
		Facing the kitchen	Money and health are flushed away.	Install a full-length mirror on the outside of the door.
		Facing the bedroom	Digestive problems.	1 Install a full-length mirror on the outside of the door. 2 Hang a crystal ball between the bed and the bathroom.
		At the end of a long hall	Ch'i is funneled too quickly; intestinal and fertility problems.	Hang a curtain, wind chime, mobile or crystal in the hall to disperse ch'i.

ROOM POSITIONS

The positioning of rooms can affect a home and thus the fortunes of its residents. See opposite for positive and negative room positions, and cures where necessary. As a rule, the master bedroom should be in the opposite corner to the entrance door, behind the central meridian of the house. This "commanding" position will facilitate maximum control in life and a greater sense of peace and security at home. Being near the front door is less settling. If the master bedroom is in the front half of the home, hang a mirror behind the central meridian, facing the bedroom, to symbolically draw the bedroom into the more secure rear area.

Particularly problematic is a master bedroom sited in an L that juts in front of the entrance (see page 112) creating the unsettling sense that a couple is sleeping outside their home and possibly leading to a divorce. If a kitchen or dining room is in this wing at least one member of the family will regularly eat out and stay away from home for longer and longer intervals. This situation, too, may end in divorce. But this L is a good location for living rooms, studies, home offices and guest bedrooms. A room in the front wing can be remedied by hanging a mirror inside the front-door line of the house, facing the bedroom, kitchen or dining room, to symbolically bring the room into the main part of the home.

The center of a home is associated with health. Avoid placing kitchens and bathrooms in the middle of a house or apartment, or residents' health will suffer along the central lines of their bodies. If a bathroom is centrally located, residents' health, luck and money will be flushed away. If the kitchen, a source of heat and drainage is in the center it should be wide, spacious and well-ventilated, allowing the lives and finances of residents the opportunity to develop and advance. A small, narrow kitchen, however, will not be able to balance the oppressive force of the stove, oven or microwave's "fire," creating bad influences and making the cook irritable. The family fortunes will slowly go up in smoke.

MOVABLE PARTS

The placement of furniture within a home can modify the flow of interior ch'i and thus enhance or hamper residents' lives and luck. This section offers a room-by-room approach to arranging furniture in order to further harmonize living environment and life. No matter what the taste of the occupants, or the style of furniture, the feng shui expert will pay attention to the placement of beds, stoves and desks—which tend to impact upon a family's fortunes and ch'i more than other objects.

Bedroom

A bedroom is one of the most important feng shui considerations—it definitely affects our well-being. It is where we spend a good third of our lives, where we rest, relax and regain our strength, where many of our dreams pass before us and where we start our day.

It offers different facets to consider: how the bed is placed and its alignment with the door and windows, the view from the room, and even the shape of the bed—a film director sought to save his rocky marriage by trading in his king-sized bed for one with rounded corners, to take the "edge" out of his marriage. In another instance, a feng shui expert suggested to a couple who had constant rifts that they bridge their marriage by exchanging their twin beds for a solid king-sized one.

How a bed is built can affect the people who sleep in it. Platform beds are considered less fertile ground for conception, as some

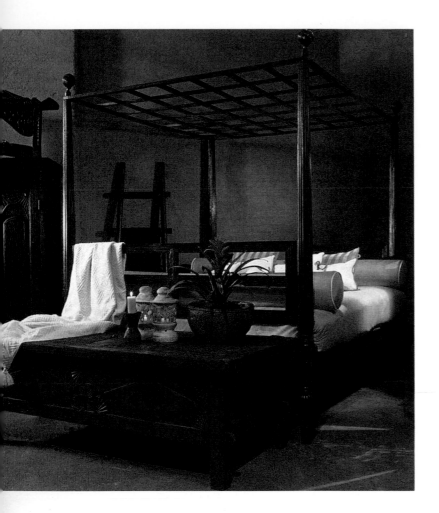

This bed is auspiciously sited. The occupant can view the door and thus read, sleep and relax comfortably.

in a miscarriage or infertility. Loft beds are discouraged, as the movement of people beneath them will disturb the flow of ch'i and make their occupants disturbed and nervous. They are also too close to the ceiling for ch'i to circulate properly.

Bunk beds can be problematic for both the person on the top, who will feel insecure, and the one below, who will feel oppressed. Make sure the mattress in the upper bunk is wide enough, or that there is a safety barrier, as the occupant will feel as though he or she is about to tumble out of bed. A flute placed directly on top of the bed frame (below the mattress) will help to symbolically secure them. The occupant of the lower bunk will feel less pressurized if a mirror-like reflective plastic cover is placed underneath the bottom of the upper one.

A bed's headboard symbolizes emotional and personal support. It should always be higher than the footboard and tightly in place. A loose headboard signifies instability and shaky foundations.

The first consideration is where to place the bed, as this can be pivotal to the occupants' physical and emotional health as well as their overall outlook on life. Its position determines their sleeping and waking ch'i, performance and mood. Generally, the bed should rest against a wall or they may find life unstable and will have little to rely on.

Chinese believe that *ling*, embryonic forms of ch'i, float around the atmosphere and bedroom, then under the bed, waiting for a chance to enter a woman's womb to give life force to a fetus. They also avoid sweeping under the bed of a pregnant woman (or one hoping to conceive) for fear that ling will scatter, resulting

Ideally, the bed should be diagonally across from the door, but positioned so that the

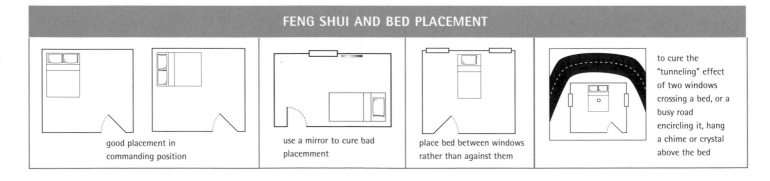

FENG SHUI AND BED PLACEMENT

good placement in commanding position

use a mirror to cure bad placement

place bed between windows rather than against them

to cure the "tunneling" effect of two windows crossing a bed, or a busy road encircling it, hang a chime or crystal above the bed

occupants can see anyone entering the room, thus ensuring smooth, balanced ch'i flow. This "commanding view" gives them a greater sense of control over their environment and lives. With a bed in this position, they will enjoy greater calm and a more enlightened overall perspective (see below left).

If the bed is not in the commanding position, the occupants will not be able to see the door and anyone entering, and their ch'i will be unbalanced. They may be startled, making them jumpy, anxious and nervous, leading to health and personality problems. As a result, their personal relationships and productivity and effectiveness at work will suffer.

If your bed is next to a door which creaks, when you read, watch television or sleep you will feel as though someone is entering the room. You will acquire an unnecessarily heightened sensitivity, and the effect will be to unbalance your mental stability—your heart will beat faster and you will be more excitable. The bed should be moved away from the door to the commanding position. If this is not possible, a mirror placed so that you can see the door will alleviate this—but the creak should nevertheless be fixed!

Another arrangement to avoid is the mortuary position. When the foot of a bed directly faces a door, this is considered reminiscent of a corpse waiting for burial. To resolve this, install a strategically placed mirror and hang a crystal ball halfway between the foot of the bed and the door.

Be aware of door and window alignment, too. If a window is directly opposite another window, or a door, and the bed is in between them, the occupants may sleep poorly and suffer from constant illness. An example is a doctor who suffered from insomnia because the highrise he lived in was skirted by a major road that seemed to come in through one window, cross his bed and exit through the other

window. A feng shui master prescribed hanging a wind chime between the two windows, and it worked like a sleeping pill. In another instance, a young woman whose bed was sited between a door and a window suffered from intestinal and fertility problems where the line of ch'i flow crossed her bed. After surgery, and when the ch'i flow had been dispersed with a crystal ball, her symptoms abated and afterwards she conceived, giving birth to a son.

Light and views further improve a bedroom and the ch'i of its occupants. Lighting should be soothing, but there should be access to a good reading light—allow for one to be placed behind or beside the bed. Including a subdued

In the upper picture below, a child's bed is auspiciously placed in the opposite corner to the door. Blues and greens were used to aid development, the brown of the wood features provide stability. In the lower picture, poor bed placement is adjusted by the strategic hanging of a mirror; while lying in bed, the child can see anyone entering her room.

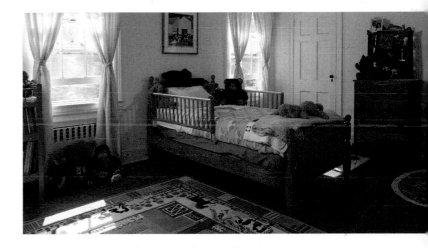

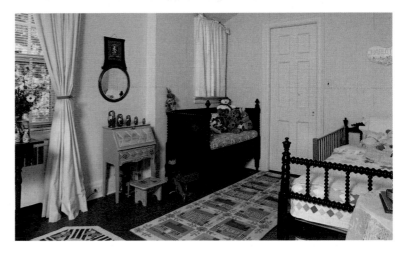

light in a bedroom scheme will encourage a romantic and intimate mood. If a bedroom overlooks a garden, park, terrace or body of water, a mirror hung in a strategic place will draw the nurturing effects of nature over the bed and thus enhance the ch'i and fortunes of its occupants. Generally, in cold climates carpets are good, creating a warm atmosphere. Carpeting and rugs should feel comfortable to bare feet, so avoid sisal or rough surfaces in master bedrooms.

Proportion is also important. The bed should not be too large for the room. Large bureaus, wardrobes and tall chests of drawers don't belong in small rooms. If the room is large enough to handle any of these, make sure it is sited away from the bed or doorway or it will unbalance occupants' ch'i and equilibrium, inhibiting body movements and unbalancing internal harmony.

This is particularly important in children's bedrooms, as children's ch'i, minds and bodies are more impressionable.

Child's bedroom

Just as a couple's relationship and careers can be affected by the feng shui of their bedroom, so too can a child's development be nurtured by the way his or her bedroom is laid out, and its colors and atmosphere.

As with adults, the bed should lie diagonally across from the door. Avoid placing heavy pieces of furniture near it, as the child may suffer from physical and emotional imbalances, leading to spills and broken bones as well as mental problems. Colors can enhance development. Pastel blue and green are particularly nurturing.

In addition to the general feng shui guidelines for bedrooms, some specific methods will help children's health, curing their maladies, as well as personality and physical problems. For example, while a

chronically ill child should have medical attention, feng shui seeks to reinforce medical cures. The application of positive colors— green, light blue and pink (good for any bedroom)—in decorating the child's room will emotionally bolster the cure. In another instance, an overactive child will moderate his behavior positively if his bedroom is decorated with white, brown, gray and/or other subdued or serene shades. A reclusive child, on the other hand, will be more outgoing if the room is primarily decorated in red or green.

Feng shui offers other methods to adjust a child's behavior. If he won't study, place a small mirror on his desk where he can see his reflection. This affects the optic nerve, which in turn stimulates the brain to think.

A bully or a rude child may become more considerate of, and sensitive to, others if background music is played softly, or he is encouraged to sing. Oranges or fragrant flowers placed in the child's bedroom so that he smells something good and sweet when moving around will soften abrasiveness. An intense child can be relaxed if the bed is auspiciously placed, and a wind chime with a crystal ball at the bottom is hung from the center of the bedroom.

Teenager's room

A teenager's room usually has both a bed and a desk. Place the bed diagonally across from the door, and hang a mirror so that it reflects the door back to the teenager when he or she is studying at the desk. Colors can also help to adjust an adolescent's behavior. A wild and unruly young person can be reined in a bit with black, dark green or navy-blue decoration, while a shy teenager will be bolstered by pink, red, blue and green. A lazy adolescent can be enlivened with an aquarium stocked with eight (or multiples of eight) black fish and one (or multiples of one) red fish to create a total of nine (or a multiple of nine). For example, a fish tank with sixteen black fish and two red ones should do the trick. In addition, place three bamboo flutes to create the Chinese character for "man" [人] between the teenager's mattress and the springs of his bed.

Kitchen

The layout of the kitchen is crucial to the health, finances and happiness of a family. The kitchen is considered a source of wealth, as well as health, by the Chinese, as their word for food sounds the same as the word for wealth:

ts'ai. The stove therefore becomes the place where food/wealth is created, and is very important.

The kitchen should be laid out so that the cook is not startled while at the stove: he or she should be aware of anyone entering the room. The cook should face the door. A "cook top" on a kitchen island works well. If someone who is cooking is startled, a negative chain reaction can occur affecting family health, harmony and finances. For example, a husband may get angry if he is preparing dinner and his wife surprises him with a hug while he is at the stove

When a cook cannot face the door to the kitchen, install a mirror as a splashback to reflect anyone entering as shown here and on page 174. The cook will be less jumpy and more comfortable, and the household will be more peaceful. The mirror will symbolically improve finances, doubling the amount of food—which connotes wealth—being prepared.

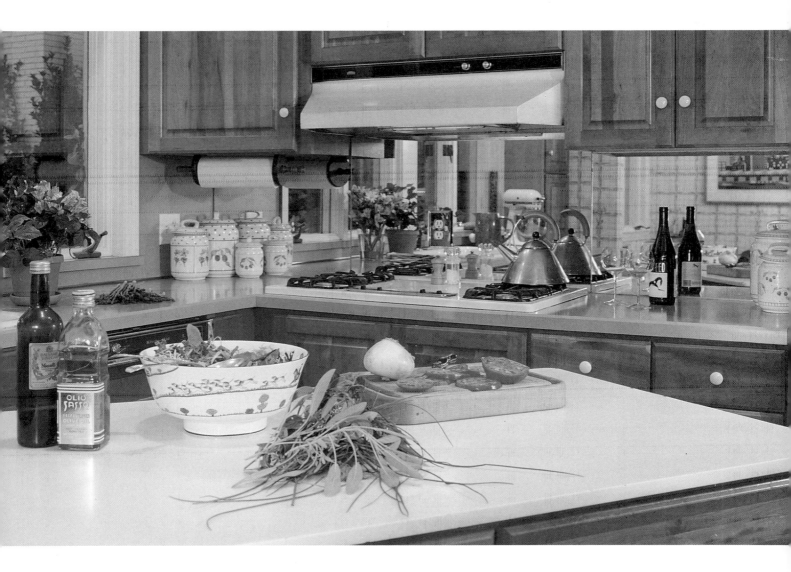

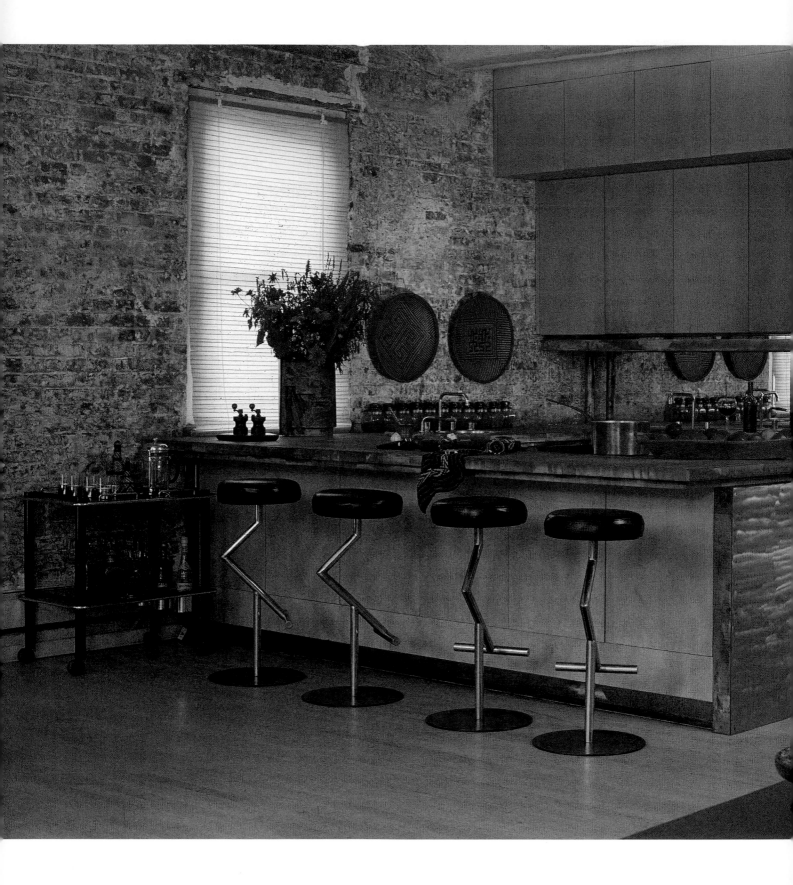

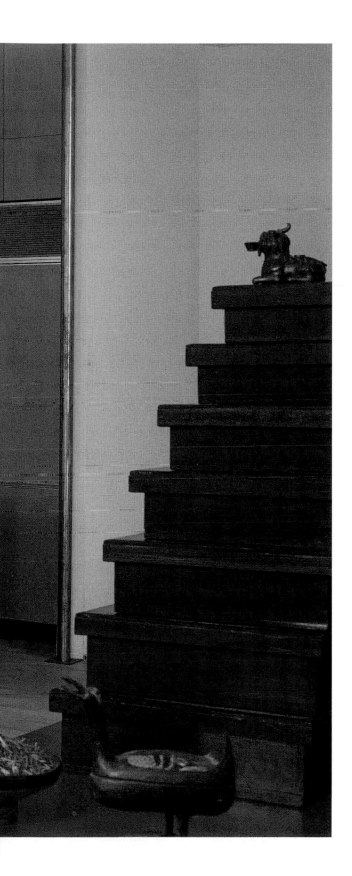

KITCHENS

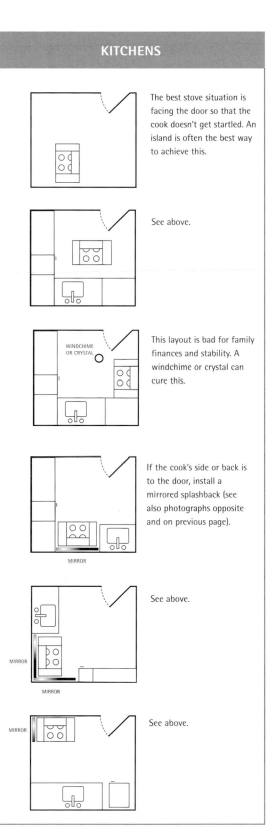

The best stove situation is facing the door so that the cook doesn't get startled. An island is often the best way to achieve this.

See above.

This layout is bad for family finances and stability. A windchime or crystal can cure this.

If the cook's side or back is to the door, install a mirrored splashback (see also photographs opposite and on previous page).

See above.

See above.

A kitchen in a loft apartment. Although it does boast an island for food preparation, the cook will still have his or her back to the room when working in the rear area. To remedy this, the back wall has been mirrored.

**GOOD DINING
TABLE SHAPES**

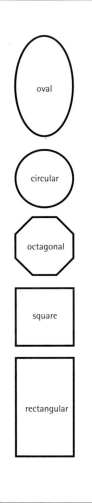

oval

circular

octagonal

square

rectangular

or chopping vegetables. This reaction will unnerve both of them, upset their relationship that night, and affect work at the office the next day. A mirror installed behind the stove will resolve this, as it will reflect anyone entering and make the cook aware of them. Symbolically, the mirror will also help family wealth to grow, as it appears to double the amount of ts'ai being created. When a stove faces a door directly, bloody accidents may ensue. It is also negative to have a stove between two aligned doors. To cure both situations, place a copper wind chime between the stove and door(s). See previous page for diagrams of best stove positions.

In addition, the cook should work in a clean, well-lit and well-ventilated space.

The best color for a kitchen is white. White symbolizes purity and cleanliness and acts as a canvas to show off the various colors of fresh and prepared food. On the other hand, red, associated with the fire element, creates too much heat and can cause combustion in the form of family fights. But avoid all-black kitchens because black, associated with water, puts out fires. (Red and black accent colors are fine, however.) Dark green is the best color for a stove.

Dining room

Along with the kitchen, the dining room is associated with a family's wealth because of the ts'ai. It is where they eat and entertain. The Chinese pay attention to the shape and position of the dining table: ideally, it should be a regular shape—square, round, oval or rectangular—and not too long and/or thin. Avoid one with missing corners, such as a rectangle with its four corners lopped off or an elongated hexagon. An octagon, however, symbolizing the perfection of the *I Ching* and the universe, is auspicious. A dining table should also have ample room for guests to sit around it comfortably. Avoid crowded seating,

This relaxed environment on the near right is fine for informal dining, with soft, inviting seating, well-presented food, and candlelight for intimacy. In the much more formal dining space opposite, extensive use is made of natural materials, and the circular mirror draws views across the regularly shaped table, which can seat many guests comfortably.

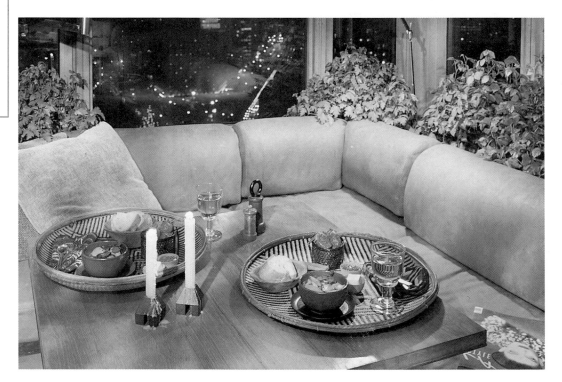

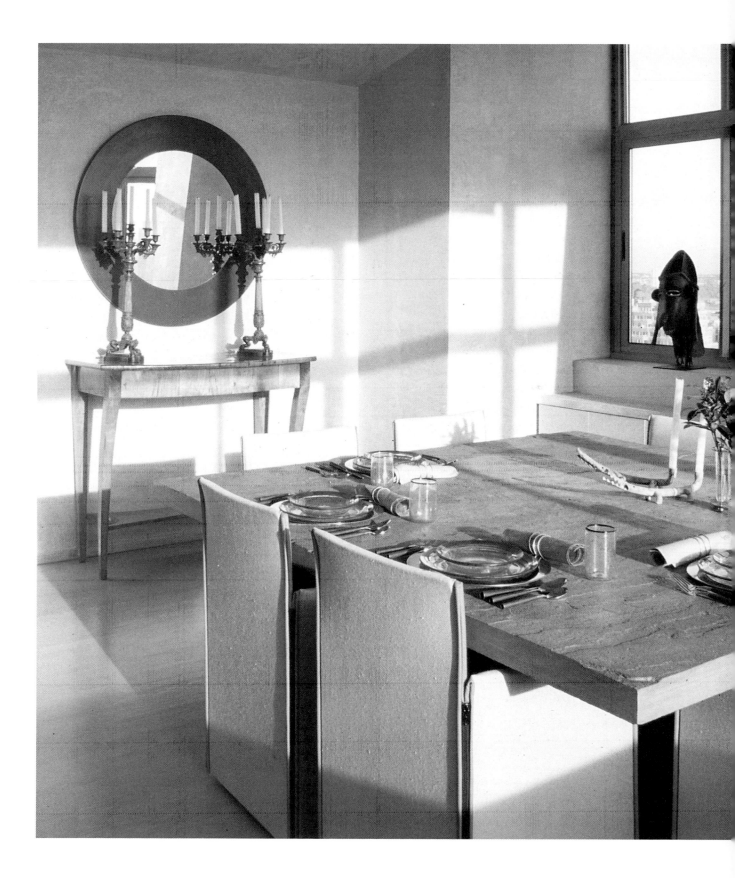

as the alimentary canal will feel constricted. When seating is comfortable and unconfined, diners will enjoy themselves, they will relax at work, deal positively with pressures that face them and good happiness will ensue.

Beware of being able to see the stove when seated at the dining table. This can be rectified by placing two flutes on the dining room side of the kitchen wall in the shape of a moustache. The best place to sit, and thus to seat an honored guest, is in the commanding position with a view of the door. The worst is one where your back is to the door.

As a symbolic source of financial health, the table should be sited with care. It should not be under a beam, as lent money will not be repaid. If the dining-room window affords a view of water, hang a mirror to draw the water, representing money, over the table.

The dining room should have light, bright colors, such as pinks, greens and blues to stimulate the palate. Black and white dull the appetite. If the members of a household are overweight, however, a black dining area can help them to lose weight by suppressing the desire to eat. For night-time dining, the lighting can be more subdued than in the rest of the house, but sufficiently bright to appreciate the food. A subdued light will also be more flattering.

For informal dining this curved table, fruit and flowers, together with a warm color palette, create a comfortable eating environment. As a living room, this arrangement employs positive, curved shapes, accent colors and ch'i-enhancing plants. But the space should preferably not be used for the two purposes.

Living room

A living room should be a warm and welcoming place to entertain guests. Hosts and guests alike should sit on sofas or chairs placed at a distance from, but facing, the door. Guests should be in the best and safest seat, in the commanding position, giving them the broadest view of both room and doorway.

Sofas, chairs and love seats should be arranged in a conversational cluster for relaxed, informal entertaining, or geometrically for more formal receptions.

Colors can enliven the atmosphere of gatherings. Blue or green, pink, white or off-white—ecru, beige or tans—as well as multicolors are good for entertaining. And an array of accent colors—on cushions, in paintings or decoration—will please a variety of guests and stimulate lively and varied conversation. Lighting should be soothing, yet there should be accessible bright lights to suit the occasion.

A living room should preferably not be used as a dining room, secondarily or not. If this is unavoidable—in a small apartment or studio, for example—a screen can be used to define and separate a dining area.

Although a fireplace is a positive and auspicious source of warmth, it must also have the appropriate setup for safety and luck. As a partial opening to a home, it should, ideally, be balanced with a mirror above it, drawing residents' ch'i upwards. Plants or flowers on either side of the fireplace will enhance the energy. Avoid placing furniture too close to, or directly facing, a fireplace.

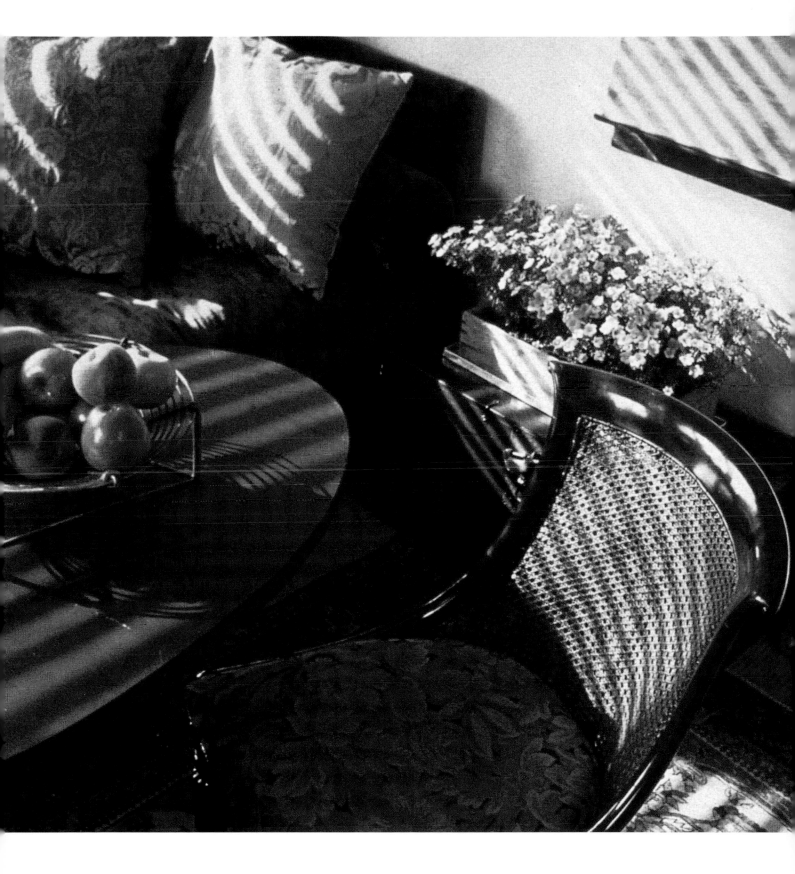

Home office or study

A home office should follow the rules of business offices, with the desk placed diagonally across from the door, so that all intruders—big or small, human or animal—can be seen and the flow of ch'i is not blocked. It should have a different ambience to the rest of the house, so that when the worker walks in he or she is entering a new world, and his mind can shift away from home matters to work. Positive business mementos should be nicely arranged in full view. The room should be set up as an office. If it is arranged for other uses (such as a guest bedroom) the space will

not be sufficiently conducive to serious concentration and work.

It should be clean and organized. Mirrors placed on all four walls will help to develop the worker's sensory faculties and ch'i as they increase the field of vision, and work will be unimpeded, informed and enlightened. Lighting should be appropriately bright. The rules for placing computers in businesses also apply to home offices (see page 136). The best colors to use are pale blue-green, brown or pink.

Library

A library should be bright and spacious. Chairs should be comfortably wide and spaciously arranged, ideally in small groups. As in a study, the best colors to use are pale blue-green, brown or pink. Dark woods encourage deep thought and stability. The room should be well lit, for reading.

Family room

This should be laid out in a similar way to an informal living room, with the best seats facing the door, in a conversational cluster. They should not be close to the television set, as proximity to the screen will harm the eyes. If there is disharmony in the family, nine vases of verdant plants will adjust the feng shui. The lighting should be soothing. If there is a predominant color in the room, others should be added as accents, to tone it down or enliven it.

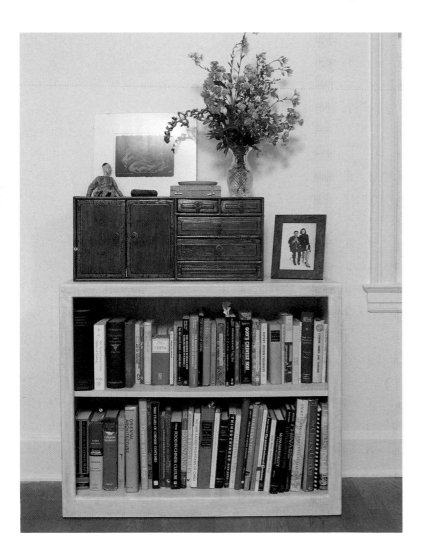

This bookcase of often-used reference works and a sketch by an artist client draws the occupant of this home-based office into the room, reminding her to fulfill her tasks.

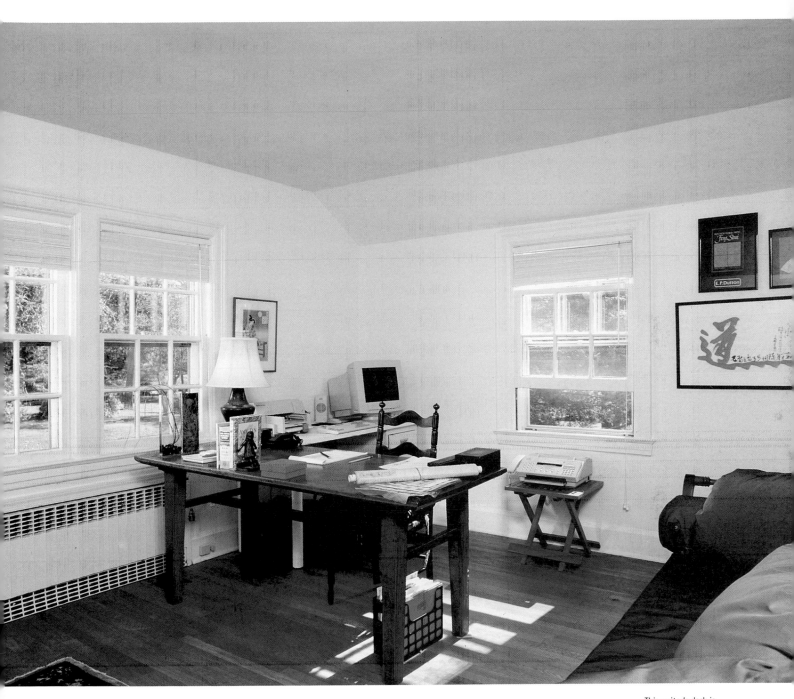

This writer's desk is auspiciously placed in her home office or study. Ideally, the computer monitor, if often used, should enable her to face the door. But the room's occupant is computer-illiterate, and prefers to write longhand on the desk.

Bathroom

As the location where water enters and exits, the bathroom symbolizes residents' finances as well as their internal plumbing. It therefore affects the family wealth and health.

As mentioned before, an important consideration is its position within the home. Avoid having a bathroom near the entrance, the kitchen or dining room, or at the end of a long hallway. If it is sited in the wealth or marriage areas of the ba-gua (see page 44) this can be problematic for family finances and marital harmony.

Within the bathroom, the position of the toilet is important. One that is hidden from view is best; the next best situation is the farthest point from the door. Avoid having it in full view, directly opposite the door, as residents may suffer miscarriages and find money and health drawing away, symbolically flushed down it. The bathroom door should also be kept shut.

To correct a poorly exposed toilet, construct a cubicle or curtain to shield it, or hang a wind chime between it and the door. Alternatively, hang a full-length mirror on the outside of the door.

The bathroom itself should be well-lit and spacious. But, while it should certainly not be cramped, avoid one that is so large that it is given too much significance in the household, influencing residents' interests and activities, and making them preoccupied with the bathroom and prone to time-consuming and self-absorbed preening, obsessive hand washing, or intestinal problems.

A cramped bathroom is problematic, too. It is awkward to move around in a confined space and this will encourage accidents. Its cramped nature will make it uninviting, creating for residents an aversion which can be detrimental to the digestive system. However, the room can be symbolically opened up and cured by installing mirrors on all four walls.

While pastel shades—such as pink, peach, light blue or green—in a master bathroom encourage family and marital harmony, black and white or a black-and-white mixture are also good bathroom colors, especially if they are accented with bright towels and accessories. Gray is also an acceptable color.

Ideally, the toilet should not be visible from the bathroom door. The two drawings on the left show appropriate placement. In the picture opposite, the toilet sits behind the bath area, out of direct view. The room is decorated in pastel shades appropriate for marital harmony.

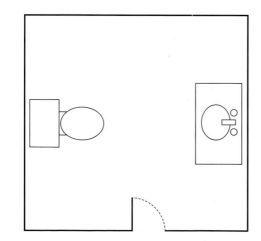

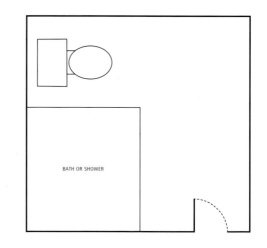

BATH OR SHOWER

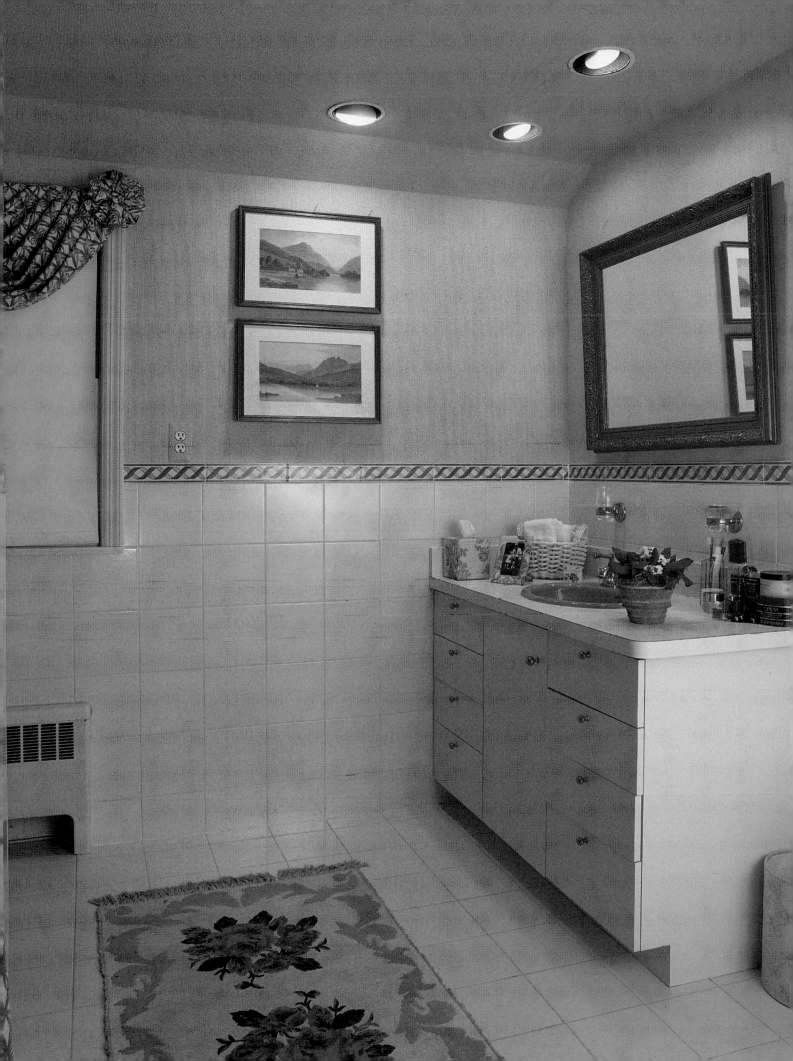

CHAPTER IX

Feng Shui Cures

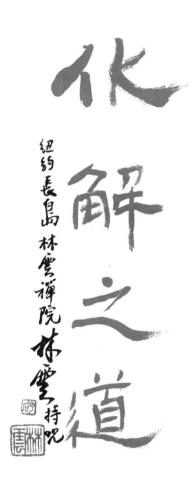

Feng shui operates on two levels: sying and yi. Sying encompasses the material and visible rules and cures of feng shui, while yi addresses its more transcendental and intuitive practices, such as blessings, meditations and rituals. The body of this book covers sying, while this chapter and Chapter III cover yi. In general, sying cures are tangible ways to manipulate the environment to improve ch'i and fortunes, while yi cures seek a spiritual and psychic transformation of ch'i and luck from negative to positive.

Three Secrets Reinforcement

A simple, ritual way of strengthening a cure, an active blessing or meditation, and is a combination of three mystical ingredients: body, speech and mind.

1 Body This is a ritual gesture—often a hand gesture (mudra)—to express a wish or feeling. For instance, the Blessing Mudra expresses homage, offerings or blessings; the **Heart Mudra** (below) calms the mind and the heart;

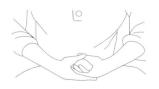

the **Exorcism Mudra** (above) expands and improves ch'i, or dispels malign spirits and bad luck.

2 Speech This is a chant—mantra—whose sound brings forth a positive and beneficial influence. For instance, the **Six True Words**: *Om Ma Ni Pad Mi Hum*; or the **Heart Sutra**: *Gatay, Gatay, Boro Gatay, Boro Sun Gatay, Bodhi So Po He.*

3 Mind This is the power of the mind, our conscious intention which can range from wish or prayer to visualization, to enhance or help ourselves or others.

Tracing the Nine Stars

This is used both to rid a home or an office of ill fortune and bad ch'i, and to transform and adjust it into positive energy. It is superimposed on the ba-gua of a room or a building.

1 Perform the Heart Sutra (see above).

2 After entering, start at the jen (family) area and direct your ch'i (by walking, talking or meditating), tracing the Nine

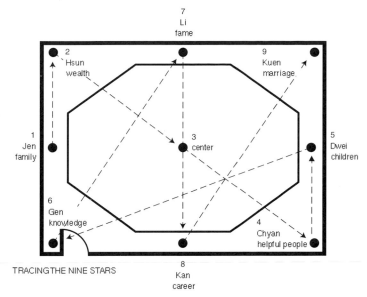

7
Li
fame

2
Hsun
wealth

9
Kuen
marriage

1
Jen
family

3
center

5
Dwei
children

6
Gen
knowledge

4
Chyan
helpful people

8
Kan
career

TRACING THE NINE STARS

Simultaneously, register a first impression formed by intuition and chance as to which fortune you actually stepped on.

3 If you stepped on one of the seven other fortunes, locate where "life" is, and then visualize turning the wheel to bring "life" to the front door. (Novices can walk over to "life," and then bring it to the entrance.)

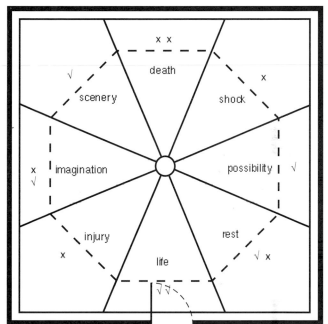

Stars in sequence and sending blessings to all corners of a house and garden, room or building—spiritually penetrating walls if necessary. The sequence is as follows: **a** direct your ch'i at jen (family), envisioning the house and family's ch'i improving; **b** proceed to hsun (wealth); then **c** to the center (health); **d** chyan (helpful people); **e** dwei (children); **f** gen (knowledge); **g** li (fame); **h** kuen (marriage).

The Eight-Door Wheel

This adjusts the ch'i of a place, be it a building, a room, yard or a garden. It is a dynamic feng shui exercise involving intuition, knowledge and meditation. The Eight-Door Wheel consists of eight possible fortunes—both good and ill—that constantly revolve within a space in sequence: life, injury, imagination, scenery, death, shock, possibility, rest. Of these fortunes, "life" is the best and "death" is the worst. "Rest" and "imagination" connote bad giving way to good. The process goes as follows:

1 When you enter a space, envision two octagons—one stationary and one, the Eight-Door Wheel—turning on the floor.

2 While stepping into the space, seek the gate of "life" and hope it is at the entrance.

4 Envision grasping the seven other fortunes and pulling them over to "life," and walk to each door depositing the essence of "life" in the sequence described in Tracing the Nine Stars. (Another method pulls the trigrams of the stationary ba-gua through "life" in this nine-star path, starting at jen.)

Yu-nei (interior blessing)

This is used both to adjust ch'i and to resolve an unbalanced shape, be it building or room.

1 Divide the space into rectangles.

2 Connect each corner to the center points of the opposite sides, as well as to the opposite corner.

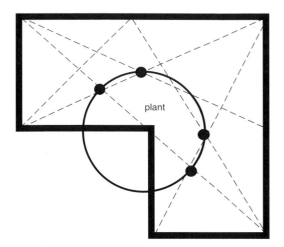

3 Within the crisscross pattern of bisecting lines an inner space is formed. Place a wind chime, crystal or living plant within this space.

Yu-wai (exterior blessing)

Yu-wai is an exterior ritual using rice both to encourage new growth and to send away bad ch'i, spirits and luck. (Rice symbolizes new growth of happiness, luck and fortune.)

1 Bless the rice, held in the palm, with the Three Secrets (see page 184).

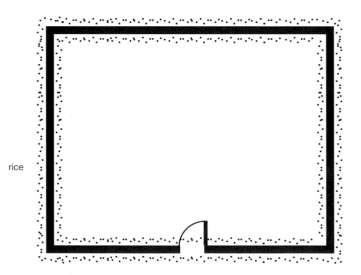

2 Sprinkle the rice first around the inner perimeter of the building and then around the outside of the structure.

Constantly Turning Dharma Wheel

The Constantly Turning Dharma Wheel is a meditational blessing to cleanse and improve the ch'i of a place.

1 Enter the space only briefly. Leave after an initial look around. Perform the Heart Sutra.

2 When re-entering the building, bring good intentions and blessings—envisioned with a higher being, such as the Buddha—for the occupants.

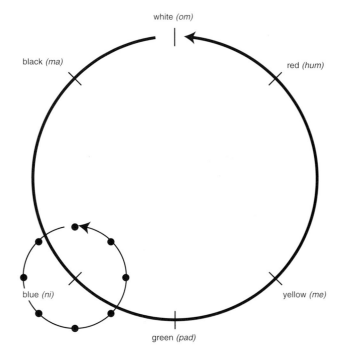

3 Imagine a wheel—the Dharma Wheel—turning before you. This wheel consists of internal sight, sound and thought. Within your mind, envision a wheel of six turning balls each with a color (the Six True Colors, see page 53) and a sound (the Six True Words, see page 184). Each ball is a universe in itself, spinning counterclockwise, and surrounded with six more colored balls, each of which is encircled with six more colored balls, and so on.

4 Take the wheel throughout the place as a cleansing and blessing, supported by your own intentions and that of a higher being.

House History

The history of a business or a home—whether its residents prospered or failed—is important to the Chinese, who believe that history may repeat itself. They investigate the previous occupants' situation and reason for moving, for they feel one adopts the habits, fortune and destiny of one's predecessor within two to three years. A house where the occupants thrived—financially, socially and professionally—and wanted to move to bigger and better quarters through good fortune is desirable.

On the other hand, the following situations may cause concern: if the former occupant died or suffered injury; downsized their work or living quarters; divorced; went bankrupt, was fired or demoted. Be aware that a low-priced property might harbor a sad or desperate past. Some Chinese, to be safe, avoid older, historic homes.

Sealing the Door

This is both a mystical cure for an unlucky place and a mystical way to protect a home or business from robberies.

1 In a bowl, place one teaspoon of ju-sha, add drops of strong liquor totaling your age plus one, and mix with your middle finger.
2 Dot the inside of the bedroom door, the entrance to the home or business, and the back and side doors, as well as the garage door. Reinforce with the Three Secrets (see page 184).
3 Flick the remaining mixture around the rooms and reinforce with the Three Secrets.

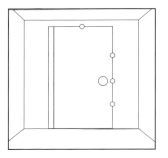

Inhale/Exhale Exercise

Use this cure to improve personal ch'i flow. It can help a multitude of disorders: if your ch'i, emotions and thoughts are choked in your throat; if you are generally unlucky; if you suffer from an unusual illness or mental disorder; or if you are so pressurized and troubled by professional, financial, social, political or familial concerns that you feel you cannot hold your head high.

While standing, place your hands in the Heart Mudra position and chant the Heart Sutra (for both, see page 184) nine times. Take a deep breath, then exhale eight quick breaths, then a ninth, which should be long and total. Repeat eight more times. This can be performed three times a day for nine or twenty-seven days.

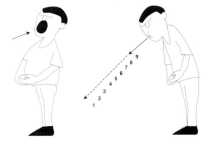

When you inhale, imagine good luck, positive emotions, spiritual powers, wisdom and good health entering through your mouth and proceeding through the throat, trachea, heart and throughout the body.

When you exhale, envision all bad luck, evil ch'i, bad karma, depression and illness being expelled.

Rooster Feather Protection

This ritualistic cure can protect you from the evil intent of negative or petty people and back-stabbers. The cure's ingredients include three rooster feathers, one teaspoon *syong huang* (realgar powder), a pinch of ju-sha (cinnabar powder) and a cup of distilled liquor from a newly opened bottle.

1 Between 11 A.M. and 1 P.M., soak the feathers in a mixture of the powders and liquor.

2 Hold the feathers and wave them in all directions, reinforce with the Three Secrets (see page 184), visualizing that all those negative people known to you, as well as unknown ones, keep away. They can no longer harm you, and perhaps eventually will become friends.

3 Then place one feather a) in your wallet or handbag to carry with you at all times; b) under your pillow or between your mattress and its base or box spring; and c) in the drawer of your desk at home or at work.

Gathering Auspicious Ch'i Method

This method of enhancing one's luck and ch'i requires the assistance of a couple engaged to be married (the ch'i of a newly married couple is known as "happiness ch'i"). On the day of their wedding, prepare nine nonconsumable personal possessions, such as a bracelet, pair of eyeglasses, a pen, watch, earrings, tie clip, hair clip or other intimate effect.

1 Wrap the nine items together in a red cloth, and have the bride and groom personally touch or use the objects.

2 Quietly don each of the items yourself, and reinforce with the Three Secrets (see above), visualizing the newlyweds' auspicious ch'i being absorbed into your ch'i.

3 After the wedding, use or wear these items often.

Wealth-Gathering Methods

These are two methods to facilitate the accumulation of wealth.

The Treasure Box Method

1 While holding your breath, write with a brand-new pen on a round piece of red paper the following: on the front, "Treasure Box" or "Ju Bao Pen"; on the back, your or your company's name.

2 Paste or tape the red paper to a piggy bank, jar or box, with the front facing out.

3 Place the bank, jar or box under your bed, directly beneath the area where your hands rest.

4 Select a particular denomination of coin to set aside each day, and place it in the container each night. Make a conscious effort to put aside all those coins of that denomination that pass through your hands. Before bedtime, put

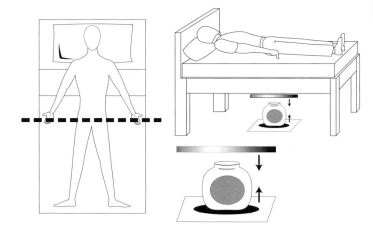

all the coins in the piggy bank, and reinforce with the Three Secrets (see page 184), visualizing wealth pouring into your hand. Repeat for twenty-seven days.

To strengthen this method, place a piece of red cloth under the container and add two mirrors facing each other—one on the floor facing up and one attached to the bottom of the bed facing down.

Inviting the God of Wealth Method

This method of increasing wealth should be performed between 11 P.M. and 1 A.M. on Chinese New Year's Eve (the 5th, 9th or 10th of the first lunar month), or the 1st or 15th of a lunar month.

1 Exit your front door holding an incense stick, or with your palms pressed together. Walk 100 steps in any direction, envisioning that you are approaching the god of wealth. (Traditionally, the Chinese walk 100 steps towards the southeast.)

2 Announce your name and address to all three dimensions—heaven, earth and man— and all ten directions—east, north, south and west, southwest, southeast, northwest and northeast, top and bottom. Visualize inviting all the gods of wealth from the three dimensions and the ten directions to come home with you for your worship and offering.

3 On the way home, no matter if you cross the street, enter an elevator or walk through a door, continue to visualize the gods of wealth walking before you. Be careful not to close the doors too quickly, as this will lock the deities and their treasures out.

4 Once inside your home, show the deities around, eventually inviting them to settle down in either a shrine or the room reserved for your sincerest worshipping.

Aromatic Cures to Adjust Ch'i

These three fragrant methods are to improve and purify a house and personal ch'i.

1 Carry nine round pieces of orange peel with you.

2 Break nine round pieces of orange peel into smaller pieces and scatter them throughout the house or office using the Giving Mudra (left) and the Sowing Mudra (right). Visualize auspicious ch'i filling the entire interior, eliminating unlucky or negative ch'i.

3 Place fragrant flowers in the main living areas of the house. Change the flowers every three days for a total of twenty-seven days— nine times in all.

Red Egg Rebirth or Golden Cicada Shedding Its Shell

The Red Egg Rebirth is a potent ritual both to drive away bad dreams, negative ch'i and ill luck and to replace it with positive ch'i, good dreams and auspicious luck. Symbolic of spiritual rebirth and cleansing, this ritual seeks to purge negativity and sadness, allowing for a fresh, positive start. It can be performed between 11 P.M. and 1 A.M. or 11 A.M. and 1 P.M. on your birthday, Chinese New Year or whenever you feel you need to exorcise nightmares or expel bad ch'i or ill fortune.

1 Purchase a teaspoon of ju-sha (cinnabar powder), an unopened bottle of liquor and a carton of eggs. Don't let anyone disturb, touch or see the eggs after you have bought them.

2 Hard-boil one egg, not letting anyone see or disturb it.

3 Put the ju-sha in your palm, and with your middle finger mix in a number of drops of liquor to equal your age plus one. Roll the egg in the mixture until it is completely red. Gently put the egg down.

4 Rub your palms together nine times to dry them, thus sealing them from ill fortune and evil ch'i.

5 Carry the red egg outdoors to a place higher than your dining table. Peel the egg and keep the pieces of shell in a paper bag or napkin so as not to drop any of them on the ground. Visualize a golden cicada shedding its shell, and that you are shedding your own old misfortune. Imagine a new shell forming, and that you are spiritually reborn and unhindered by bad luck; you return to your original, pure self. Eat the whole egg, or at least part of the white and the yolk, and discard the remains (minus the shell) in four directions, envisioning that you are feeding hungry ghosts. Sated, they depart.

6 Walk 100 steps away from your home, crush the eggshells and throw them in four directions. Reinforce with the Three Secrets (see above), visualizing all bad luck, ch'i and karma being thrown away.

7 Walk home, carefree, and avoiding stepping on the eggshells.

Touching the Six Points

This is a way to strengthen one's own ch'i as well as driving away bad luck and malign ch'i. It applies the Six True Words (see page 184) and their corresponding colors to the body to enhance ch'i.

1 Between 11 A.M. and 1 P.M., create the Exorcism Mudra (see page 184) with your hand and place one teaspoon of syong huang (realgar powder) on your palm.

2 Add a number of drops of strong liquor to your palm, equaling your age plus one.

3 Mix the ingredients with the middle finger of the opposite hand (see table).

4 Dot the six points of your body (see diagram), chanting the Six True Words and envisioning the Six True Colors. Reinforce with the Three Secrets (for all, see page 184).

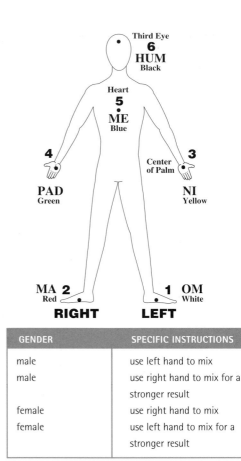

GENDER	SPECIFIC INSTRUCTIONS
male	use left hand to mix
male	use right hand to mix for a stronger result
female	use right hand to mix
female	use left hand to mix for a stronger result

GLOSSARY

ba-gua: pronounced "bar-gwar," *Ch'ing*, overlaid with eight trigrams and eight life situations.

ch'i: pronounced "chee" and translated as "breath," refers to cosmic, earthly and human energy or life force.

chu-shr: pronounced "chew-shur," that which is irrational, unproven, beyond our realm of experience, such as illogical, metaphysical cures.

feng shui: pronounced "fung shway" and translated as "wind" and "water," the Chinese art of placement and harmony with the environment.

guo-bai: pronounced "gwo-by" and translated as "pass-through," a perspective of sky or void usually framed by architecture.

ju-sha: cinnabar powder used in mystical feng shui cures and rituals. Ju-sha (red mercuric sulfide) is poisonous, so care must be taken when applying it.

ming t'ang: bright hall or cosmic court, a sacred, defined space where humans—or the emperor—communicate with heaven.

ru-shr: pronounced "rew-shur," that which is rational, proven, within our realm of experience, such as logical, practical cures.

sying: pronounced "shing," relating to appearance and form. The material and visible aspects of feng shui, what can be seen, felt or moved. Sying encompasses earth configurations, landscape, man-made structures and furniture placement.

sze-he-yuan: pronounced "shay-hey-whan"; "four-sided courtyard," the traditional arrangement of four buildings around a central court.

tao: pronounced "dow," a philosophical concept of unity and harmony of opposites.

ts'ai: a Chinese word that sounds both like "food" and "wealth."

yi: pronounced "i," relating to the more transcendental, intuitive aspects of feng shui. Yi is an intention, a wish or a will, in the form of a blessing, a ritual or a meditation, to reinforce the more practical sying cures and to improve and adjust the ch'i of a place or person.

yin-yang: two opposites that unite in tao.

THE CHINESE DYNASTIES AND HISTORICAL PERIODS

Shang	*c.*1766–*c.*1123 B.C.
Chou	*c.*1122–256
Ch'in	221–207
Han	202 B.C.–A.D. 221
Six Dynasties	221–581
Sui	581–618
T'ang	618–906
Five Dynasties	907–960
Sung	960–1279
Yuan (Mongol)	1260–1368
Ming	1368–1644
Ch'ing (Manchu)	1644–1912
Republic	1912–
People's Republic	1949–

BIBLIOGRAPHY

-Eliade, Mircea. *The Sacred and The Profane*. Translated by Willard Trask. New York: Harcourt, Brace, 1959.

-Eitel, Ernest. *Feng Shui or The Rudiments of Natural Science in China*. Hong Kong: 1873.

-Feng Yu-lan. *A Short History of Chinese Philosophy*. Translated and edited by Derek Bodde. New York and London: The Macmillan Company, 1948.

-*I Ching, or Book of Changes, The*. 2 vols. Translated by Richard Wilhelm, rendered into English by Cary F. Baynes. Princeton, N.J.: Bollingen Series, Princeton University Press, 1950.

-Inn, Henry and Shao Chang Lee (ed.) *Chinese Houses and Gardens*. Honolulu: Fong Inn's Ltd., 1940.

-Keswick, Maggie. *The Chinese Garden*. New York: Rizzoli, 1978.

-Lee, Sang Hae. *Feng Shui: Its Context and Meaning*. Doctoral Thesis, Cornell University, 1986.

-Li, Dr. Zhisui. Translated by Tai Hung-chao. *The Private Life of Chairman Mao*. New York: Random House, 1994.

-MacFarquhar, Roderick. *The Forbidden City: China's Ancient Capital*. New York: Newsweek, 1978.

-Meyer, Jeffrey I. *Peking as a Sacred City*. South Pasadena, Calif.: E. Langstaff, 1976.

-Needham, Joseph. *The Shorter Science and Civilization in China*. 2 vols. Cambridge, Eng.: Cambridge University Press, 1980.

-Rossbach, Sarah. *Feng Shui: The Chinese Art of Placement*. New York: E.P. Dutton, 1983.

-Rossbach, Sarah. *Interior Design with Feng Shui*. New York: Arkana, 1991.

-Rossbach, Sarah, and Master Lin Yun. *Living Color: Master Lin Yun's Guide to Feng Shui and the Chinese Art of Color*. New York: Kodansha America, Inc., 1994.

-Steinhardt, Nancy Shatzman. *Chinese Imperial City Planning*. Honolulu: University of Hawaii Press, 1990.

-Steinhardt, Nancy Shatzman. *Chinese Traditional Architecture*. New York: China Institute, 1984.

-Sze, Mai-mai, trans. and ed. *Mustard Seed Garden Manual of Painting*. Princeton, N.J.: Bollingen Series, Princeton University Press, 1963.

-Waley, Arthur. *The Analects*. New York: The Macmillan Company, 1938.

-Waley, Arthur. *The Book of Songs*. New York: Grove Press, 1978.

-Waley, Arthur. *The Way and Its Power*. New York: The Macmillan Company, 1958.

NOTES

Chapter II p. 26: Arthur Waley, *The Way and Its Power*, p. 151; p. 28: Feng Yu-lan, *A Short History of Chinese Philosophy* New York and London, p. 235. **Chapter IV** pp. 63, 65: Arthur Waley, *The Book of Songs*, London, pp. 282-83; p. 65: quoted in Roderick MacFarquhar, *The Forbidden City: China's Ancient Capital* New York, p. 72; p. 66: Chang, Kwang-chih, *Shang Civilization* New Haven and London, p. 159, quoted in Nancy Shatzman Steinhardt, *Chinese Imperial City Planning* Honolulu, p. 32; p. 67: Dr Li Zhisu, *The Private Life of Chairman Mao* New York, p. 76, translated by Professor Tai Hung-chao. **Chapter V** pp. 90-91: Mai-mai Sze, trans. and ed. *Mustard Seed Garden Manual of Planting* Princeton, p. 13. **Chapter VI** p. 98: Associated Press, *NYC Metrowire*, Beth Duff Brown, October 31, 1994.